Youth
and
Social Capital

the Tufnell Press,

London,
United Kingdom

www.tufnellpress.co.uk

email contact@tufnellpress.co.uk

British Library Cataloguing-in-Publication Data
A catalogue record for this book is
available from the British Library

ISBN   187276777X
ISBN-13   978-1-872767-77-2

Copyright © 2007 Helena Helve and John Bynner

Printed in England and U.S.A. by Lightning Source

Youth
and
Social Capital

edited by
Helena Helve and John Bynner

Youth and Social Capital
Contributors

Helena Helve,
Research Professor, University of Kuopio and Adjunct Professor, University of Helsinki; she has been a Visiting Research Fellow at the Centre for Longitudinal Studies, Institute of Education, University of London and a Coordinator of the Nordic Youth Research of Nordic Council of Ministers and President of the Finnish Youth Research Society 1992-2005 and the President of International Sociological Association, Research Committee of Youth Sociology 2002-2006; currently directing the Finnish Academy research project *Behind the Scenes of Society (BeSS): Young People, Identity and Social Capital*; recent publications include *Contemporary Youth Research, Local Expressions and Global Connections* with Gunilla Holm.

John Bynner,
Emeritus Professor of Social Sciences in Education, Institute of Education, University of London. and Director of the independent think tank Longview; until retirement was Director of the Bedford Group for Life course and Statistical Studies, the Centre for Longitudinal Studies, the Wider Benefits of Learning Research Centre and the Joint Centre for Longitudinal Research, with responsibility for the 1958 and 1970 birth cohort studies; directed the Economic and Social Research Council's *16-19 Initiative*; recent publications include co-authored books on *The Benefits of Learning* and *Changing Britain*.

Namita Chakrabarty
Senior Lecturer, School of Education, University of East London, teaching arts modules; she is also a creative writer and performer.

James Côté,
Professor of Sociology, University of Western Ontario; founding editor of *Identity: An International Journal of Theory and Research*; currently Vice-President for North America (2006-2010) of the International Sociological Association's Research Committee (34) on the Sociology of Youth.

Janet Holland,
Professor of Social Research, London South Bank University; Co-Director of both the *Families and Social Capital Group*, and *Timescapes: Changing Relationships and Identities though the Life Course*, a five year qualitative longitudinal study.

Markku Jokisaari,
University of Jyväskylä; research interests include social networks and organisational socialisation.

Arniika Kuusisto,
Researcher, University of Helsinki, departments of Comparative Religion and Applied Sciences of Education, in the *Behind the Scenes of the Society: Young People, Identity and Social Capital* (BeSS) group.

Jari-Erik Nurmi,
  Professor of Psychology, University of Jyväskylä; Director of the Finnish Center of Excellence in Learning and Motivation Research; publications focus on topics such as motivation, adolescent socialisation, coping, and life-span transitions.

John Preston,
  Senior Lecturer in citizenship and education, University of East London (UEL); Co-Convenor of the CREATE (Community, Resistance, Education, Activity, Traditions, Equality) research group; most recent publication, *Whiteness and Class in Education*.

Tracey Reynolds,
  Senior Research Fellow, Families and Social Capital Group, London South Bank University; publications in the field of gender and ethnic studies including *Caribbean mothering: identity and experience in the UK*.

Ricardo Sabates,
  Senior Research Officer and NIACE Fellow, Institute of Education, University of London.

Katariina Salmela-Aro,
  Professor, University of Jyvaskyla; fellow, Helsinki Collegium for Advanced Studies; member of the Centre of Excellence in Learning and Motivation; member of Academy of Finland's Council for Culture and Society.

Ingrid Schoon,
  Professor of Human Development and Social Policy, Institute of Education, University of London; recent publications include a study on *Risk and Resilience: Adaptations to changing times*.

Tom Schuller,
  Head of the Centre for Educational Research and Innovation (CERI), OECD, Paris; formerly Dean of the Faculty of Continuing Education and Professor of Lifelong Learning, Birkbeck, University of London; and Co-Director of the Centre for Research on the Wider Benefits of Learning; recent publications include *Understanding the Social Outcomes of Learning* (with Richard Desjardins).

Tarja Tolonen,
  Research Coordinator for YUNET (Youth Research University Network), Department of Sociology, University of Helsinki; her post doctoral studies focus on young people and their spatial and social transitions.

Susie Weller,
  Research Fellow, London South Bank University; currently researching the changing nature of children's lateral relationships as part of the ESRC *Timescapes: Changing Relationships and Identities through the Life Course* programme of work.

Contents

Part 4   Social networks in education

Part 5   Transitions and potentials

Preface

The ideas for the book *Youth and Social Capital* were brought to fruition in a series of papers presented at a two day conference of Finnish and English researchers held at the Finnish Institute in London on 10-11 October, 2006. The contributors were affiliated to research programmes in their respective countries concerned with social capital in various ways: in Finland, based in Finnish Academy research programme project on social capital, *Behind the Scenes of Society* (BeSS) at the University of Helsinki and Kuopio, and in a project at Jyväskylä University; and in England, based in London South bank University *Inventing Adulthoods* project, and projects in the Institute of Education, University of London and London City University. It was agreed that the range of high quality papers made a significant contribution to understanding young people's development of, and use of, the different forms of social capital. The research papers based on these projects make a significant contribution to understanding young people's development of and the use of the different forms of social capital. They have been brought together as chapters in this edited collection for publication.

We would like to address our thanks to the Finnish Institute in London for hosting the seminar and Tufnell Press for publishing the book.

Helsinki and London 23 May 2007
Helena Helve and John Bynner

Part 1   Introduction

Chapter 1

Youth and social capital

Helena Helve and John Bynner

Social capital and young people

Since the pioneering efforts of James Coleman and Robert Putnam in the U.S.A. and Pierre Bourdieu in France in establishing the idea of social capital few people in policy, social science and social science circles need convincing of the importance of trust-based relations in social and economic life. The cohesive quality of trust and the opening up of opportunities and mutual support through social networks is now seen as a form of capital that all societies need to promote. But it is also recognised that such 'bonding' social capital needs to be tempered by 'bridging' and 'linking' social capital to ensure that cohesion is fostered between as well as within social groups. The Canadian psychologist James Côté takes the idea further in seeing the different forms of social capital as significant components of what he describes as 'identity capital'. This encompasses a role for social capital in the expressions of identity and active agency, which are at an increasing premium in a rapidly changing and increasingly globalised society. The loosening of borders and widening immigration present new opportunities for societal development. They also bring new forms of tension between communities defined by ideological and religious conviction. Building social capital supplies the critical means of resolving the potential conflict and ensuring positive growth.

Research on social capital has generally addressed the situation of adults and the communities in which they live. Far less attention has been directed at younger age-groups, adolescents particularly, but also children. They are typically seen as gaining the benefits of social capital in education and the transition to work largely through the social capital of their parents. However, young people in their move towards autonomy and independence from their parents transfer their allegiance increasingly to the peer group. This supplies the means of resolving identity conflicts and coping with uncertainties on the route to adulthood. Young people's social capital is therefore of major interest in its own right.

The existence of social capital in the peer groups formed by young people is one distinctive feature of their experience. Another comes from the advances in information and communications technology (ICT) and various media. For example the internet gives access to a virtual world comprising an unlimited range of groups, unconnected by geographical proximity. It also supplies a setting for experimentation with new forms of relationship and new forms of identity, if not 'multiple identities'. The somewhat disturbing aspect of some features of these developments needs to be set against the opportunities supplied for expanded networks and new horizons for example in formal and non-formal education, employment, cultural expression, political engagement and social life, i.e. bridging and linking, as well as bonding, social capital.

Contents of the book

This book, written by authors mainly from England and Finland, is intended as a source book in a non-traditional sense for students and faculty in youth studies, and it will also be of much interest to youth policy makers and practitioners working with young people. The book has been put together at a time of growing concern about the alienation of many young people in today's society and the negative consequences including drug and alcohol abuse and anti social behaviour and political apathy.

The book consists of five sections: Introduction; Youth and Capitals; Social Capital and Identity; Social Networks in Education; and Transitions and Potentials. Each section contains a response from an expert who offers his or her personal perspectives on the papers' themes. The chapters provide much in-depth analysis of issues such as inventing adulthoods, ethnic and religious identities, adolescent's goal-related social ties, education and juvenile crime, the potential for change within and across generations. The book gives youth workers, researchers, and policy makers important and timely information about young people's social capital from different life perspectives in different contexts. Looking at issues from the perspective of England and Finland deepens our understanding as well as giving us new ideas about how to engage with young people's interests and concerns.

The Youth and Capitals section is divided into four topic areas focusing on issues related to social, cultural and human capital especially in studying youth and adulthood from a number of different perspectives. The chapter by Janet Holland draws on a unique qualitative longitudinal study which has involved following a group of young people, using various methods but mainly repeated biographical interviews, over a ten year period. The young people live in five locations in the U.K. varying by socio-economic status: inner city, leafy suburb, disadvantaged northern estate, rural area, and a contrasting location in a city in Northern Ireland. The study focuses on the emergence of distinctive forms of adulthood, shaped by social class, gender, locality and ethnicity, and related to the type of social capital available to the young people in their differing communities. Drawing on the ideas of Pierre Bourdieu the author regards social capital as a resource available to the young people in the study, along with economic and cultural capital. Access to these resources and agency in recognising and deploying them, play through the biographies of the young people, entwined with personal, family and community factors, and subject to individual, social and policy contingencies.

Tarja Tolonen in her chapter also uses Bourdieu's concepts of social and cultural capital, in pursuing her interest in the social stratification of Finnish society and how individual young people are positioned in their social fields. She has observed the processes through which social capital is being created and used by young people in certain cultural, socio- economic locations: What kinds of social relationships do young people have, how are they formed and what meanings do these relationships have for young people themselves? By social capital she refers to social networks, skills and recognition as well as to the emotional support and responsibilities carried by adults or children within these networks. Her data includes interviews with young people with different life histories made in different locations in Finland.

Namita Chakrabarty and John Preston focus on Putnam's *Bowling Alone* text in which Putnam grieves for the death of sociability through both generational change and the threat of the socially isolated exhibiting the 'dark side' of social capital. *Better Together* is an expected line of flight from his earlier text in which Putnam makes social capital 'perform' to bring together class, race and gender divisions. Starting with Putnam's *phantasies* of the social, they use the work of Deleuze and others to consider the possibilities of anonymity, loneliness and nomadism to de-territorialise the 'over-coded social body'. Using the events around 7/7 in London as a springboard and an ethnographic study of youth drama in two London sites, they consider the role of the anti-social, eccentric and 'evil' in subverting conventional practices of youth drama. In their conclusions they consider that in emphasising the 'performative' nature of social capital, Putnam reifies a limited form of human sociability. They consider the revolutionary possibilities of alternative forms of social organisation which do not fix youth as a predominantly social or anti-social entity.

In his discussion chapter of the papers *Youth and the provision of resources* James Côté distinguishes between the interpretation of young people's situation by Holland and Tolonen, with broadly Marxist undertones and that of Chakraparty and Preston's post modernist account. They share in common a sense of oppression of the young in which social capital as conceived by Puttnam and Coleman particularly—less so Bourdieu—is an instrument. Côté disagrees with this analysis, seeing its emphasis on bonding social capital as locking young people into disadvantage as patronising of working class communities. He also argues vehemently for more recognition of the role of parents and adults more generally in the 'guidance' of the young preferring to see them as a crucial resource in young people's development rather that as an obstacle that has to be overcome. In his terms the heightened complexities of the situation of young people in late modern society demand the development of identity capital, in which the resources of the family and the community are central to identity achievement.

The second topic, Social Capital and Identity (three chapters) embraces the more general topic of ethnic identity through a case study of Caribbean young people in Britain and religious identity through a study of the Seventh -day Adventists in Finland. In her chapter Tracey Reynolds shows how young people utilise social capital to develop and sustain friendship networks and how these networks inform the young people's thinking concerning ethnic identity formation. The analysis explores different aspects of young people's experience to illustrate how bonding and bridging social capital are drawn on to establish ethnic specific or multi-ethnic friendship networks. She is also interested in identifying in what arenas and contexts the young people are choosing their friendships (i.e., through schooling/education, employment, kinship networks and membership of social interest groups) and the social resources they acquire through these networks. By drawing on various case studies of the young people in the study she highlights the different types of and categories of friends characterised by different levels of emotional closeness, trust and caring reciprocal relationships. There also exists a clear demarcation between 'work friends' and 'associates' and these categories of friendship are generally racialised (also class based). The paper is based on research findings from her project 'Caribbean families, social capital and young people's diasporic identities'. This is one of a number of projects within the Families and Social

Capital ESRC (Economic & Social Research Council) Research Group, led by Rosalind Edwards and Janet Holland at London South Bank University. This project critically investigates how Caribbean young people in the U.K. construct ethnic identity, and the ways in which they utilise family and kinship networks and relationships as important sources of social and material capital to do so.

Arniika Kuusisto examines the social capital of young people who have grown up affiliated with a religious minority, the Seventh-day Adventists in Finland. Her study indicates that the denominational network serves as a social capital generating social structure. It brings several benefits to young people and their families; both intangible things like lasting relationships and social support for developing and maintaining a value system and religious identity, and concrete benefits such as finding a summer job or a place to live. Social ties and networks can support religious identity by reinforcing the socialisation process, for example, learning values and helping young people maintain the denominational value system. Parental attitudes and religious socialisation in the home are of principal importance for religious attitudes; after all, it is a rule rather than the exception that there is continuity in religious identity between generations. Thus significant others, especially parents, have a monopoly on forming children's habits and beliefs. Learning from parents is tied to: a) the children's dependence and the parents' power over them; b) perceived authority of the parents; c) love of the parents, and identification with them. In addition to these, parents are also in a good position to influence children's social contacts with others. A religious minority provides an interesting context for research. The value system in a minority, especially a small minority like the Adventist community, is not only more cohesive—both in terms of value system and social networks — but it may also be more effective in producing social capital. Whereas parental values are increasingly fragmented in contemporary postmodern society, within a more coherent minority setting the culture and lifestyle are more uniformly defined and child-rearing practices typically vary less.

In the discussion chapter by Helena Helve the focus is on the identity and social capital of religious and ethnic minority young people. In her chapter she raises new questions: How do relationships and social networks enable minority young people to increase their social capital? Is social capital inherent in the structure of religious or ethnic family relationships, particularly intergenerationally? How does this differ for majority young people, and how do these minority young people form cohesive social and moral norms of trust and co-operation? Are strong family and kinship for them more important in their identity construction and formation of social capital than they are for other young people. Does the concept of social capital for these young people differ from that of majority young people?

Even if it seems that minority young people still form their social capital in 'traditional' families and community relationships, the 'individualisation' identified with late modernity means that ethnic or religious minority young people also have their own life courses, values and beliefs, which contribute to the formation of their identity and social capital. In the minority position the term 'identity' seems to refer to individual identity, group identity, and social identity of the minority group, which means integration with the minority group with a strengthening of boundaries between 'us' and 'the others' i.e. 'bonding' rather than 'bridging' social capital. In the transition to adulthood strong bonds to the family and to the minority communities can be negative leading to social exclusion within the wider society. In contrast, bridging social capital can lead to social inclusion in wider social networks and social integration and participation in society. Furthermore we need to know how important are family and family relationships to the well-being and transitions of minority young people when building bonding and bridging social capital.

The third topic area (three chapters) focuses on Social Networks in Education. This section draws upon the findings which explore how both children and parents use their networks and resources, broadly their social capital in England and Finland, and how education can have a potentially large influence on individual propensities to offend. Susie Weller's research into secondary school choice in Britain over the last few years has increasingly included 'social capital' in its framework of analysis. This work has often focused on parents' perspectives with regard to the nature of complex admissions processes and it is widely viewed as a stressful and challenging time for many families. Nevertheless, this body of research rarely considers how children learn friendship and use their own social capital to manage the transition from primary to secondary school. The chapter draws upon the findings from a three-year research project which explores how both children and parents use their social networks and resources—broadly their social capital—to find and locate schools, gain school places and settle into secondary school. In particular this chapter focuses on children's friendship and familial networks as social resources which enable them negotiate the transition to secondary school. The study has been carried out in areas of high deprivation, such as in London, the South-East and the Midlands, where access to highly esteemed secondary schools is very limited.

Katariina Salmela-Aro focuses on adolescents' goal-related social ties and changes in them during school-related transition. She examines in her chapter the extent to which bonding would be more typical during the transition period. It has been suggested that social capital changes during life transitions. In consolidation periods, social capital is more meaningful than psychological capital, while at a crisis point the psychological capital counts more. In her study she examined adolescents' goal-related social ties and changes in them during transition from comprehensive school with questionnaires twice, at the end of the comprehensive school and one year later. The results showed that the most often mentioned goal-related social ties were to parents. The next often mentioned were ties to friends and siblings. After the transition from comprehensive school the results showed that social ties to mothers, peers and boy/girlfriends strengthened. In addition, the results showed that adolescents' with higher GPA (Grade Point Average), and those on the academic track mentioned social ties with parents more compared to those with lower GPA or in the vocational track. Girls mentioned mother and peers more often than boys, while boys mentioned fathers more often than girls. In addition, the results showed that in divorced and non-divorced families mothers were mentioned as often, while in the divorced families father was mentioned less often as a social tie than in non-divorced families.

In his chapter on *Education and juvenile crime: understanding the links and measuring the effects* Ricardo Sabates explores the relationship between education and crime at the level of the LEA (Local Education Authorities). In doing so, he first reviews the empirical evidence on the relationship between education and crime and on the possible mechanisms linking education to crime outcomes. He then uses the random variation provided by the area-specific provision of EMA (Educational Maintenance Allowances) to estimate the effects of the educational programme on juvenile crime rates. Results show that juvenile conviction rates for burglary fell in areas that introduced the EMA initiative relative to other LEAs. This was not the case for convictions for thefts or other minor offences. In conclusion, there is an indication that the EMA programme has external benefits in terms of burglary reduction, but the lack of effects on other type of offences lead him to conclude that this may be partly because EMA works with other interventions targeted at reducing crime.

The fourth topic area (four chapters) focuses on Transitions and Potentials in England and Finland. Across most societies the timing of transitions into adult roles has extended from the early to the late twenties, or even into the early thirties. The average age of primary employment, marriage and family formation has been pushed back, as more education and skill development is required to take on adult roles. The period of preparation for adulthood has been elongated, especially for those who can afford to invest in their human capital, bringing with it a polarisation between fast and slow track transitions. Early life transitions such as young motherhood can have developmental consequences, setting in motion a chain of cumulative advantage and disadvantage, with implications for subsequent transitions in other life domains. Adopting a 'life course perspective', the chapter of Ingrid Schoon examines the pathways linking experience of early social disadvantage, timing of life course transitions and associated adult outcomes capturing social exclusion or inclusion in mid adulthood. The study draws on data collected for two British birth cohorts, comparing the experiences of over 20,000 individuals born 12 years apart in 1958 and 1970 respectively. Many young people show the capacity to meet and overcome challenges and use them for growth or maintenance of adaptive functioning. There is great heterogeneity in responses to adversity, which correspond to the contingencies of social environments experienced by young people, and the risks encountered therein. Without enduring protective structures and opportunities even the most resilient individuals will not be able to maintain their adjustment. This leads to the conclusion that the crux in understanding how individuals navigate developmental transitions and challenges lies with the availability of relevant personal and structural resources.

Markku Jokisaari's chapter examines the role of social capital in the transition to working life in Finland. For example, how different network mechanisms, i.e. for young people, who you have access to and how you gain access to them, might be related to successful transition from school to work. In addition, based on a longitudinal study, he presents results which are in line with social capital theory. For example, the results showed that recent graduates' social ties and resources were related to getting a job and salary level after graduation.

In his chapter Tom Schuller offers reflections of a general kind on issues surrounding the status and utility of social capital as a research and policy concept. His focus is specifically on the gender-social capital link as a key dimension of young people's transitions; and his chapter offers some comments on young people's engagement in civic institutions. His approach tends to focus on the links between social capital and education or human capital. He distinguishes between instrumental and intrinsic forms of social capital, and reflects on how these might apply to young people's transitions into adulthood.

Gender differences in educational achievement have been one of the most remarkable trends in education over the last decade, and one which is certainly already having a major effect on youth transitions.

John Bynner's chapter focuses on the arenas where different roles of young people are demanded—for example in the leisure context. Young people are connected with the new media and communications technology to which they have increasing access; the links extend globally and to the virtual world as well. With the growth of internet-based systems for the creation of communities and communications that are entirely self-determined, bridging, takes on new forms. For example social capital resides in a system that offers new democratic forms with great liberating potential, but also the possibility of new forms of coercion.

The papers making up the content of the book offer an exceptionally rich array of evidence to illuminate its major themes. They also highlight the challenges to conventional thinking and the methodological issues that future research and theory in the field of social capital needs to address.

What have we learned about young people's social capital

The strongest message is that young people's networks and trust-based relationships are not only a manifestation of growing up as a 'sub-cultural response' to the oppressive structures and instruments of coercion of the adult world, but a vital means of demonstrating how society can shape up to the new. In seeking to weaken, if not to sever, the strong ties to family that are the hallmark of childhood, adolescents find their own modes and strategies for relating to each other and the wider world, which in many respects matches modern realities better than those of adults. Their social capital is thus not only of immediate value in supplying a kind of security in the teenage world but through use of new technology—mobile phones and the internet—offers models that may be of vital importance to effective adult functioning now and especially in the future.

Thus young people's social capital is not just a product of the social capital of their parents—the means of hoisting them up the ladder of achievement, as the founding fathers of the subject tended to believe, but as a vital means of renewal and development for society as whole. This is not to deny the strong ties of the family which will continue to play a part in the choices and developmental opportunities with which young people have to engage. Family, by mixing the generations, will continue to supply the most effective means of achieving intergenerational solidarity, of especial value at times of societal crisis and stress. Teachers will also continue to offer major inspirational models both in emotional and identity terms as well as didactically in supporting identity achievement.

It is too easy to see the younger generation as oppressed by the adult world. Better rather to see them within the family (at least) as offering the potential for continual dialogue about what the future should be. In the world of work, which is changing at an ever increasing rate, young people should not be seen as simply some kind of problem but as one of the major means of re-invigoration—a resource through which the strong and weak ties of community and workplace can be renewed.

Although the theoretical challenges may be surmountable at least in the short term, the methodological challenges raise issues that will continue to bedevil social science. The pace of social change suggests that few, if any, of the traditional stabilities in the family or the community or the workplace can be taken for granted. We need repeated cohort studies on a massive scale to monitor the new ways the transition to adulthood is being differentially shaped, and re-shaped, across gender, socio-economic status, ethnicity and community (regional, urban and rural) with the passage of global time.

At the same time we need to understand the configurations of events and contexts in young people's lives that prompt particular decisions about the pathways to pursue. Ethnographic studies of closely knit groups of young people will continue to supply the essential means of access to the thought processes, values and bonding mechanisms of the coming generation. They can also help us to enter the much more difficult territory of the extended networks and weak ties on which effective functioning in the modern work place is built. Surveys, though valuable for mapping the broad picture of changing transitions, can never capture all the nuances of individual—context interaction through which change processes are expressed. Better perhaps to draw on the modern methodology of web-based data collection and analysis to capture a range of real and virtual scenarios through which the different options available to youth of the future might be understood.

Over all we think the book takes a valuable step towards understanding the largely uncharted territory of young people's social capital. By doing so it opens the doors to the new programmes of research and action that will be central to supporting the achievement of identity and effective functioning in the late modern world.

Part 2   **Youth and capital**

Chapter 2

Inventing adulthoods: Making the most of what you have

Janet Holland

Introduction

Each generation tends to think that they are living through changing times, but some social theorists consider that this is a period of particular, even spectacular change, with the supports for traditional ways of organising people's lives eroding and falling away. The individual is left to take responsibility for her/his own life. And young people do seem to accept that, they expect to do well by their own efforts. Discourses of social improvement and social mobility are particularly strong in both social policy, and the informal cultures of young people in the U.K. This is despite the fact that opportunities for social mobility for young people from disadvantaged backgrounds are fewer today than twenty years ago, and expansion in further and higher education has benefited the 'not-so-bright' middle-class rather than academically able working-class young people (Schoon et al., 2001, Blanden et al., 2005). So there is a mismatch between the relatively optimistic views of young people, and the restrictions they actually may face due to their social and economic background. Furlong and Cartmel (1997) have pointed to an 'epistemological fallacy' where individuals make sense of social inequalities in terms of personal failings, and Evans (2002) has illustrated a particularly British orientation towards opportunity and success, which is characterised by a very individualised attribution of failure. This chapter is about transitions and intergenerational transmission in the context of an accidental qualitative longitudinal study in which the aim was to examine the lives and experiences of 'ordinary' young people, not the spectacular or problematic as has often been in the case in studies of youth. I will describe the study and outline our longitudinal, biographical, holistic approach. I will then briefly describe changing youth transitions and discuss the theoretical background of the study, which itself has changed and developed over time, most recently focusing on the concept of social capital. I will then draw on the data in the light of this theoretical stance, to discuss advantage and disadvantage in relation to family background in the biographical pathways the young people have followed.

Inventing Adulthoods: A biographical approach to youth transitions

The Inventing Adulthoods qualitative longitudinal research project funded by the ESRC in the U.K.[1] has followed a sample of young people drawn from five sites in England and Northern Ireland (NI) since 1996, when they were aged 11-18 (Holland et al., 2000; McGrellis et al., 2001). The sites were chosen to capture socio-economic differences and other diversities, and are: a leafy commuter town (largely middle class and white[2]); an inner city site (working class and ethnically diverse); a disadvantaged estate in the north of England (working class and white); an isolated rural area (mixed social class—professionals, rural labourers, farmers) and a city in Northern Ireland (communities mixed with respect to social class and religion) (Thomson and Holland, 2002). Location and community and their effects on young people's lives were very important for us, as increasingly has been temporality.

The methods employed include questionnaires (1800), focus groups (60) and individual and repeat biographical interviews (493), memory books and lifelines (Thomson and Holland, 2003; Thomson and Holland, 2005). Recently we have focused on families, communities and social capital in the context of a large programme of research with the Families and Social Capital ESRC Research Group at London South Bank University (Edwards et al., 2003; Holland, 2007; Holland et al., 2007). A further project, *Making the Long View*, is producing a showcase archive from the longitudinal study, for secondary analysis of the dataset[3].

Our concern throughout has been to investigate: agency and the 'reflexive project of self' (Giddens, 1991); values and the construction of adult identity;

1   Three studies have become one over 10 years: (Inventing Adulthoods): Youth Values: A study of identity, diversity and social change, ESRC funded (L129251020), Inventing Adulthoods: Young people's strategies for transition, ESRC (L134251008); Youth Transitions, part of the *Families and Social Capital ESRC Research Group* at London South Bank University (www.lsbu.ac.uk/families). The core research team from whose work this chapter is drawn are Sheila Henderson, Janet Holland, Sheena McGrellis, Sue Sharpe and Rachel Thomson.

2   The dense information provided by our long-term contact with the young people gave multiple sources of assessing class location, and the picture has become complex. Based on this knowledge we attached a social class location to each, using the categories: embedded working class (ewc), respectable wc (rwc), lower, middle and upper middle class (lmc, mc, umc). For brevity here we use wc and mc, but stress the variability in the sample, including changing circumstances of work, economic situation and family form.

3   (www.lsbu.ac.uk/inventingadulthoods).This work will continue as part of a large-scale qualitative longitudinal study, *Changing lives and Times: Relationships and Identities through the life course (Timescapes)* to be undertaken by a Consortium from five universities (Leeds, London South Bank, Cardiff, Edinburgh and The Open University) starting in February 2007 for five years.

and how the social and material environment acts to shape the values and identities that young people adopt.

Table 1: The sample over time

Inventing Adulthoods	Total sample	Age	M	F	Eth[4]	Wc	Mc
Youth Values 1996-1999	Interview 1 54	11 -17	25	32	4	44	13
Inventing Adulthoods 1999-2001	Interview 2 121	14 -23	58	63	19	85	36
	Interview 3 98	14-24	40	58	12	66	32
	Interview. 4 83	15-25	38	45	11	53	30
Youth Transitions 2002-2006	Interview 5 70	17-26	28	42	9	43	27
	Interview 6 64	19-28	26	38	9	39	25

Wc = working class Mc = middle class

The value in the approach adopted in the study lies in it being longitudinal, biographical and holistic. *Longitudinal* in that we walk alongside these young people through the changes and vicissitudes in their lives. Young people are faced with the task of 'inventing adulthood' because material and social conditions have shifted significantly in the course of a generation. *Biographical*, in that we listen to their narratives of self and lives, narratives that develop and change over time in the construction of self and identity. *Holistic* in that we do not fragment these young lives into categories, education, work, health, crime, drugs, but are interested in all aspects of their lives and how they interact in a dynamic process. We have tried to gain insight into the relationship between the unique life (biography), the context within which it is lived (structural dimensions), and the processes of which it is part (for example history, social mobility, intergenerational transfers) (Henderson et al., 2007; MacDonald et al., 2005; Coles, 1995, 2000; Du Bois-Reymond and Lopez Blasco, 2003).

4 The minority ethnic groups included African-Caribbean, Vietnamese, Mixed Race, Black British, African, Mauritian and Southern European. We increased the sample size in the second study to 16% of the total, and it has hovered between 12% and 14% since 2000.

Changing transitions

Traditional transitions in the U.K. followed social class lines, from school to manual or work low in the occupational hierarchy for the majority and for a minority an extended period of education, training and then non-manual work in the higher reaches of the hierarchy. The literature on youth transitions indicates that the social class and educational background of their parents has always been and remains the major consistent element affecting the education, work and life chances of young people (Machin and Blanden, 2004; Metcalf, 1997). This clear intergenerational pattern continues today with some variations in relation to some minority ethnic groups (Modood and Acland, 1998; Platt, 2005; Platt and Thompson, 2007). But social and economic change has characterised the last three decades—recession, technological change, a major restructuring of the U.K. economy, with a move from manufacturing to service industries, and from full- to part-time work, including an influx of women into the restructured labour market. In this period the youth labour market collapsed and the destination for traditional transitions particularly for working class young men, became increasingly out of reach (Morris, 1994; Johnston et al.; 2000, MacDonald and Marsh, 2005).

There is a general consensus in youth studies and Europe wide that youth transitions have become fragmented and stretched, although distinctions remain between north and south Europe. Jones (2005), drawing on a range of work in the U.K. and elsewhere together, has characterised these changes as making young people's transitions to adulthood:

- more extended: with economic independence deferred
- more complex: there is no longer a conventional timetable, dependence and independence may combine and critical moments make a difference
- more 'risky': involving backtracking, risk taking and parent/child conflict
- more individualised: young people have more choice but are not equally able to capitalise on it
- more polarised: with inequalities more sharply defined in relation to more elite 'slow track' transitions and more risky 'fast track' (see too Goodwin and O'Connor, 2005).

Du-Bois Reymond and Lopez Blasco (2003) talk of 'yo-yo transitions'. They suggest that there is a mismatch between the policies developed to help disadvantaged and excluded young people across European countries and the (post)modernised transitions that they now experience. And we see these types of fragmented transitions amongst the young people in our study, as well as some more traditional routes.

Theoretical background for the study

Theories of post or late modernity and critiques of these approaches have influenced our study and data, as well as the concept of social capital. We also developed concepts in interaction with our data, including that of critical moments that have consequences in young people's trajectories (Thomson et al., 2002), and a biographical model. This model identifies the fields of activities—education, work, the domestic arena and leisure—in which young people build their identities and adulthoods through the exercise and recognition of competence, and consequent investment in the field (Thomson et al., 2004). We have considered Giddens'detraditionalisation', where traditional institutional supports for belonging and identity are eroded and people are free to engage in a reflexive project of self, responsible for constructing their own identity. This has similarities with Beck's 'individualisation'. Here a transformation of the relationship of the individual to society leads to a process of moving from 'normal biographies', with pre-existing roles and life plans, to 'choice biographies' where we are responsible for who and what we become. Beck recognises the enduring nature of inequality, but explains it at the individual rather than the group or class level. He also recognises the formation of new inequalities in new times:

> The reflexive conduct of life, the planning of one's own biography and social relations, gives rise to a new inequality, the *inequality* of dealing with *insecurity and reflexivity.* (Beck, 1992, 98; original emphasis)

Drawn into youth studies, these approaches emphasise intergenerational change, where the predictable patterns of the past, powerfully shaped by gender and social class are eroded. But there are critiques of this position within the field. Nilsen and Brannen (2002) for example argue that the distinction between normal and choice biography is too simplistic and bring structural factors, in particular social class back into the frame. They draw attention to the continuing significance of structural inequalities, gender, social class, ethnicity, which provide the parameters within which individual choices are made.

Walkerdine and her colleagues have another more psychosocial take on the continuing importance of social class, suggesting that the choice biography should also be understood in terms of self regulation, where 'the most seductive aspect of self invention of all lies in the possibility of the working class remaking itself as middle class' (2001, 121). From their longitudinal study of the educational trajectories of middle- and working-class young women over 20 years, Walkerdine and her colleagues conclude that:

> The production of subjects from all classes and the way in which they live their subjectification centrally involves a constant invitation to consume, to invent, to choose, and yet even in the midst of their choice and their consumption class is performed, written all over their every choice. ... And ... the living out of these marks of difference is filled with desire, longing, anxiety, pain, defence. Class is at once profoundly social and profoundly emotional and lived in its specificity in particular cultural and geographical locations.
>   (Walkerdine et al., 2001, 53; see too Reay 2005)

A general theme in critiques of theories of late modernity is that whilst there have been fundamental social changes in the recent past, these have led to the reconfiguring and reworking of class, gender and ethnicity and related inequalities, rather than their erosion or eradication. Although we returned to the ideas of Giddens and Beck, working with and against them to make sense of changes over time and differences between young people's lives, we also drew on increasing critical scholarship in relation to these theories in the area of gender studies (Adkins, 2002; Walkerdine et al., 2001; McLeod and Yates, 2006) social class (Skeggs 1997, 2004; Reay et al., 2005; Reay and Lucey 2000; Gillies, 2005) 'race' and ethnicity (Alexander, 2000; Nayak 2003, 2006) as well as a growing body of debate within the field of youth studies as to the value of late modern theory (Furlong and Cartmel, 1997; Cohen and Ainley, 2000).

Throughout the study we have used Bourdieu's typology of capitals, economic, cultural, social and symbolic as an analytic frame to understand the access to resources that characterised the young peoples lives and trajectories. For Bourdieu, as well as being part of a constellation of capitals all of which are translatable into the core economic capital, social capital does not arise automatically in networks of association as in other conceptualisations of the idea, but must be worked for on an ongoing basis. It is

> the product of investment strategies, individual or collective, consciously or unconsciously aimed at establishing or reproducing

social relationships that are directly useable in the short or long term.
(Bourdieu, 1986, 251).

It is also crucially about the production and reproduction of power and inequality. More mainstream versions of the concept stress social cohesion, and the collective goods of reciprocity, trust and co-operation, features of social organisation, such as networks, norms and trust, that facilitate action and co-operation for mutual benefit (Putnam, 1993, 35).

Putnam has elaborated the concept to include bonding and bridging social capital. Inward looking 'bonding' social capital focuses on relationships and networks of trust and reciprocity that reinforce ties within groups—families and communities. Outward looking 'bridging' social capital focuses on connections outwards, across different heterogeneous groups. From this perspective, bonding social capital is negative and associated with social exclusion, and bridging social capital is positive and links with social inclusion. In the Families Group in general, in nine or ten projects we have critiqued and elaborated on these mainstream concepts, often in connection with the lives and experiences of children and young people (Holland et al., 2007).

Recently there has been a move to bring social capital and late modern perspectives together to capture empirically and describe everyday practices of 'sociality', how people do 'people work' or social affinities, shaped as has been suggested they are, by situated class cultures (Bauman, 2000; Franklin and Thomson, 2005). So Valerie Hey (2005) writes about the 'offensive' sociality of the new middle class (involving self conscious networking) and the 'defensive' sociality of the disadvantaged in which practices of sociality first secure survival, and can then reinforce exclusion. This shift in distinction echoes that between bridging and bonding social capital, but the shift in language reflects a political shift from understanding inequality as located in individuals and communities towards an understanding of how inequalities are made and remade.

Our longitudinal, holistic, biographical method has enabled us to gain insight into how such resources are accessed in practice, shedding light on how their recognition and exploitation are entwined with personal, family, community and local factors, and subject to individual, social and policy contingencies.

Disadvantage and opportunity

The disadvantaged estate in the north of England in our study was in the top ten per cent most deprived local authorities in the U.K., and the inner city area was in the top twenty (Index of Deprivation, 2001 Census, U.K.). They stand in great contrast with the leafy suburb, which was in the bottom five per cent of the Deprivation Index. So we had in the sample some of the most and least disadvantaged locations and communities in the U.K., and we found intergenerational transmission of inequalities. The generations could in fact succeed one another rather rapidly, since the most available feminine identity, which would confer an understandable adulthood in the disadvantaged estate for example was that of mother, through relatively early sexual activity. Many of the mothers had been teenaged parents, and so were their daughters. The community is inward looking; people are often reluctant to leave, even to socialise, and the location is geographically isolated. Family is central to the local culture and reconstituted families were the norm; families were entangled, to the extent for example that a father of one of our participants was living with and then married the mother of another. Mothers were at the core, children revolved around them, and male partners might come and go. Poverty, illness and bereavement, unemployment, drugs, crime, gangs and violence were endemic on the estate, and integral to the young people's lives. The route to adult *masculinity* was through a hard man stance. What singled out some of the young people in our sample from this area, particularly young women, was their rejection of the estate, and realisation that to get on they had to get out, where others felt that it was impossible to escape from the bubble or seemed to have no desire to do so. While most developed the bonding social capital that bound them to family and community and would help them get by and cope, others sought bridging social capital, and a route out through education.

Our study induced reflection in the participants, we would return periodically and reflect with them on their lives since we last saw them. Some people dropped out of the study at one round of interviews, and back in later. We sometimes felt that this might be because things were going badly at certain points. This was particularly so on the northern estate where it was hard for us to keep everyone on board. But we would hear stories, or snippets about some of our missing participants as we spoke to others. Several of our young men disappeared into the miasma of the estate and we lost track. Two who remained with us have disabilities, which tied them to family and community even further, and made employment a problem. One of them did gain independence through state provision of a home and facilities, and at the time of writing was living with a girlfriend and her baby. Two of the young women took the route of early sexual activity and became mothers, while another rejected children until she was older, and was training to be a beauty therapist, (a position obtained through her sister) but saw herself as totally committed to her own mother and the community:

> *Int*: And is there—I mean, there must be a reason why you think it's more important to stay in (local community).
> *Sandra*: That's where I was brought up. Yeah, this is me.
> *Int*: This is where you belong?
> *Sandra*: Yeah—my home, around here
> *Int*: You would never even contemplate leaving it?
> *Sandra*: If me Mum weren't here.

Over the years we have visited, the estate itself was an endless target for state intervention in relation to social exclusion, and efforts to boost access to education for the excluded—housing regeneration schemes, education maintenance grants to encourage young people to remain in education beyond the statutory leaving age, mentoring whilst at school, taster visits to nearby universities. When we first arrived, the school our participants attended was considered to be one of the worst in the country, despite the care, commitment and hard work of the teachers. Although the young people were bright, voluble and entertaining, given their circumstances we could hardly imagine any going to university, and many of *them* imagined a future bounded by family and community. But time was to prove us wrong, at the last count four young women had managed to get to university. They did not have an easy route, it was often beset with setbacks, and changes in direction, since as Maisie pointed out:

> But some people—not everyone—but you have to really struggle. And it's a shame because it's like they make it so hard for you to go. Really hard, and I just really think—but I don't think normal people are supposed to go to university, the way they work it out.   (Maisie, 20, 2003)

Although family support and provision of material resources enabled three of the young women to attempt the educational route to social mobility, Maisie herself received none. She was in fact an emotional, physical (in terms of domestic labour) and financial support for her separated and rather ill mother, and her wayward siblings. Responsibility for and duty towards them wove through her later interviews. She was in employment in the low paid service sector throughout her school and university career to support herself and family, and her interrelated work and educational trajectory reflects the place of the working class in the new economy. It is argued that the new economy is becoming increasingly more virtual, reflexive, flexible and networked, and characterised by data, knowledge and service intensity (Adkins, 2005a; Castells, 1996; Lury, 2003; Thrift, 1998) through a process of economic postmodernisation (Hardt, 1999). Maisie's experience also reflects the changing nature of work, the blurred and shifting boundaries between different forms of work—public and private, paid and unpaid, and the embeddedness of work in other social relations (Pettinger et al., 2005).

Maisie recognises the value of social capital built in networks of association, and has used her multiple jobs to generate such networks:

> *Int*: Well do you think you've got more networks than people you know?
> *Maisie*: I think it's just because I've got so many jobs, and I've had so many jobs, you know. ... Because I've got friends at (sports club where she works part-time), I've got friends at my new job, I've got friends that I know from the (hotel where she worked), I've got friends from College, from school, from uni –

Despite her felt ties to the community, she has a driving need to leave:

> when I'm the one that's got a nice job with like loads of money and a nice car and don't live round here—I'll be the happy one won't I, not them little scallies on the dole? (laughs) ... And like I'm not saying that it's that bad around here but, I don't know if you understand what I mean, it's just like I just don't want that, I just really don't want that. And it's just not anything that I'd ever want.   (Maisie 20, 2003)

Two of the other young women had contrasting pathways. Lauren's route was riddled with ambivalence, with the pull of community and a lack of motivation to resist it on her part playing a strong part. Her interviewer commented: 'A sense of instability and chaos, linked to rapidity of change underpinned all Lauren's interviews' (Researcher Notes). Like many from her background, she struggled to get onto and maintain an educational route, and at a certain point her mother had explicitly drawn her back into the community and away from the education that would lead to a career, suggesting she was 'not a paperwork person'. We were unable to interview Lauren between 2001 and 2004, but caught up with her in 2004 and things had changed again, she had reinvested in education and was in the second year of a Nursing Diploma at university. The strategy that Lauren has pursued also suggests that she is working within the confines of the possible within her locality.

In contrast, over the years Maureen showed an increasingly steely determination in pursuing education and a profession, and a realisation that she needed to get out of a disadvantaged community in order to get on, with all the costs that entailed. With the support and encouragement of her separated parents (giving her the advantage she felt of two households since both were re-partnered) she resisted ties in the community, including deferring active heterosexuality and womanhood until they held less of a threat to her desired future. After a gap, we caught up with Maureen again in 2004 and she was in the second year of a law degree. Her interviewer commented: 'She seem to be making her own way now, supported by the 'friends for life' that she has made at university' (Researcher Notes 2004).

The policy focus on building social capital as a route to community and social cohesion, stands in sharp contrast to a policy discourse of social mobility and individual success in which educational achievement is central, particularly in the lives of young people. Each of the young women here revealed a different balance between individual and wider resources, and access to support and social capital, demonstrating that for young people from economically disadvantaged backgrounds, individual resources of ability and ambition do not easily translate into success. The 'costs' of social mobility, and community oriented values, investments and identities (bonding social capital) may militate against social and geographical mobility.

Advantage and opportunity

Amongst the more middle class young people in the study we can still find 'traditional', slower, more elite transitions for both young men and women. These young people have greater access to material and economic resources, and considerable social capital through their parents', and during the course of the study, their own networks. We can see some signs of the instrumental use of social capital, and perhaps the offensive sociality that Val Hey refers to. Keith, of mixed class background from the rural site, with useful cultural and social capital from his mother, and a skilled deployer of social capital himself over the years, was surprised at university to find people much more middle class than he. He observed that they did not bother much with university work, nor indeed other work, and expected to slip into Daddy's business after university. In his account, they spent much of their time aggressively creating networks that would be of use for them in the future. He himself, however, thought that degrees were 'two a penny' but did value the contacts and social capital he had gained at university, which would enhance his career prospects in his chosen field of the creative arts.

From their children's accounts, many of the middle class parents in the study put considerable emphasis on a successful progress through education for their offspring, in order to provide them with the best life chances, and provided considerable support of all kinds to facilitate this. Many of the middle class young people moved relatively smoothly along this path. Our longitudinal, biographical approach enabled us to explore cases when the path was not so smooth, due to unexpected eventualities, the uncertainties of new times. There might be family break-up, depression on the young person's part, perhaps as a result of the pressure of their own and their parents' expectations, or other critical moments in their paths. Robin from the rural area narrowly escaped expulsion from school for drug use thanks to his parents' frantic efforts to mobilise their contacts. Samuel in the leafy suburb dropped out of university because he had got everything that he wanted from it, useful contacts and networks for his planned career in the entertainment business, for which he saw a degree as unnecessary 'It's about who you know not what you've done.' He indicates an instrumental approach in distinguishing between his true and his networking friends, and when asked who he would go to for career suggestions and ideas says:

> *Samuel*: Friends again—I'd say more my networking friends than my close friends, because all my networking are usually friends for reasons. And there are a lot of people for a certain reason—not because I don't—not because I'm using them—but just because it helps to have friends in—not so much high places, just in places.

Edward and Nat both from the leafy suburb, faltered in their university career due to depression and in Nat's case family breakdown, but did finish their degrees.

Bonding and bridging social capital

The well networked in our sample have tended to be middle class young people, albeit in a range of circumstances, and with both themselves and their families experiencing some of the uncertainties of new times. They tended to be flexible and their networks span different age groups and communities—local, family, educational, work, leisure—and a range of activities, from bell-ringing to volunteering, bridging social capital. They are often well resourced by their family.

It seems also that it is the predominantly working class sites that generate bonding, and possibly negative social capital. But young people in such settings can also develop networks of support and concomitant social capital that enable their lives in the community as has also been pointed out by others (Raffo and Reeves, 2000; Leonard, 2004). MacDonald and colleagues (2005) in a longitudinal study of a disadvantaged and excluded community in the U.K., agree that supportive local networks do enable young people to cope with poverty, inequality and exclusion. But they argue that these local networks become part of the process in which poverty and class inequalities are reproduced:

> Paradoxically, while local networks helped in coping with the problems of growing up in poor neighbourhoods and generated a sense of inclusion, the sort of social capital embedded in them served simultaneously to close down opportunities and to limit the possibilities of escaping the conditions of social exclusion. (MacDonald et al., 2005, 873)

In an example from our data, sectarian families and communities in Northern Ireland could exert a strong hold on the young people. A number of young men in the study from both republican and loyalist working class backgrounds were totally embedded in those sectarian cultures, and all their social capital came from those associations and networks. They discussed their involvement in violence and how their reputations and family background 'trapped' them in their communities, and in situations that depended on their use of violence, as well as exposing them to its consequences (McGrellis, 2005). On the other hand, in Northern Ireland bonding within communities as a result of community and political activism could generate networks that made links out of the community, or could initiate broader changes within that could create progress for the whole community.

We also found forms of networking and association for the working-class young people, through their families and communities, that can support them more generally in their activities in education, as entrepreneurs, and in terms of work and travel opportunities, helping them to bridge out into the broader community. These often have a diasporic element, with contacts amongst those in our sample in the U.S.A., Caribbean, Australia and elsewhere. Similarly, Tracey Reynolds (Reynolds this volume; Holland et al., 2007) argues from her study of social capital and Caribbean young people in England, that they drew on ethnic-specific resources and experiences of bonding within family networks and communities to bridge out and gain access to resources and friendship networks outside their group during transitions to further/higher education and work. The security of a basis in family and community and concomitant ethnic identity, necessitated by the prejudice and exclusion experienced by Caribbeans in the U.K., provided a platform for bridging into the wider society. Along with colleagues in FSC Group and others, we would argue that the move from bonding to bridging social capital is more complex than envisaged by Putnam. Exploring transitions in young people's lives highlights how many draw upon their social networks as resources to negotiate these passages. For some bonding social capital provides a solid base from which to bridge out to new networks, whilst for others bonding social capital is more constraining.

Young people's views on intergenerational continuities and social mobility

In the fourth round of interviews in 2002/3 when they were aged 18-24, we asked the young people about change over the generations, and expectations of social mobility and 91% (64/70) responded. They did see considerable change between their parents' generation and their own, largely in relation to increased opportunities, particularly for education, although this tendency was greater amongst the working class young people. Of those at university, nine were working class, eight of whom were women. Most of these were the first in their family to go to university, so it could be said that this group has benefited from the expansion of higher education in the latter part of the 20th century in the U.K., and the improvement in access for women.

When asked if they thought they would do better than their parents, most of them thought they would, many linking it to education and opportunity. Matching their progress to university, almost all of the working class young women from whatever site thought they would do better than their parents, who were often separated, with mothers largely in low paid work. A number of these had considerable support from parents, particularly mothers, in their ambitions. Shannon (wc, NI) thinks 'I probably will do very well', Cynthia (wc, NI) is 'Aiming high' as is Jade (wc, inner city) 'I'm aiming really high, I think. Even if I don't reach exactly where I wanna be, I'll still be up there somewhere'.

The working class young people recognised the burdens that their parents, particularly mothers had laboured under, getting married and having children too young, lack of opportunity, poor and broken relationships with the father, poverty, ill health. Many, both male and female, admired what their parents had been able to achieve under difficult circumstances:

> I can never be better than my parents because OK, my mum left, and my dad raised four kids ... that's better than a degree, raise four kids alone see, on social benefits you know, ...keep them all happy. From him not having money he can look back on what he achieved. ... I don't think I'll be able to do better. (Nam, 20, 2003)

Parents had provided the motivation for some in their ambitions for social mobility. Corine (wc, NI) does not like to make the comparison with her parents, but thinks they wanted to do better themselves, and this spurs her on:

> ... It's given me that extra kind of push maybe to do better for myself because they wanted to do better and they just, you know what I mean, the opportunities weren't there when they were growing up. There's so many opportunities here now for us ... there's so much out there. (Corine, 21, 2003)

Shirleen (wc, inner city) does it for her mother:

> I just hope I can do better really. Cos I know that is what my mum wants for me, ultimately that's why she helps me so much.

Over the years of interviewing, it became clear that Shirleen's cultural and social capital is drawn from her strong identity as a black woman in an extended intergenerational family of strong black women. She has considerable support from her family, particularly financially from her mother, all of which is critical and motivates and enables her to pursue her ambition to become a barrister. It is a family (and generational) affair (Thomson, 2004). In an earlier interview she had commented:

> I try and work hard because like I wanna be something that, cause like when people in my family, they just, they don't get to be that prestigious, have lots of money, not rich or anything, so I just wanna kind of turn it around. … I really do wanna get somewhere, I really do cause like some people in my family they just end up in jobs they don't like.

Many of the middle class young people also thought they would do better than their parents, this young man assertively so:

> A lot better than my own parents, a lot better. In the sense of money … I wanna do better in business, definitely a lot more money and make better decisions about my money, and not borrow money …I think I will be a better parent than my parents, definitely. Just 'cos we've grown up in different times. (Richard, 20, 2002)

There was a tendency for the middle class young men to want to do better and young women to be happy to be the same as their parents. Naz wants to move up and pass on wealth and position to his children, as his parents did to him, and Heather would be happy to be the same:

> Hopefully I'll do better anyway, hopefully I want to progress … Move up a step aye move up a few steps and hand to my kids and stuff.
> (Naz, 21, 2002)

> I think they're both doing quite well at their job and everything, yeah. They travelled a lot like when they were married, before they had us, so yeah, I think I wouldn't mind sort of following in their footsteps.
> (Heather, 21, 2003)

Four young women (two wc, two mc) valued highly the long, happy and successful relationships that their parents had had, Maeve (mc) encapsulates her hopes and expectations in relation to her parents' lives:

I think they've done pretty well really. I suppose in different aspects if I found someone, a person to spend the rest of my life with, I'd be quite happy. I'd be over the moon, because they're so happy with each other, if I followed them in that way I'd be grateful. But career wise I suppose they're very stressed out with their jobs, but I suppose I will be too.

(Maeve, 19, 2002)

Four other young people mentioned the risk and insecurity of new times Monique (wc, inner city) thinks anything might happen and you cannot predict the future, giving some negative examples: 'I might break my legs tomorrow, I might end up with brain damage'. George (wc rural area) thinks that the wider choice available nowadays makes decisions more difficult 'but at least you've got more choice in the first place'. Neville (mc, NI) wants to be like his father, but considers that jobs for life no longer exist: 'getting good jobs, you know, maybe not have a job for 20 years like he has, cause I think those days now just passed at the minute, all round'. And Francis similarly compares himself with his father in that respect:

It's certainly less certain, but I'm more qualified I suppose, so hopefully I should be—I'd have more chance of getting the fewer jobs that are out there. But um I don't know. Yes it's certainly a bit more nerve racking for me I think. (Francis, 21, leafy suburb)

Conclusion

The main themes emerging from this analysis are that times have and are changing, and with them young people's transitions into adulthood, which have become extended and potentially fragmented. These transitions are still heavily influenced by class, gender, ethnicity and other inequalities, which may be being reconstituted in new ways. Processes of detraditionalisation, individualisation and disembedding, do not appear to have been so thoroughgoing as has been argued by late modern theorists, and family and family relationships remain critical to the well-being and transitions of young people. Access to social capital is an important resource for young people, with bonding social capital more prevalent amongst the working class and bridging amongst the middle class in general. The policy pressure to create social capital in excluded communities to enhance social and other mobilities may contain the seeds of its own destruction in obliging the individual aspirant for social mobility to break with the support and inclusiveness of the community in order to pursue that path. Forms of bonding social capital can reinforce exclusion, but other forms can provide a stable identity and support and enable disadvantaged young people to bridge out of their communities to more heterogeneous groups.

Chapter 3

Social and cultural capital meets youth research: A critical approach

Tarja Tolonen

Introduction

In this article I will discuss the relationship of youth research to concepts of social and cultural capital. Firstly, I will critically examine the much-used concept of social capital, which, I suggest, not only functions as a concept but as a strong metaphor for interpreting young people's lives (cf. Field, 2003, 11-40).

Secondly, I turn to Pierre Bourdieu's theory of different forms of capital and examine its strengths and weaknesses while applying it to youth research. Bourdieu's analysis consists of several types of capital, which are closely interconnected. I suggest that their interconnectedness makes the theory potentially useful, since the social and cultural capital which young people have access to is surrounded by (if not converted into) certain material conditions—economic capital. According to Bourdieu, economic capital refers to wealth and financial assets, while cultural capital consists of embodied, body/mind dispositions and goods as well as education. Social capital refers to resources based on connections and group membership; symbolic capital is the form that the different types of capital take, once they are perceived and recognised as legitimate (Skeggs, 1997, 8; Bourdieu, 1997/1986).

The article attempts to explore theoretical arguments concerning social and cultural capital in studies on young people. I will, however, refer to my own empirical analysis on social and cultural capital from the research project *Young people's social and local transitions,*[1] to illustrate problems related to the concept of capital. My data consists of 61 interviews with young people (from 17 to 23 years of age) in four different areas in Finland. Some of the interviewees[2] attended local schools, others I reached through social services. I have attempted to observe the

---

1 This research 'Social and Spacial Transitions in Young People's Life course' has been funded by the Youth Research Network, University of Helsinki and Academy of Finland.
2 Most of the young people selected for this study were currently studying. A total of 26 out of 61, i.e. over one third of the interviewees were studying in polytechnics or vocational schools, and they were primarily from working-class or middle-class families with some vocational or professional education.

Ten interviewees had academic backgrounds, and most of them were either applying to or studying at university. Four young people with vocational education had a permanent job. In addition, 21 young people were studying or unemployed.

processes of how social capital is created and used by young people in certain cultural, social and economic locations (Tolonen, 2004; 2005a and 2005b).

Social capital as a metaphor

Theories of social capital and other forms of capitals have been much discussed and strongly criticised in recent years. Some authors explicitly wonder if there is any use for the concept at all (for example Adkins, 2005b; Siisiäinen, 2003; Smith and Kulynych, 2002). In the field of sociology, in social capital analysis three major strands are most prevalent at the moment: Coleman's, Putnam's and Bourdieu's analyses (see introductions in Field, 2003; in Finnish, Siisiäinen, 2003). All situate social capital more or less in social networks, but there are also plenty of differences among the three. In Coleman's analysis the formation of social capital takes place in a relationship, for example, between parents and children: in his analysis of the educational success of young people, he tracks down how social capital (in this case, parental support) helps to create human capital (or cultural capital). At the community level he uses the notion of 'closure', which means tight relationships (and norms) among parents and between parents and young people: for example if parents know each other, this may lead to joint norms and sanctions. As a result, social capital is generated in the community (cf. Coleman, 1988, 106; Field, 2003; Portes 1998; Seaman and Sweeting, 2004). According to Field, Putnam's analysis mainly addresses the formation of social capital at the community and State level (Putnam, 2000; Field, 2003 and Siisiäinen, 2003).

In Coleman's analysis social capital is also treated as something public rather than a private entity, and it is argued to be both abstract and functionalist (Field, 2003, 26). Putnam's analysis includes the same problems: he places social capital in social networks, and his analysis emphasises the decline of social capital in American 'civic' society, a view based mostly on a certain degree of concern and a romanticised image of society (Field, 2003, 38-9, also critical overviews in Portes 1998 and 2000; Smith and Kulynych 2002, 158). Much of this analysis is also claimed to be uncritical about time and history, and conservative in its views on gender and families. Single motherhood is cited as a deficit of social capital, as well as women's involvement in working life (Field, 2003; and Edwards et al., 2003). The most serious criticism, perhaps, is that the concept of social *capital* views social relations with economic terminology, and social networks are seen as exploitative, as if they were commodities to be traded. Social capital is seen as a very loose concept theoretically, and at times the analysis may lead to tautological statements (that the successful succeed, Portes, 2000, 5). It has led to numerous different endeavours and developments in studies of young people (Shaefer-McDaniel, 2004; Seaman and Sweeting, 2004; Raffo and Reeves, 2000).

Social capital may be a loose concept theoretically, but nevertheless it works as a strong metaphor for reading young people's lives. Lakoff and Johnson write: 'The essence of metaphor is understanding and experiencing one kind of thing in terms of another. [...] The concept is metaphorically structured, the activity is metaphorically structured, and, consequently, the language is metaphorically structured' (Lakoff and Johnson, 1980; Lefebre, 1991; Gordon et al., 1995). In addition, Smith and Kulynych (2002) have analysed the language of capital from Roman times up to the 20th century, and draw serious attention to the consequences that the use of the concept may have in social sciences and policy making:

> We believe that the use of the language of social capital is more than reflection of an already existing world. The term social capital also helps to create and sustain that world: the language itself has pernicious consequences [...] every time when the inequities of income and wealth of actually existing global capitalism are skyrocketing [...] has been explosion of [...] literature that views [...] social problems in terms of social capital. Such a view suggests that all parties can gain access to capital, just in different forms, and that appropriate 'investments' in social capital will compensate for gross inequities in financial capital.
> (Smith and Kulynych, 2002, 166-167).

With this example I want to highlight that metaphors thus bring a certain point of view into the picture, and simultaneously, also hide some other elements (or policies). In this article I suggest that describing young people's lives through the notion of social capital may lead to an emphasis on a certain kind of analyses while hiding other things, such as inequalities concerning young people's lives.

Youth research and social capital

While studying young people through the concept of social capital, several problems may appear, including youth research and studies of social capital seeming to come from different research traditions. Highlighting the differences of these approaches is revealing: researching young people makes the problems of theories of social capital visible in a certain way.

There are several kinds of developments in research on social capital and young people, some of which refer to Putnam and Coleman (Shaefer-McDaniel, 2004; Seaman and Sweeting, 2004; Raffo and Reeves 2000). Nicole Shaefer-McDaniel (2004) is developing a theory referring to Putnam's notions, where social networks and sociability, trust and reciprocity, as well as the sense of belonging are included in the analysis (Putnam, 2000). Seaman and Sweeting (2004) base their analysis on Coleman's view of social capital: they study the parental structure of families (criticising Coleman's conservative notions of family life), and they add agency and material conditions to the analysis. Carlo Raffo and Michelle Reeves are also trying to develop a new social capital theory for young people, which they call 'individualised system of social capital'. They highlight that young people make decisions individually but these decisions are made in social networks that draw from different material and symbolic resources available for young people. (Their theorisation actually comes quite close to Bourdieu's notions of social and cultural capital, in the end.) James Côté (2002) introduces the term identity capital, which highlights agency and personal resources over structures in late modern surroundings such as universities.

When young people have been included in the study of social capital, traditionally, especially in Coleman's analysis, the main focus of the research has been likely to position them as members of families, communities, school or the state, which is a very interesting analysis. The problem lies with the point of view that young people are treated as those receiving social capital rather than creating it themselves (cf. Coleman, 1988; and critics in Morrow, 1999a, 747 and Ellonen and Korkiamäki, 2006), even though some youth researchers have broken down this canon (McLeod, 2000; Stephenson, 2001; Bullen and Kenway, 2004, 2005). For example, Coleman's analysis of 'closure' is quite revealing. It means that if parents know each other, a closure exists in the networks, with the consequence that there is much social control in their children's lives. The phenomenon is mainly looked at from the perspective of the parents: I call this type the *upbringing* version of social capital (Coleman, 1988; Morrow, 1999a, 747).

Youth cultural research, on the contrary, is grounded on a strong analysis of teenage peer culture and groups. The kind of youth research that is commonly applied in the Nordic countries has its roots in the Chicago School, adapted through the Birmingham School (Hall and Jefferson, 1986/1976; in Finland cf.

Puuronen, 1997, 64-70). Youth research following this tradition has focused on young people's cultural meanings and their values, styles and behaviours (Willis, 1978; Griffin, 1993). Often young people and children were treated as agents and subjects of meaning production (cf. Jenks, 1996). It is assumed that young people are able to create their own worlds and cultures, styles of dressing, music, modes of success in schooling and attitudes towards the adult world. The subjects of this type of youth research were often groups of young people and their way of living, or for example some subcultural styles (Hebdige, 1979). In this type of research the families of young people were treated as the background of the study. However, in some of the analysis, youth subcultures were seen as a part of class cultures (which has also been criticised), (Willis, 1978).

This kind of terminology had a strong influence on youth research in the Nordic countries until the 1990s, before postmodern readings of youth cultures became the dominant discourse in Nordic youth research (cf. Tolonen, 2005b). Muggleton calls this recent period in Britain 'post-subcultural studies' which concentrates for example on club cultures and consumerism. These were considered through change, individualism, fluidity, neo-tribalism and hybridisation (Muggleton, 2005, 214-217; Blackman, 2005). Nevertheless, these studies continue to explore (and value) the meanings of different types of youth cultural phenomena and agency, and not, for example, how profitable these practices (and capital) are for young people in the future or how integrated young people are into their communities, with their social capital.

Cultural and social capital

Using Bourdieu's concept of cultural capital as a tool of analysis has been quite popular in European sociology of education for some years. This kind of analysis has paid attention to single students and their school success: these are explained by school culture and family background (Vanttaja, 2002; Metso, 2004; Tolonen, 2004, 2005b in Finland, Skeggs, 1997; Allatt and Bates, 1994 in Britain; McLeod, 2000 in Australia). In my own work I have been using Bourdieu's version of social and cultural capital, since I have been interested in the social stratification of Finnish society and how individual young people are positioned in this social order. I have been studying individual students, whom I see as possessing, creating or having attained more or less social and cultural capital (Tolonen, 2004, 2005a, 2005b). I find Bourdieu's theory the most applicable to young people's life histories because the analyses include different modes of capital instead of just one (see also Field, 2003; McLeod,

2000). Next, however, I will explore some problems concerning the concepts of social and cultural capital when applied to the lives of young people, and in this case, to my data.

Bourdieu states that social capital is accumulated through durable networks which are based on mutual acquaintances or recognition. In late modern societies this accumulation mainly takes place outside the home (for example at work, in neighbourhoods or in various kinds of social clubs). Social capital has also been closely connected to symbolic capital, which means in practice that those with more power have access and are able to use their social networks to their advantage more than those individuals with less power in society. (Bourdieu, 1997/1986, 51-52; Siisiäinen, 2003, 210; Portes, 1998)

Ilari, a 23-year-old studying in two faculties at university is perhaps good example of the accumulation of social capital. Ilari also studied subjects such as economics, which are likely to enable him to qualify for more advanced positions in society (with a high amount of cultural, but also economic and symbolic capital) later in life.

> *Ilari:* ... I just get appointed to these student activities [many at his present studies T.T.], [...] I really would not have time [...] But I've made many good acquaintances through these activities [...]not just the people who are studying the same year's course, but others as well [...] There are lots of people I know.

According to Bourdieu, cultural capital is acquired in childhood families through 'habitus'. Bourdieu's notion of *habitus* refers to an unconscious way of making decisions: it is embodied, learned in the childhood family (although the learning continues) and taken as self-evident (Bourdieu, 1990, 53-65). Those who have a high amount of cultural capital also can take it also as self-evident, like Ansa in my data, a young woman and a university student of 22 years of age, who had a clear understanding of her background:

> *TT:* [...] How have your educational decisions been influenced and who has influenced them? Can you say, I mean was it your friends or your family or?
> *Ansa:* Mmm, I suppose that I have had the kind of upbringing that leads to university study. [...] It is not that anyone ever told me what to do. I suppose it is just like the habit they all have—my parents and their

acquaintances—have graduated from university. It is like the only option that came to my mind.

Generally in the empirical data it is quite easy to find a great amount of the right kind of cultural and social capital in the lives of those young people who can be considered to be successful in some areas for the time being.

Bourdieu's theory has, however, been criticised in many ways. First, even his theory is rooted in economic capital (other forms of capital convert into economic capital) and second, he believes that all action is interest-oriented (Smith and Kulynych, 2002, 176-177). Third, agency is seen to be missing or underdeveloped in his theoretical thinking (McNay, 2004, 182). Fourth, his theory is inclined to hierarchies among people through the analysis of distinctions, and therefore his theory undermines 'horizontal' relationships (Siisiäinen, 2003, 214; Field 2003, 18-19). Fifth, his theory is seen as elitist. Only those young people who already have much social capital (who belong to the right networks) are able to benefit from it. However, social capital may not be only available to the privileged. As Field states: 'There was no place in his theory for the possibility that other, less privileged individuals and groups might also benefit in their social ties' (Field, 2003, 20; also Tolonen, 2004). Sixth, Bourdieu's theory is also seen to be biased: analysis on gender and ethnicity is either missing or insufficient (cf. Adkins and Skeggs, 2004).

While working with my data and interpreting the transitions of young people (for example, from school to work, moving from place to place) it is evident that the analysis of different forms of capital is not so clear: there are flaws regarding individuals' pathways and decisions, as well as differences among the capital of siblings of the same family, and there are also individuals who do not seem to have very much capital of any kind. Thus we may ask what is wrong with the theory of capital if it does not allow us to see all the strengths and resources available to individuals (Field, 2003, 20). Next, I will demonstrate this, discussing the situation of Heidi, a 20-year-old from a small town (for a more detailed analysis see Tolonen, 2005b). She grew up with her siblings and practically without any parental support. She had completed comprehensive school a few years earlier. During the time of the interview she had a temporary job and was dreaming of higher education. When she talks about her past she claims she was the one 'who kept the house standing' while only eight-years-old:

Heidi: It was like I would take care of my sisters and my brother so that nothing would happen to them.

TT: You were afraid of that?

Heidi: I had to be there all the time. If I were not, it would be like my fault if something happened to them [...]

Heidi: At the moment, it's with the rest of the bunch [meaning siblings T.T.] that I feel that I am most at home, wherever we are [...] not feeling responsible any more [...]

TT: How did you live your own life then?

Heidi: I didn't have a life of my own back then. I lost four or five years when I did nothing with my life. I mean, I did go to school, but I only spent my time there. I didn't do any schoolwork. The whole of comprehensive school went by just like that.

It would have been easy to suggest that Heidi did not have much social or cultural capital in the context of capital theory: Heidi did not have high cultural capital with her interrupted education, neither did she have many social contacts which could be converted into economic capital later in life. This type of theory of capital does not allow us to see that she took care of her siblings during her childhood (care work of women, and siblings as a source of social capital) and learned to be a responsible young working-class woman (local culture and identity work) (Skeggs, 1997, Kovalainen, 2004, 156). Caring seemed to be a rich resource for her. Also her siblings can be seen as her social and emotional resource in a difficult life situation; thus both young people and children can and do create important social capital among themselves, especially in situations where parents are not available (Pösö, 2004: Törrönen, 1999).

Many feminist researchers (who include the experience and complicated processes of women in the analysis, cf. Adkins and Skeggs, 2004) have combined cultural and social capital in their work; for example, in Britain Beverley Skeggs' research (1997) on young working-class women and Diane Reay's (1998, 2000) study on mothers and their children's pre-schooling. In Australia, Julie McLeod (2000) used these terms to study young people's class, subjectivity and educational institutions. Elizabeth Bullen and Jane Kenway (2004, 2005) have focused on young women and education and have criticised underclass theories through capital analyses. The above mentioned analyses are based on further readings of Bourdieu's thinking. These authors suggest that it is important to localise and contextualise the notions of social and cultural capital in order to make a gender-sensitive analysis in which agency is also explored (Skeggs, 1997; McLeod 2000, in the Finnish context Tolonen, 2004, 2005a and b).

Therefore, analysis using cultural capital alone, or combined with social capital has perhaps been more popular than studies which have solely used social capital in the research of young people's education or lifestyles. Cultural capital seems to be more fluid and easier to apply to the different social fields. Cultural capital has also been developed further in the context of youth studies in recent years. In her study of the Norwegian Radical Nationalistic Underground Movement (1991), Katrine Fangen interprets the members of the movement as having 'subcultural capital', which means proper 'stylish matters' and 'ideological knowledge' (Fangen, 2001, 45). Sarah Thornton's research on club cultures also plays with the notion of subcultural capital, which, like Bourdieu's version of it, can also be objectified and embodied. Subcultural capital is embodied in the form of being 'in the know', such as using current slang (Thornton, 1995, 11). Thornton also claims that subcultural knowledge can be converted into economic capital, since it may help one to attain or maintain work within club culture or the business of club culture, or, for example, working in the media using one's knowledge (Thornton, 1995). However, one might argue that this is not similar to the kind of economic capital developed in Bourdieu's theory (see critics in Qvotrup Jensen 2006).

One of my interviewees Jukka, who I knew since he was a 15-year-old, had developed and created various kinds of social capital through relationships while 15 years of age. He was one of the 'kings' ruling the social life in his school at that time (Tolonen 1998, 9-11) and in this context he had plenty of 'subcultural social capital'. He also was using drugs at the quite early age of 14 in which these contacts also played an important role. However, when I re-interviewed him as a 23-year-old young man, he had found that these social groupings were not very supportive later in life. He had had trouble with the law and had difficulty finding and sustaining work relationships.

> *TT*: We met last time in your grammar school. How is your life now?
> *Jukka*: Well the tape won't be long enough if I tell you everything [...]
> I don't know. After comprehensive school my life did go in a quite bad
> way [...] I had trouble with the law and I had to do community service
> for 40 hours [instead of going to a juvenile detention centre T.T.]. That
> finished on the last day of 1998.. In 1999 I went in the army and finished
> an education of a 'medical assistant' there. Since then I have tried to find

a job. This year I have been in my second job, but only for two days, since
I did not like it there.

While Thornton (1995) and Fangen (2001) have introduced the term
'subcultural capital' in their work, here I propose the notion of 'subcultural
social capital'. The concept emphasises social contacts and networks that are
valued within youth cultures, and is used to discern contacts that may not be
seen to be useful perhaps, later in life. This type of capital could be considered
as the 'dark side of the social capital' (Field, 2003). I do agree with Thornton
and Fangen that the term 'sub' is important when studying the cultural and
social capital of young people. Young people create capital in the context of all
kinds of subcultural activities among themselves, even though from outsiders'
(or parents') perspective this does not seem to be the right kind of capital for
coping later in life.

Gender, the economy and social capital

Gender is also a significant issue in the debate on capital (Adkins and Skeggs,
2004). For example, in an analysis of gender and power it is crucial to note who is
included or excluded in social networks, or if social capital is an accurate term to
describe the activities of women (Adkins 2005b). Producing social and cultural
capital is also a gendered and local process (Skeggs, 1997; Reay 2000; McLeod,
2000; Tolonen, 2005b). Here, I will concentrate on the issue of combining social
and economic capital in the analysis of young women and men.

Social capital, with its close connection to symbolic capital (Bourdieu,
1997/1986; Siisiäinen, 2003, Field 2003) seems to be burdened with the
presence of power, and further, economic power, which often is only attainable
by adults (and, easier by men than by women). In Bourdieu's theory, one either
has or does not have social capital (which can be converted into economic
capital), and therefore social capital is a ready-made category. In late modern
societies where young people are involved with several alternative life-spheres,
this concept is too static. In her critique of the concept of social capital, Lisa
Adkins (2005b) claimed that the economic situation has changed, and that 'the
social capital concept is inappropriate for postmodern economies' (2005, 208).
She notes that in new economies the information flows and their control is vital,
and 'axes of difference are being reworked *vis-à-vis* relation to these flows', and
that 'attention should focus on how, in [...]economic postmodernisation the
social is being reworked (Adkins, 2005, 209).

Adkins also states that there is a gendered subtext in the theories of social capital. Referring to the work of Molyneux (2002) she argues that 'social capital theorists overwhelmingly associate social capital with (domestically defined) women, where domestic femininity acts as a sign of social capital' (Adkins, 2005b, 199). She worries that by criticising social capital as not taking into account local and contextual situations, research tends to only theoretically correct conceptualisations of social capital and furthermore places women (or within youth studies, young women) even deeper into the domain of the social, and keep women there instead of placing them as agents within the postmodern economy (Adkins, 2005b, 201).

In their recent Australian study of 'underclass' young women and their experiences of education Elisabeth Bullen and Jane Kenway (2005) base their analysis on Thornton's (1995) use of the term subcultural capital. They broaden their analyses to include social, economic and symbolic capital to what Thornton called subcultural capital: '[...]our usage encompasses social and symbolic capitals as well as cultural capital.' Their work also refers to material conditions, and they state that 'Subcultural identity is not constituted solely through consumption' (Bullen and Kenway, 2005, 53).

Are young women in Bullen's and Kenway's analyses thus captured in the domain of the social as Adkins (2005b) claims this type of analysis might be? Perhaps not: the aim of their analysis is to overcome the difficulties that underclass theories have in interpreting young women's lives. They build a sensitive picture (as opposed to simplifying theories of the underclass) of the experiences of school life of young girls who are at risk of leaving school early, experiencing teenage pregnancy, and have poor employment prospects. 'The cultural, social and symbolic capitals they deploy have currency within their social groupings, providing resources and strategies for survival in the classroom and the schoolyard, indeed, for surviving the positional suffering they experience there' (Bullen and Kenway, 2005, 52-53). In Bullen's and Kenway's analysis, therefore, sub*cultural* capital is taken into account, but so too are social and material conditions, which does not exclude them from the domain of the economy as Adkins suggests. I agree with Bullen and Kenway that especially with young people at the risk of marginalisation the situation is economic, but social and cultural contexts need to be explored carefully too.

One of my interviewees, Marja, is a 22-year-old working-class young woman, who works temporarily at a local shop. Her parents divorced when she was very young, and ...

Marja: [...] when I was little our mother always had violent boyfriends [...] and it was pretty bad when she left us alone for many days when we were about two or three-years-old. And later she might just go out to have a beer. And then she would come back after a week or so. We were eight and nine-years-old [...] we had little food, and there were empty bottles from mother. We took them to the food shop and bought something.

And later:

Marja: I want to go on to higher education and study economics [...] I tried once but didn't succeed [...] I was going to do that again this spring, but couldn't since I didn't have the money to buy the books needed for entrance examinations.

TT: You don't have anyone to help you? Parents of any persons who would support you?

Marja: [...]first of all my mom is unemployed and I have not had any contacts with my father for several years. And there is no one like that [who could help, T.T.]. And now when I am working, the social services don't help, and my wage is really low, and I will get it next month, which is too late anyway.

‒‒‒‒

Marja: Well generally it could be said I grew up too early. But somehow [...] I am pleased that I learned to be so independent so early [...] I learned very early to work and take care of my own affairs.

Marja sees herself as a survivor and she relies on her own actions and agency. On the other hand, she does not think of herself as very successful, not yet: she would like to become an economist later. In her case her personal cultural capital was relatively high (with well-completed upper secondary school) but the material and social resources supporting her were quite low (see more detailed analyses in Tolonen, 2005a).

With young people facing difficult social situations of the past or present particularly, it is important to include both social and economic capital when conducting analyses on gender issues, since all the forms of capital (social, cultural, economic and symbolic) intertwine. It is also important politically, since if only one form of capital is explored, for instance social capital, one might end up in a situation where appropriate "investments' in social capital will compensate for gross inequities in financial capital' (Smith and Kulynych, 2002, 166- 167).

Critics and possibilities of the term capital

I think the most serious criticism against theories of social capital is that economic terminology is used and that people are expected to profit from all their social relations: this is a very different approach compared to traditional youth research with youth groups, valued for what they are and what they do, as well as the meaning production embedded in them. Despite heavy criticism, many researchers do use these concepts when interpreting the lives of young people. In recent years much of the criticism actually refers to the use of the concept of social capital, and many youth researchers actually either use cultural capital or combine the analysis of social capital with different forms of capital. I think the analysis of social capital is most fruitful when it includes an analysis of economic and symbolic capital (e.g. power and wealth), that is where the strength of this theory lies.

However, using an analysis of social, cultural, economic and symbolic capital in the sphere of youth studies may have some positive outcomes. It is currently one sufficient way to analyse social class, the existence of which can not be overlooked in Finnish or other European societies today. Critical arguments of capital theories also bring to light some fruitful subjects: for example the discussion concerning the dialogue of agency and structure in young people's life is important (Raffo and Reeves, 2000). Addressing questions of changes in the economy and their effects on young people's lives and the employment of young people is also important. One significant criticism of capital theory (by Bourdieu) is its elitism: empirical youth research can address some very critical questions to a theory which can not include the experiences, resources and networks of less privileged members of society and see them as valuable. These young people are the ones who mostly challenge the theories of elitist social capital. While analysing these young people it is important to place them not only in the domain of the social (since economic capital is usually low) (Adkins, 2005b) as there is a danger of expecting social capital to replace the lack of economic capital (Smith and Kulynych, 2002, 167). So in this case the theory needs to be changed.

To avoid the 'strong use' of the metaphor of capital in youth research—and to make the theory more explicit and applicable to this research—certain questions need to be asked: On what level is the formation of social capital primarily placed? (the level of the state, community, networks or individuals?) (Field, 2002) Social capital is always local and contextual (McLeod, 2000). Who is able to attain social capital? Who is creating social capital and how and where? How are young people situated in this kind of analysis? (Morrow, 1999a; Holland et al., 2007) How are things such as gender and the family, or ethnicity conceptualised in the theory? (Edwards et al., 2003; Adkins, 2005b) And in the end: What is left outside this kind of analysis? What are the limits of this kind of research? For example, inequalities are not sufficiently addressed (Smith and Kulynych, 2003).

If the theory of capital is reformulated, this may have consequences in many fields.

In the social political field, for example, this theory may potentially treat children and young people as creators of social and cultural capital, not just victims of their past experiences or the wrongdoings of the social services (cf. Stephenson, 2001, Tolonen, 2004, Ellonen and Korkiamäki, 2006, 246).

In this article I have presented many critical comments on the theories of capital. Putnam's theory of social capital seems particularly to be very often opposed with quite a critical tone. Bourdieu's theory, however, is seen slightly in a different way, even though some critics also subscribe to his theory. In feminist critique his theory is taken further on to the ground of the social; capital is seen to be in relation to localities and social contexts. However, Lisa Adkins (2005b) is doubtful of this move. She thinks analysis of women should be in relation to postmodern economies. I agree with both feminist arguments: with the first one that social and cultural capital needs to be carefully contextualised in local social relations, and with the second, that women, or in my analysis both young women and men, should also be studied in relation to their economic situation; however, one should do this with caution. In the end, I think it is important not to apply overly ready-made concepts to the lives of young people but to seek how and through what kind of processes young people's social relations are created, and what kinds of other possible capital, wealth, skills and knowledge can be intertwined in these processes.

Chapter 4

Putnam's pink umbrella? Transgressing melancholic social capital

Namita Chakrabarty and John Preston

Introduction

Better Together is an expected line of flight from his earlier work in which Putnam makes social capital perform to 'bring together' class, race and gender divisions. Starting with Putnam's conception of the social, we use the work of Deleuze and others to consider the possibilities of anonymity, loneliness and nomadism to de-territorialise the over-coded social body. Using the events around 7/7 as a springboard and an ethnographic study of youth drama in two London sites, we consider the role of the anti-social, eccentric and 'evil' in subverting conventional practices of youth drama. We conclude that youth are unpredictable and defiant of categories, including those of social capital theory. This unpredictability represents a point of enfolding interest for those interested in developing praxis with youth drama that does not necessarily preclude the use of social capital theory but does not attempt to understand it in those terms alone.

Social capital as theatrical text

We want to consider social capital as a text and look at the implications of 'reading' youth through social capital in terms of dangers of the possible over-coding of youth cultures and the desire of researchers to constantly 'explain' youth. We make no claims for or against the empirical validity of social capital but wish to counter some of its more rhetorical features particular in terms of its scientific style. Social capital is activist in nature but tends to privilege those forms of community activism which support the status quo. Indeed, Putnam is often criticised for harking back to a form of 1950s U.S.A conservatism which in securing middle class suburban 'whiteness' had disastrous implications for class and race equalities. Rather we ask whether forms of social capital (or even anti-social capital) could be renewed within an activist tradition, perhaps even within a CRT (Critical Race Theory) framework.

Firstly, we reflect on the literary styles which are used by Putnam et al. in their latest work, *Better Together* (2003). The focus on the literary is not to necessarily undercut the strength of Putnam's theoretical arguments but rather to focus on their rhetorical and literary power. Whatever one may think about Putnam as a social scientist, his books are well written and above all readable. Through doing this, we consider that in writing social capital as 'performance' Putnam makes use of allegorical and rhetorical techniques. In particular, Putnam makes use of both melancholia and sentimentality in considering social capital. These are Putnam's *phantasies* of the social—his fears, hopes and dreams—which are embodied in the form of social capital.

We then move to briefly consider the work of Deleuze and Guattari (2004), drawing on the applications of his work by Tamboukou (2004) in order to critique the over-coding of youth through explanations such as 'youth culture' or 'social capital'. We consider that although structural considerations of youth are important, it is also necessary to consider the ways in which youth is characterised by concepts of nomadism and escape. Substantively, we use these insights in an ethnographic study of school drama, making use of literary techniques and non-temporalities. We consider the ways in which youth break out of the expected routines of school drama and seek to destroy networks and social capital through acts and activities which might be considered to be 'anti-social'. We speculate that another way of 'reading' these interventions by youth might be to consider that these are nomadic activities, transgressions and re-writings. In conclusion, we consider that the advancement of school drama calls for subversion rather than sustainability. It requires a critical engagement with class and race rather than recourse to an ahistorical theory of human sociability (e.g. naïve versions of social capital). We do not reject social capital, but consider that we need to explore its connections with radical, rather than reactionary, forms of pedagogy, by seeing the epicentre of social capital in the perceived youth trauma as enacted on the streets.

Better together: Dramatising social capital

Putnam's works are not confined to academic libraries but are found in airport lounges and high street shops. Putnam is the social scientists answer to Tom Clancy. His name appears on the cover of his books as large as the title. He is a prolific generator of literary social science texts. *Better Together* (Putnam's most recent book) dramatises and romanticises social capital. As Putnam and Feldstein (without irony given the title of their previous book) remark:

> The performance in the bowling alley is both funny and serious.
>   (Putnam et al., 2003, 67)

In the transition from *Bowling Alone* (Putnam, 2000) to *Better Together* (Putnam et al., 2003) Putnam shifts from perlocutionary (naming and defining social capital) to illocutionary (creating it by the act of naming it) hails on social capital. Both texts (like this paper, like all social science papers) are social scientific fictions. That is not to say that the social science in either is false (although the claim that the quantitative evidence in *Better Together* was tested '... against evidence as rigorous as could be discovered' (Putnam et al., 2003, 6) is hyperbole). Rather that Putnam uses the tropes and rhetoric of fiction to make his case. This is not a weakness of Putnam's work, in fact it makes the work immensely readable and popular, but it is instructive to observe how these tropes work. The performative nature of social capital in *Better Together* is hidden and revealing this aspect of social capital is instructive in terms of what social capital theory itself obscures—fundamentally the inherent difficulty of speaking of the subject.

Bowling Alone is a science fiction story. It is a dystopian tale (being the antithesis of Putnam's solidaristic and trusting utopia) of how humanity in highly technological civilisations lost community and became social isolates. It is in turn utopian in that humanity can rediscover community through using the most basic social technologies (social capital) to create bonds, bridges and links between themselves. It is a perlocutionary text, a text that aims to have an effect. Putnam is trying to affect the social scientific community, policy makers and individuals in taking action to restore social capital. A task in which Putnam has been hugely (for some worryingly) successful.

Better Together is a travelogue, heartwarming and sentimental:-

'In *Better Together* we invite you to join us on a journey around the United States. You will visit big cities, suburbs and small towns and meet people engaged in a wide variety of activities. You will see bustling branch libraries in Chicago and an evangelical Church in Southern California ...'
(Putnam et al., 2003, 1)

It illustrates the reality of *Bowling Alone* through an omniscient Putnam who states that:

To write this book we descended from the statistical heights of *Bowling Alone* to ground level, entering into the living room of Catherine Flanery, a long time resident of Roxbury, Massachusetts, who has seen her neighbourhood unravel and then knit itself together ...

(Putnam et al., 2003, 5)

Each of the chapters in this journey (except for the introduction—a primer on social capital and the conclusion—some interesting thoughts on social capital and diversity) is an account of a social capital performance. *Better Together* is an illuctionary text, through writing it brings something into being. That is, the stories of people and communities are made to be social capital. It puts social capital on the stage, the words and actions of individuals are theatre, but the meta-theatre is Putnam's. Putnam, the theorist, makes social capital act through those words and actions. Although this is true of all qualitative research that uses a theoretical frame what is apparent in the performances, in each chapter, are the absences. As Butler (2000) states where there is performance there is error, there is the possibility of misinterpretation, there is the chance of resistance. In the performativity of *Better Together* there is little. As the actor, social capital follows a number of set routines perfectly (bonding, bridging, linking—sometimes the reverse of these, and sometimes the racialised and racist alter-ego of social capital as Putnam calls it 'the dark side').

For example, in the chapter *The Shipyard project: building bridges with dance* Putnam describes the town of Portsmouth, New England as the setting for a community dance project. The town is 'divided' in terms of a gentrified, bohemian and retirement area (with 'green lawns') and a military shipyard (where you can see the 'orange and slate-blue girders' and the 'matt black hull of a nuclear submarine' (Putnam et al., 2003, 55). There is a perceived need by community artists in the area that the shipyard and its workers needed to explain themselves to the more recent arrivals in the community—a desire for an arts project 'that would reveal and explain it to the city and maybe bring the two communities closer together' (p. 56), that the working class ship workers could 'make art from their experience' (p. 59). A community dance practitioner (Liz Lerman) is invited to create various pieces of public dance involving current and past shipyard workers. Labour and the nature of labour is a feature of the performances:

All through the week gestures discovered during conversations and rehearsals play out in dance: the gasping, sweeping, pulling and gathering motions of work; the fluttering, sweeping, and diving notions of hands and arms that suggest the sea and submarines; the raised arm imitation of shipyard cranes. The gestures are not mime. That is, they are not meant to create the illusion of real work with invisible objects. These are not people pretending to do things. Stylised and repeated, the gestures communicate something about the human elements of the work, the concentration, strength and precision it requires, the grace and dignity of purposeful physical skill.

(Putnam et al., 68)

This distinction between real work and performed work ('people pretending to do things') is artificial. Performed work is as real as physical work, both are labour. However, although we could make points concerning the essentialist use of 'labour' in the chapter or the patronising way in which the working class are interpolated to represent themselves to the middle classes in this scenario, we are more concerned with the performative nature of social capital in the book, rather than the performance of individual actors. As Putnam states in the chapter '... the performance in the bowling alley is both funny and serious' and this duality of performance is what is not grasped in the chapter, in Putnam's theory of social capital, and in social capital theory more generally. In making social capital 'perform' the ability of performances to transgress social capital are made impossible. If all human activity is reduced to that which bonds, bridges, links aside from a category known as the 'dark side' then there is little room for activities which transcend these simple performatives. In the performative narratives of *Better Together* there is no posturing, no activities which fall outside of social capital. Given the way in which Putnam portrays social capital could there be?

Over-coded youth and social capital

We would state that aside from considerations of power, which has been well discussed, social capital needs to be approached critically as *performative and literary*. Naming others as social capital is a performative activity as is 'building social capital'. We would like to suggest that in (implicitly) emphasising performativity, the role of posturing in social capital has been downplayed. Transgression, subversion and resistance to social relationships are not the 'dark side' (Putnam, 2000) of social capital but rather ways in which historical changes may be effected.

In terms of youth, social capital is another way in which youth and youth cultures can become over-coded (as social, anti-social, individualistic). This over-coding of youth (burdening young people with another form of representation), indeed over-coding in general has been criticised by the French post-structuralist Giles Deleuze. Deleuze considers that 'escape' from over-coding and over-representation is a valid political project for individuals and societies to undertake. Deleuze discusses 'escape' from over-coding through the concept of what he calls a 'Body without organs' (Deleuze and Guattari, 2004).

> 'Deleuze and Guattari's anti-Freudian project is an attempt to create an anti-essentialist, yet scientist (in its use of concepts such as field, force, waves) political project which privileges the schizoid, the unstable and the nomadic. The Body without Organs (BwO) is not an entity, but '... a practice, a set of practices' (p. 166)—which can fail (p. 169). It is a doing, rather than a being. In typical schizoid style, there is little relation between cause and effect in the construction of a BwO '... it is an inevitable exercise, already accomplished the moment you undertake it, unaccomplished as long as you don't' (p. 166). The types of BwO which Delueze and Guattari consider (the hypochondriac body, the paranoid body, the schizo body, the drugged body) are 'Emptied bodies, instead of full ones' (p. 167). The BwO is not '... a site, a scene, a place' (p. 169) but a 'meat circuit' (p. 169) through which 'Only intensities pass and circulate' (p. 169), the project is the end of the human—'... the enemy is organism' (p. 175).'
>
> (Preston, 2007, 89)

The concept of the BwO seems to be closely related to the postmodernist project in terms of the decolonisation of categories and the escape from embodiment. There are pre-modern elements in the construction of such a body—it is a ritual ('a practice', 'an exercise'), the becoming of spirit ('where ... intensities pass and circulate'), animalistic. Recently (2004), Tamboukou has used Deleuzian concepts to interrogate work by Ball, Maguire and Macrae (2000) on youth trajectories which she critiques as being over-burdened by concepts such as race, class and gender. Rather, Tamboukou re-reads the trajectories of the youth described as escaping such categories—using the Deleuzian concept of nomadism ('wandering' between, within and without categorisation).

In terms of social capital, we would apply the concepts of BwO and nomadism to young people. The identification of youth as a category is a relatively recent development which is connected both to the identification of youth as a market (and the creation of 'youth cultures') and the pathologising of youth as a problematic transitional phase. This has led to an over-coding of youth as being overtly social (possessing social capital) or anti-social (low social capital or the 'dark side' of such capital). We view young people through the lens of an overtly social category—'youth'. In contrast, we would like to emphasise transgressions of youth in terms of sociability, the 'wanderings' which young people make away from 'the social' and hence the decolonisations of their over-coded bodies. Young people can be lonely, anti-social and crave anonymity as all human subjects can.

In our ethnography (below) which is also written in a literary style (including parodying the conventions of ethnography in terms of the fictionalising (re-naming) of 'characters' in other educational ethnographies) we show how young people pursue 'lines of flight' away from efforts to reinforce their sociability. In doing so we also make use of *storytelling* techniques employed in critical race theory. This may seem to be somewhat of a contradiction in terms of Deleuze and Tamboukou's emphasising of 'escape' from categories such as race. However, we hope that in doing so we might illustrate not only the tensions, but also the possibilities in combining post-structuralism with Critical Race Theory (CRT). By CRT we are referring to the use of counter narratives within a framework of social analysis that places 'race' or, more properly, the 'racialised other' centre stage as an alternative to majoritarian discourses which are produced by white narrators. This approach has been recently transferred from CRT studies of law to those of education (Ladson-Billings, 2004). CRT emphasises activist forms of research rather than academic critique alone. However, this should not be uncritical activism, but informed by praxis—the meshing of theory and practice.

The pink umbrella and the mask: an ethnography

The timing of the ethnography was during the autumn term after the bombings in London of 7 July 2005, the subsequent failed bombings of 21 July and the tragic shooting, by police, of an innocent Brazilian man on 22 July 2005. Although London had returned to perceived normality, gone were the masses of police with guns all over the city for example, something had changed, a feeling of awareness that transgression is possible and that it is seen as inherently evil. In terms of this ethnography we explored site and the possibility for individual transgressions. Thus we entitle our ethnography 'the pink umbrella and the mask' as we found the site of posture, in the theatre of the depressed (how we

shall term the drama produced at this time), within the stage properties claimed
by the students and within the lyrical use of theatre skills. However we would
view all locations of ethnography as sites of posture and terror, beginning with
us as observers of lessons, and ending, as it turned out in School 2, all of us,
students, researchers and Teacher 2, under the post-empire gaze of Teacher 3,
the ultimate power in that particular site. The writing of this ethnography uses
some of the techniques suggested by critical race theory.[1]

Site—inside the schools

School 1 harnessed black and urban culture towards empowering school
performativity: graffiti/spray-paint/text-speak (txtspk) were displayed to deliver
school rules to seemingly nomadic pupils moving between lessons. It felt in a
funny kind of way rather like the sixties adventure playgrounds, those urban
spaces made by adults to appeal to young people but in their very makeshift
qualities became rather quickly abandoned. There was a feeling of the absence of
authority being an over-riding feature of this type of social organisation—until
break time when we were waiting in the staff room a member of staff came
in and shouted out 'need to clear a few kids away' demanding for staff to help
(this recalled for us Sarkozy's talk of *racaille* (scum) referring to the young black
populace rebelling against the police)[2]. I wondered whether this was the part
of school that you cannot take out of school—that there is no escaping that
school-student equation is about control, despite the posture of txtspk.

School 2 inside felt the very essence of a traditional school—dark curtains,
school hall, the smell of school lunches, signage in traditional text and subdued
colours, young people being told to be quiet, whereas School 1 had more of a
working buzz about it with its student welcome desk at the front of the school
and students approaching staff with questions in an easy manner. The site of
School 2 therefore emphasised the place of students as being the lower level of a
hierarchy, educating students for their place in society and against transgressing
boundaries, reinforcing the all pervading view of youth as anti-social.

---

[1]   This paper is a step for us towards writing in the area of Critical Race Theory which employs experience,
       storytelling and scholarship to reveal the truth that capitalist societies are *constructed* on the basis of racism,
       and to suggest confrontational strategies by which white supremacy and other systems of oppression can
       be overthrown (Ladson-Billings, 2004).

[2]   The events termed 'riots' by politicians and the media catalysed in Birmingham by the transmission by
       a Radio DJ of an unsubstantiated allegation of rape of an African-Caribbean young woman by a group
       of Asian men; in Paris the deaths of two young men running away from police and the labelling of the
       ensuing demonstrators as *racaille* by Sarkozy, French interior minister, and repeated across various media
       ignited the explosion of events.

The theatre of the depressed

When I[3] taught drama in the nineties in a North London school I got rid of the outside, (by curtain and sound proofing), and freed the inside from the school environment by getting rid of all desks, most chairs, and all shoes. The imagery I used consisted of photos of drama productions, drama books and some theatre museum posters (e.g. an image of Paul Robeson). I also taught to the classic drama menu of warm up, stimulus, exploration of task or rehearsal, performance and evaluation. A particular key I felt important was the teaching of skills e.g. accurate mime, how to fake death and a fall. The latter, interesting in retrospect, in terms of the time in which we are living.[4]

Both School 1 and 2 studios and lessons turned out to be quite alien to me on a number of levels, in particular that both lessons started with the students sitting at tables around a board (2) in a circle but near a board (1). There was no warm up in either lesson. Both studios were decorated in recognisable drama lexical and pictorial vocabulary which seemed to demarcate the areas of interests for the specific teachers within the realm of the exams they teach to—(1) Edexcell[5] GCSE/Btec/A level—so a range of influences from Boal to Aristotle; (2) Edexcell vocabulary and the stills from Casablanca. In School 1 there were no curtains so there was light and the concrete of the surroundings, in School 2 we could see the memorable image of a council block, which had been shown on the news during the hunt for the 21/7 would-be bombers, that is until Teacher 2 drew the curtains. (One of my thoughts later was is it possible to draw a curtain and erase reality—should school drama be doing this? Doesn't this erasing transgressions take away intelligent theatre reflection—like the government not holding an inquiry[6] would not erase the events or the possibility of future ones?)

In both schools the students wore a kind of uniform, in (1) the uniform of the street—a mixture of labels, jeans and sweats, influenced by *gangsta* rap, the one girl in the group wearing big dangly gold jewellery. This group of students wore the gestures of that fashion too—the arms hidden in sleeves and sweats

3   Namita Chakrabarty
4   During the writing of this the Iraq war continues and is labelled a civil war by many, the war in Afghanistan is also dominating the visual news media as the situation worsens, that is more troops are killed—this we witness via the western media by named individuals returned home—what is missing, but as a drama educator I think about what are the names of those who fall on the 'other side' who remain nameless, their stories and the scenes which led to these uncounted deaths.
5   The examining body.
6   During the week of the first anniversary of the 7 July bombings there were calls by survivors for an independent inquiry into the events, this has been rejected by the government

pulled out of shape to change body shape, to hide flesh. This transgressive body play reflects the breaking away from the norm, the individual shaping themselves inside their clothes and away from the shape of the furniture and the site. Interestingly this type of gear translated well for the mask work during the lesson as it allowed the body to move quite freely and this reflected the key words on the board of body isolation, exaggerate, stylised. The teacher at School 1 also inhabited the world of her studio in the manner of a record producer—stressing that the work was going to develop for performance, for a particular audience, and she used the term 'hip hop rap' when introducing the students to the origins of the cussing terminology of 'your mum' to Sophocles' Oedipus. She also led the students to different areas within the room with ease, to the display on ancient Greek theatre, to the bench when we watched the performance, or gesturing to the mask display on the wall.

So in Lesson 1 the teacher seemed to harness the site specific terminology of the school site, or London as a multicultural site, in drawing the students in to the world of the mask, and in doing this she was culturally specific in terms of pinpointing the use they were to make of it in western European theatrical origins rather than the mask of African oral or dance traditions. To return to the record producer metaphor, the lesson brought together a number of elements of the pop video—short performances using masks—which could easily have been used in videos of music at the moment in the way that they sought to use specific cultural stories of our times- the marionette and its master, the Matrix fight scene, the drugs supposed suicide/crime scene. We could say that the cultural product reflected the site as directed by the teacher, as producer, and the students as products of the locale. Or another way of looking at this would be to say that the teacher as shaper of social capital harnesses the seemingly transgressive elements of the sites to produce an acceptable product for the *status quo*.

In School 2 there was a traditional school uniform of blazer and tie, that restrictive clothing rejected by many neighbouring European countries, and reflecting this there was a more traditional student-teacher interaction (students were told what to write, prompted with key words—this was very much to produce the written coursework for the Edexcell Unit One paper), and Teachers 2 and 3 seemed to reinforce these traditional aspects, Teacher 2 the male a more experienced teacher soft voiced but in control and suited (he was referred to by us all as Mr—), whereas female Teacher 3 used a louder voice and more anxious to get the right words on the page (she was referred to by her first name). For a large part of this lesson the site of the lesson seemed to be in the coursework—a worksheet to record the previous lessons work—the performative nature of this lesson being examinative rather than theatrical as this part of the exam involves students and teachers recording what happens (students via writing and images and teachers via video and writing up a timed record of the students' work during the session).

However this feeling of control seemed to be undercut by the students' use of props/objects during the work on a Bob Marley[7] recording. As introduced by the teachers (as one of a series of lessons using this particular song as a stimulus towards a narrative on a young man being trapped by 'the system'—the melancholic cycle of violence and tragic deaths, families caught within a system where they have no hope of escaping this environment and so young men are seen to be influenced by this death drive). The students' task was to produce three key scenes from the narrative of the song, using movement but little sound, to fit to the recording. The objects/props involved included a pen that was tapped quite a bit, a number of mobile phones, and a pink umbrella. The pink umbrella was very much a girlish toy-like umbrella, think my little pony or Claire's Accessories usually associated with stereotypically feminine pink accessories. It belonged to one of the boys in the group. He used it to tap the floor when others were generally sitting head in hands listening to the song. (This is actually the kind of object a lot of teachers would have got put away on health and safety grounds, being an umbrella, also, of course, many drama teachers would encourage mime and so would have dissuaded the use of props, in this case it was actually very interesting as a transgression by both student and teachers!) The song's seventies melancholic atmosphere was very much reflected in the words of the students later when explaining their scenes to me: 'it's a vicious circle ... it's the street, it's what happens ... the dad thought he was Tupac, he got killed, the son has to avenge his death, then he gets killed'. In the scene by Group 2 the mobile as prop was a central sign in their performance: the murderers of the father see the father talking on his mobile, he is talking to Johnny's (the son) mother on the phone. He gets killed (for the phone). The mother hears the murder on the phone. She tells Johnny when he gets older who murdered his father, and he kills them using a mobile as a gun (or knife?), then Johnny gets killed too. I now realise from my notes (it was very fast and flowing, to the words of the song) that I'm confused as to who got killed by the mobile as gun/knife and who got killed by a gun as hand gesture. The student

7   Marley, B. (2001) Johnny Was, taken from the CD *Rastaman Vibration* (New York, Island Records)

who played the father played the death in a very balletic way, it was beautiful in the way of the destined to die gun culture type death of *gangsta* rap. This death ritual dance was the site of the posture of what Foucault termed 'lyricism and religiosity', the resonances (with the killing of Jean Charles de Menezes on 22 July, the faces of allied troops shown on CNN and the BBC, the music dance death ritual music promos on MTV) only heightening the grace of the students (this was very moving theatre) in playing out the transgressive behaviour of the street within the safe environs of the drama studio, the melancholic transgression of the nomadic (current political speak about 'immigrants' and 'our country' by politicians and the BNP gains in local elections in 2006 make many of us feel like temporary citizens even if we were born in this country) dramatising youth as not anti-social but as a creature of its locale.

Inter-textuality

Teacher 3 asks the students, during the evaluation of the performances: 'What are the connections between the dad and him (Johnny) dying violent deaths?' A student (female) with a totally neutral look on her face asks, 'What do you mean?'

It's interesting that a drama teacher can ask students a question which presupposes that violent events have some kind of pattern or path between them but that the government and some media commentators of our time are adamant that no connection can be made between the U.K. joining the U.S.A. in a war on Iraq and 7/7, 21/7 and presumably 22/7—and in fact people who point out that there does seem to be some kind of a connection are deemed to be making excuses for terrorism. The students at School 2 do not engage in discussion (at School 1 there was much more of a banter between teacher and students and in that sense the discussion on masks went the full extreme from ancient to contemporary cultural references like Michael Jackson and the mask, spring-boarded very much by the students).

Teacher 3 reminded the students to 'get your ending' in the last moments of rehearsal, and Teacher 1 had told her group to shape the scenes with 'a beginning, middle and an end'. Both lessons then were promoting a kind of drama shaped by a cultural specificity—that is that things have an end, that they tell stories, that peoples' deaths can be explained, that there is a purpose to performance, and there is always a specific audience. On the other hand Teacher 3 stressed 'the system' as the force that trapped the character Johnny, and this in itself, allied with the melancholy melodic nature of the song, lulled us all in the room into a kind of collective depression. When I was inside that room I felt that everything is cyclical, I felt compelled to be within that feeling—that very Monday afternoon school feeling of being trapped in fact in a cycle that will end on Friday but begin again on Monday. In fact the inter-textuality of these two lessons, that is the mask of ancient Greek theatre and drama being an enactment of myth/'the system', connected with the song of one generation (the seventies) echoing in another generation (and another century). In the first lesson we had the neutral masks (albeit in whites, browns etc.) and in the second lesson the mask became the collective acceptance of the cycle of 'the system'—our contemporary acceptance of the fate of the Gods of ancient Greek theatre and the power of myth and prophesy translated into our contemporary individual melancholic place within the hierarchy of the global and powerful, those with weapons.

Future site

On the last page of my notes for this ethnography I wrote 'pink umbrella' and 'renaissance' in large scrawling letters; my memory of that day is dominated by the second school and the lethargy I felt from the students and the feeling of depression that we felt as we found ourselves walking towards Brixton afterwards. The one ray of light seemed to be the prettiness and comedy of the pink umbrella in School 2 and the clarity of clear mask work in School 1. Perhaps part of me wants to see the power of the theatre of the absurd in this time? I remember feeling momentarily lifted by the buzz of Brixton and the outside World.

On reflection a few days later I started to try and fight the feeling of that day and came up with the feeling that what was missing from this part of the study was a dominant group—or a group who felt dominant. This was partly because these two schools were very different from my own experience of teaching drama to young people in single sex schools or schools which were more ethnically diverse than either of these schools and a lot of exciting experimentation on gender and posture, especially in devised work, may have ensued because female students would act as male characters, and where race was generally irrelevant, for example, I remember a scene where twins were played by students of different ethnicities. What I'm grasping after here is when no one group is dominant or the players become themselves a coherent group then there seems to be a more fruitful relation to creative drama; that the eccentric, the posturing, the clowning of the Shakespearean, or the vision of Brechtian theatre where alienation meant that theatre had a purpose in its interaction with the audience to transgress theatre and to resist the social cycle—this is the kind of posturing theatre which we are striving for, and which exists on the street in queer cultured or urban radicalised spaces.

Just as Teacher 3 demanded students have a beginning middle and an end I'm wondering whether an empire requires more epic theatre, to face the epic challenge of empire—that this will be inspiring theatre, theatre in the epic mould, that takes a Brechtian attitude to ending? Where it makes the performativity evident, plays with artifice, indeed takes on the technology and masters it rather than be mastered and enslaved? What I'm talking about is bringing together, the mask (performance skills and the quintessential human rather than the specific experience to use epic theatre), and the pink umbrella (the challenging symbol, the mythic to challenge empire).

Social capital against humanity?

In its worst manifestations, social capital can seem to be the antithesis of the creative and performative responses shown by the students in our ethnography. Social capital can be overtly scientific and mechanical in nature—policy science rather than a mechanism for achieving social change. Even though social capital comes in a hundred flavours—as cause/effect, real/metaphor, as panacea/poison and all combinations in between it maintains its tendency towards privileging the existing order. It is trite to refer to social capital as a contested concept. Aside from the classic theorists of social capital (Putnam, Coleman, Bourdieu, Fukyama) there are thousands of published and lay, idiosyncratic social capital theories with '... many differences in methodology, theory and concepts despite similarities in language and, at times, mechanisms' (Fine, 2001, 97). However, there are some key points that we can make about the nature of social capital:-

---

Key points about social capital

A theory, or maybe just a convincing or good story (*Bowling Alone*) involving networks and attitudes (norms/trusts). This is more than its component parts, it is social capital (Michael Woolcock refers to this augmented form of social capital as 'networks plus')

Social capital is both solid and gas. It works like a (solid) construction set, there is bonding social capital, bridging social capital and linking social capital. These ties can be weak or strong. Once created, social capital exists in the atmosphere (like a gas) available for any to make use of it. (This is a reading of Putnam's, 2000 view of social capital)

Social capital is a universal panacea for human social problems. (Putnam, 2000)

Social capital rolls uphill in continuous virtuous circles, but can also career downhill (Putnam, 2000)

Like Pandora's Box, social capital has a dark side—use it *appropriately*—it is also in decline in the U.S.A. (but perhaps increasing in the U.K. according Hall, 1999) but both declines and increases can be reversed through policy applications.

Within these conceptions of social capital there is a sense that social capital is a modernist solution to the classical social science problem of 'social order'. It can even be said to be a technicist form of social science whilst making claims about individuals abilities to transcend their social realities through building social capital. In contrast, we would signal that CRT is rooted in the experiences of individuals but also their material conditions as racialised subjects and their creative responses to those situations, as we have discussed above.

Unpredictable youth

Through the ethnography we see points of transgression of youth beyond categories of the social—the use of the pink umbrella, the appropriation of popular culture and the questioning of 'normative' narratives of explanation. These allow us to make conclusions regarding the current nature of drama in schools (which needs to make more of these transgressive moments) but we also wish to consider the relationship between youth and social capital theorising. As we have seen, youth can be said to exist in a tension between the social and escape from the social. In both the drama classes described above we see how sociability is both reinforced and undercut by the actions of youth. Although these are not necessarily conscious projects to create BwO, there is nomadic 'wandering' between, within and without categories of the social and the individual. These should not be coded as 'anti-social' or disruptive, but rather used as points of enfolding interest for the teacher and pupils.

We must obviously remain silent on the empirical validity of 'social capital'— we can not say whether technically it represents social reality well or badly. Rather we have considered social capital as a narrative, as a successful series of Putnam's stories. What we do wish to consider is how the over-coding and over-narration of young people's lives as full or bereft of the 'social' might lead us to miss something important about youth—its *unpredictability and defiance of categories.*

Chapter 5

Youth and the provision of resources

James Côté

The chapters in this section illustrate three approaches to the understanding of the role of social networks in young people's lives. This divergence of approaches can be understood in terms of differing ontological, epistemological, and methodological metatheoretical issues involved in understanding concepts like social capital, as well as how explicitly the political motivations of the authors are revealed. Respectively, these metatheoretical issues involve (1) the existence and nature of social capital, (2) ways of understanding manifestations of social capital, and (3) how to study it.

In reference to the theoretical maturity of this area, these three chapters underscore the point that we still have some way to go before we might establish a consensus about, and a coherent theory of, social capital, replete with a taxonomy of different forms of capitals. However, it is also the case that some of those dabbling with the social capital concept are not so much interested in scientific theory so much as in political action, as illustrated by the third chapter in this section. Still, after locating these chapters in terms of their underlying metatheoretical and political assumptions, my commentary will focus on the challenge of developing an agreed-upon theory that allows us to employ a taxonomy for understanding how young people are affected by the resources that are available to them, and/or unattainable because of social structural and psychological factors. This challenge takes us beyond the concept of social capital itself, to an examination of various forms of resources and their inter-relationships.

All three chapters take issue with some ontological elements of the concept of social capital, calling into question the validity of its applicability to all youth. Both the Holland and Tolonen chapters suggest that structural differences in social networks serve to perpetuate social classes, while the chapter by Chakrabarty and Preston questions the very existence of social capital beyond a coercive means of social control. In the latter chapter, their structural concern involves forms of racial exclusion. However, this problematisation of the concept of social capital varies among the chapters in terms of degree of rejection of the project of building a theory of social capital, with the third chapter claiming an agnostic stance, while the first two chapters suggest that a reformation will resolve the barriers blocking completion of this project.

In terms of epistemology, the first two chapters do not question the utility of the concept of social capital or the benefits actual social capital can have in the lives of young people and our understandings of those lives, while the third chapter questions these very things. For example, both Holland and Tolonen argue that social class differences in this form of capital signal that the concept highlights some things (i.e. bonding capital can perpetuate disadvantages), but disguises others (i.e. the disadvantaged do not have the same access to bridging capital as the advantaged). In contrast, Chakrabarty and Preston question the utility of the concept itself in any form of understanding, while paradoxically using the concept to emphasise their problematique of Critical Race Theory.

Methodologically, all three chapters utilise qualitative methodologies. These methodologies provide illustrations of their claims, but do not allow us to generalise beyond their select samples. The first two chapters, being based more in realist ontologies and positivist epistemologies, use 'hard' categories to characterise social capital and its workings, while the third chapter offers us fluid categories, compatible with its nominalist ontology and anti-positivist epistemology.

In terms of their political relevance, all chapters explicitly take an advocacy posture toward 'youth', but the degree of this advocacy and the extent to which it allows an 'anti-adult' posture varies. In fact, the third chapter offers readers what amounts to a form of radical journalism explicitly fuelled by postmodern rhetoric where the existence of categories accepted by adults is mocked. In the case of the third chapter, we are to believe that adults should abandon their concern with guiding the young through preformed structures, and instead should provide unstructured environments in which the young direct their own development. The third chapter is thus reminiscent of earlier radical critiques of pedagogy such as those found in the free-school experiments and Marxist critics of mass education.

In reading these chapters, and observing the social capital literature in general, it is interesting to note how some of the social sciences have evolved in terms theory development. In the current era, we can witness the individualisation of the academic career and the decline of collective efforts in building theory. Perhaps because each academic must now prove her or his mettle to tenure committees, it is now commonplace for publications to justify themselves on the basis of their ability to outdo or best those who are considered 'grand theorists' or 'masters'—those who have ventured to propose broadly applicable theoretical formulations. Consequently, we now find less in the way of either truly original new theory or theory-building programmes, and more in the way of critiques that offer only limited advances of knowledge, if any advances at all. In fact, the cumulative weight of a literature based on critiques that attempt to undermine the insights of the 'masters', rather than a literature that builds on the strengths of previous advances, seems to render the social sciences rather impotent in explaining much of anything. The contrast with the some of the natural sciences is striking, or with the social sciences in the first part of the 20th century, where collective efforts are/were undertaken in an effort to advance knowledge (as in the case of medicine, for example).

Such observations undoubtedly will evoke the ire of some young academics and will be considered blasphemy by those who have drifted toward, or embraced, postmodern ideology, but I believe they are pertinent to the state of fields like social capital. I do not raise these concerns to single out these three chapters, for each does make its own contribution. I speak rather to the problem of a social science dominated by doctrinaire approaches that lead to predictable critiques and the lack of progress in developing a social science that is actually of much use to the very people it is intended to understand.

Challenges to the field

I turn now to the challenge of developing a consensus regarding a theory incorporating social capital that includes a taxonomy of the resources that might be employed by, or made available to, youth. This challenge requires us to examine the concept of 'capital' itself by going beyond the concept of social capital, to an examination of various forms of capital and their inter-relationships.

I have proposed, and written extensively on, the concept of identity capital (see especially, Côté, 1996, 1997, 2000, 2002, 2005; Côté and Levine, 2002). My intention here is not the promotion of my own work, for I leave it to interested parties to read those sources themselves, but rather to share the insights I gained in attempting to develop a theory based on this concept.

To share this experience and draw direct connections between social capital and identity capital, several points need to proposed (and debated as necessary as part of a consensus-building process among those interested in advancing the field) regarding basic concepts and their inter-relationships:

- The crux of social capital is networks, and networks are equivalent to inter-personal relationships; relationships can take many forms, such as reciprocal, hierarchical, unilateral, bilateral, or multilateral structures.

- Relationships always involve identities; people affirm or negate each other's identities through their interpersonal interactions.
- Interpersonal affirmation and negation define the parameters of, and possibilities for, identity formation—who people become in terms of social locations and what these locations mean in terms of access to resources and the possibilities for interacting with those in other social locations, or occupying other social locations.
- The content of the networks (e.g. caring, instrumental, exploitive) needs to be distinguished from the structure of those networks (e.g. bonding or bridging).
- The identities of those in the networks matter in terms of their potential to enrich a community and people in it; not all potentials are the same and not all strivings for improvements are Machiavellian.
- Social capital networks activate the relational aspects of identity, allowing for the integration of the individual into communities.
- Identity requires differentiation from others in some way, however minor, and can contribute to an agentic capacity for self-transformation, as well as the transformation of networks and resources; agency is based on a resource-based penetration of social and economic structures (cf. Emirbayer and Mische, 1998).
- Networks involving relations between adults and youth are horizontal (bonding within each generation, as in youth culture), as well as vertical (as in intergenerational relations that bridge the generations, such as guidance and resource transfer).

Capital as resources

In addition to establishing fundamental assumptions such as the above about the inter-relationship of concepts, the task of theory-building also requires a taxonomy, in this case a classification of types of resources that more concretely represent the metaphor of 'capital'. Dictionaries define 'capital' to refer to sources of profit, advantage, and power, as well as net assets and resources. As metaphors in the social sciences, the more popular conceptualisations of capital refer to various types of capital: human, cultural, and social (cf. Schuller, 2004). Some scholars prefer to use just one 'capital concept', to the effect that all resources a person can possess are called cultural capital or human capital or social capital (e.g. Catan, 2004). However, if one reflects on this preference, it becomes apparent that each such concept has its focal point, but outside that point, its ability to explain phenomena diminishes (cf. Shipman, 2002). This focal point needs to be defined in terms of context, based on the assumption that resources are context-specific. For example, the value of financial capital, as represented by a country's currency, is context-specific, both in terms of time (the market value of currencies fluctuate on a daily basis), space (currencies do not exist in some cultures), and place (e.g. if I try to spend Canadian money in Europe, vendors will not accept it and I will be sent to a bank where if I exchange it for Euros I will get only a certain percentage of the dollar's worth in Canada). This analogy suggests that there is no reason to expect that any of the other resource-metaphors should be characterised by trans-contextual universal laws.

Based on the more concrete idea of asset-based financial capital, human capital is a metaphor introduced by economists to account for characteristics of people, like educational attainment or specific technical skills, that are productive in some economic context (e.g. Becker, 1964). Although some scholars feel that the concept of human capital is all that is needed to account for the wherewithal necessary to function in industrial-capitalist societies, it is really unnecessary and ill-advised to 'rubber sheet' the concept like that—stretch it try to cover everything nearby—because doing so reduces both it conceptual clarity and scientific utility.

One very good reason not to treat human capital theory as a rubber sheet theory is that human capital is a concept developed to account for conditions in 'modernity' more so than in 'late modernity'. This point becomes clearer if we reserve the concept of human capital to refer to skills that are relevant to the workplace. In doing so, we can preserve the focal point of the concept of human capital for economic contexts, and utilise additional concepts with focal points that are more useful elsewhere. In recognising this, I developed the concept of identity capital to refer to more general contexts where identity negotiation and maintenance are paramount, many of which are outside the workplace. For example, in undertaking the individualisation process, people are confronted with the task of planning their own life courses, which includes determining their own values and beliefs (religious, political, secular, and the like), group affiliations, leisure time pursuits, as well as intellectual and aesthetic preferences. These are now primarily identity tasks, which may or may not have to do with tasks primarily associated with human capital development, namely, forming an occupational identity. Thus, a human capital analysis would not provide a basis for formulating research questions to examine aspects of late-modern functioning, such as the individualisation of tastes, beliefs, and values that constitute the bases for personal identity.

Identity capital resources

The idea for the concept of identity capital originated in research projects that attempted to understand what now happens to identity formation among those attending contemporary mass-universities, and how this identity formation influences graduates' subsequent work- and life-experiences. The initial problem was conceived in terms of the tendency for universities to be viewed as 'black boxes' (Karabel and Halsey, 1977) into which something 'goes in' and out of which something else 'comes out', but what happens in between is not well conceptualised. The same applies to sociological understandings of 'the person'. The 'person' is currently little more than a subjective 'black box' in the minds of many sociologists; consequently, disagreements and confusion over notions like 'human agency' continue (cf. Emirbayer and Mische, 1998).

This initial education-specific problem comes into clearer focus when expressed in terms of the problems encountered during the transition to adulthood in an era of declining authority, as in late modernity, and the institutional disjunctures this can create (e.g. in the education-to-work transition). That is, with a growing segment of the population rejecting traditional forms of authority, and with existing authority structures often being indecisive in terms of guiding the young, the basis of identity formation has become increasingly problematic. Under such conditions, the resources at each individual's disposal become more important, including those psychological resources that can contribute to an internal point of reference and an ability to reflexively evaluate and manoeuvre through a variety of social contexts.

A resource is an asset that people can exchange, literally or metaphorically, although this need not be seen as selfish or Machiavellian. In these exchanges, identity negotiations take place—pragmatically, symbolically, or emotionally—during contextually specific interactions, as part of a *quid pro quo* developed by the parties involved. If successful, these identity negotiations and exchanges involve mutual acceptance with another individual, an informal group, a community, or an institution. And with this acceptance, the incumbent gains identity capital—there has been an increase in some aspect of 'who they are'. In this way, people acquire identity capital on the basis of the resources at their disposal. And, as in the financial world, capital can beget capital. Conceptualised in this fashion, we should be able conduct audits or inventories of people's accumulated gains or net assets. Thus, we can refer to identity capital acquisition as representing an individual's net assets at a given point in time in terms of 'who they are' (see Côté and Levine, 2002, for a full account of this).

University students bring certain resources with them to their educational settings, but these resources can be compounded in that setting. Additional resources can be derived directly from involvements in these settings, net of initial resources. Assuming that a certain segment of the population already engages in the active accrual of identity capital resources, it is possible to study their initiatives and strategies to see which are most 'adaptive' in face of the disjunctive conditions of late-modern society.

Identity capital represents attributes associated with sets of psycho-social skills, largely cognitive in nature, that appear to be necessary for people to strategise and make decisions affecting their life courses (i.e. to individualise), especially in the absence of cultural guidance and societal norms, as in the case of late-modern societies. The process of identity capital acquisition describes how the individual invests in a certain identity (or identities) and engages in a series of exchanges with others in a variety of contexts (only some of which are economic). Engaging in reciprocal exchanges in individualistic social milieus requires certain social skills and psychological attributes, because normative structures for reciprocal exchanges are often deficit or non-existent, eliminating many default forms of exchange that might have existed prior to late modernity. These personal resources involve agentic capacities such as an internal locus of control, self-esteem, self-efficacy, and a sense of purpose in life, all of which can help people reflect on their life circumstances, and plan courses of action. Together, these personality strengths enable people to cognitively understand and behaviourally negotiate the various social, occupational, and personal obstacles and opportunities that they are likely to encounter throughout an individualised life-course. The obstacles can range from outright discrimination through to institutional voids, while the opportunities can range from the emergence of new social norms allowing for diverse lifestyles to new educational prospects among people who previously would not have obtained higher credentials.

I argue the above in full recognition of the social-structural and economic obstacles that many people face, including social class, gender, race, and age (Allahar and Côté, 1998). Thus, in addition to better understanding the role of agency in overcoming these persistent obstacles, we need to understand the identity capital acquisition strategies within each category of inclusion-exclusion (like social class) if we are to make recommendations regarding how best to benefit from available opportunities, such as those in educational systems. For example, among the largely middle-class population of university students, we know that there are different outcomes for students that can not be attributed to their class background because class background is more or less constant in this population. However, we do not really understand what differentiates those who go on to construct meaningful life-projects or embark on rewarding careers when their class background and IQs are basically the same. This is where the identity capital model should be most useful in practical terms.

Choices based on unreflective thought limit the effectiveness of those very choices in making a difference in a person's life. The likelihood of agentic action overcoming social structural obstacles is diminished if choices are based on lower-order levels of cognition, morality, and ethics. Accordingly, we cannot expect the disadvantaged to rise above adversity if they are not equipped with the personal resources for doing so—identity capital. And, even if social structural obstacles were suddenly magically eliminated, those who have lived their lives under constrained conditions would not likely have the agentic resources for functioning in unconstrained environments.

Social capital and identity capital

To return to the concept of social capital, as noted, one meaning of 'capital' is of net assets and resources. Some assets are tangible in the sense that they are relational (contingent on interpersonal relationships rather than being the exclusive property of persons). Those involving identity include such things as group memberships and various statuses (age, gender, race, etc.) that can function as 'passports' into different social and institutional spheres. These identity resources directly affect intergenerational social capital (cf. Edwards, 2004; Zhou, 1994), which refers to a *quid pro quo* between parents and their progeny and the ability of the parental generation to transfer assets (e.g. functional values and facilitative networks) to their offspring.

As rightly noted in the three chapters in this section, the ability of parents to provide assets depends on their level of affluence. However, what is missing is an understanding of the identity capital of their parents, which can make class analysis less clear and useful. What often slips into class analyses is the stereotype that the working class is to be considered 'disadvantaged'. For some, class analysis seems to evoke images of the working class being equivalent to an underclass, or some other unsavoury groups of people who threaten middle class sensibilities. The bias here may be more common among academics from the upper levels of affluent backgrounds with no direct lived experience in the working class, but the pejorative view of the working class is offensive to those of us from the working class. I have been an academic for 30 years but my working class roots and affiliations run deep. In fact, experiences derived from a dual class identity were a source of insights in developing the identity capital model. In developing that model I reflected on my own experiences associated with moving among various social contexts where one is judged on the basis of 'who one is' in terms of social-class accoutrements, like language patterns and leisure habits. Making the transition from the working class to middle class professional life can be difficult, and subsequent life in the ivory tower can be difficult in terms of deeply ingrained behaviour and language patterns. Those who change, or straddle, social classes must learn many things as adults that are taken for granted by those whose primary socialisation fully prepared them for their adult lives (e.g. those whose parents were professors or other professionals). In my case, my parents were unable to provide any anticipatory socialisation for my adult career; in fact, the status associated with my middle class career was a source of tension between us.

To return to the issue of context, it quickly becomes clear that what is effective in one context may not be in another. For example, my own academic-identity capital is negotiable in university settings, but of little value in other contexts (e.g. in dealing with bureaucracies in which I am but one of tens of millions of customers, or in getting my car repaired). At the same time, the identity capital I have in working-class circles requires a role distancing from my academic identity, and considerable work in neutralising that occupational status as a threat to my working class friends and relatives. While my working class identity may not help me in dealing with bureaucracies, it certainly helps in getting my car repaired and in getting advice and assistance from trade workers. In fact, because of my class background, and knowledge of language patterns, appropriate demeanour and the like, I can function effectively in the working class circles associated with my upbringing.

This example underscores the fact that identity capital is not context- or class-specific, and that people can possess various forms of it that appear on face value to be contradictory. Identity capital can include cultural capital (as part of a diversified portfolio) to the extent that a person believes that exchanges in high status culture are useful; but identity capital can include many other things that are specific to membership in any type of culture—including street gangs, prison cultures, the mob, or even corporate culture. In this sense, identity capital operates to access and/or preserve group membership validation and personal definition. Moreover, identity capital can involve personality mechanisms (e.g. charisma, cleverness, impression management skills) that facilitate free movement among diverse groups and contexts, including social class groupings and ethnic groups, as in the case of dual class- or ethnic-identities. The accumulation of identity capital can also facilitate the person's movement through the life course, with or without any social class mobility. Identity capital exchanges can be equal and mutually beneficial, or they can be unequal, as when people with greater resources use those resources to acquire further resources at the expense of others (analogous to capital accumulation in the economic system). Thus, identity capital exchanges can lead to: mutual validation among equals; unilateral validation, as by a subordinate to a superior; and financial or material gain, as by a superordinate from a subordinate.

When we turn to the possibilities for intergenerational identity capital transfers, these highlight what is missing from many social capital analyses, namely, that people in networks can benefit from each other's personal competencies in negotiating their way through the late-modern world, and in this case children can benefit from their parents' personal attributes. Accordingly, while knowledge of networks is important, it is helpful to understand the attributes of the people potentially sharing the bonds, in part because those attributes can determine who is allowed to share the bonds, especially as these attributes relate to social identities based on race, gender, and the like.

Conclusion

The perennial concern in sociology with social cohesion has found renewed vigour as societies have entered the late-modern period. In this sense, the idea of social capital dates back to the earliest sociological concerns (e.g. Durkheim) and types of community (e.g. Gemeinschaft versus Gesellschaft). Late modernity is apparently characterised by even more anomie than early modern societies, and sociologists are still attempting to come to grips with this problem, and how to alleviate its ill-effects. One of these ill-effects concerns the role of the adult world in forming and maintaining relationships with the young that nurture rather than control them. However, one has to wonder whether we have lost all sense of what it means to be an adult—an epidemic of identity crises around this issue, experienced by the ostensibly mature members of society—a possibility implicit in the Chakrabarty and Preston chapter. Are adults to give up all claims to authority, wisdom, and fiduciary duty, and hope that the young can create a society free of the sins of the past? Such a utopian view seems to be symptomatic of adults lost in an anomic late-modern society and the postmodern ideology that has slowly supplanted beliefs in any source of authority.

In my view, the challenge for late-modern societies is how to regain some of the intergenerational social capital lost during the 20th century, at both the first-order level of mutual cooperation (which is of immediate importance to new members of a group, like youth), and higher-order levels of reciprocity represented by the notion of 'space'. This will require that adults with sufficient identity capital (that incorporates moral-ethical integrity) to break down social class barriers, making it possible for those who have the wherewithal for class mobility to undertake that trajectory, whether it be through the educational system or some other means. The concept of identity capital is promising in this regard, because it links active forms of individualisation with increased social dividends from which the larger community benefits. For example, a person's identity capital can contribute to a larger, more global community by adding bridging value to local social capital, with identity capital operating in a manner analogous to the way in which personal economic investments in a local business enterprise can benefit a community. Much of the work on social capital and its benefits is at the first order of 'place', which is of limited benefit to the human species as a whole, because groups tend to look primarily to their own interests to the exclusion of the interests of others (see Portes, 1998). However, bridging social capital would involve identity capital invested and utilised across 'space' through networks with other groups.

As the authors of the three chapters in the section rightly point out, the implications of social capital are both conservative and emancipatory, depending on the advantages that go with the well-supported and embedded positions. However, even the most radical or libertarian social forms need social cohesion and competent people if their communities are to survive and people in them are to thrive. The problem does not lie with social capital networks, or concepts of these, but rather with the equity of resource distribution. To give up on the project of forming cohesive communities is misguided, and postmodern hyperbole seems only to divert our attention from the issue of the material conditions of existence and how capitalism produces inequalities that need to be directly confronted. Moreover, to give up on the fiduciary requirements of adulthood is a bit like the following analogy: If we know that a group of young people might become lost in a forest, should adults with decades of learned experience stand back and not offer them their accumulated knowledge of orienteering and use of technological aids, like compasses and handheld GPSs, for fear of imposing their categories on them? Should adults really leave them to find their own way out of that forest and not provide their collective knowledge in direction-finding? Should they be hesitant to tell these young people that someone long ago invented the concepts of north, south, east, and west, and that these concepts are useful, even if they have arbitrary elements (like considering north 'up' or distinguishing magnetic north from 'true' north)? I think the answer to this concrete problem is clear. It is a pity that we are not as confident in our knowledge of more abstract problems like the provision of nurturing networks, and the importance of individual competencies, in making deliberate and planned transitions through the life course, especially for young people from those backgrounds with the densest forests to traverse.

Part 3   Social capital and identity

Chapter 6

Judged by the company we keep: Friendships networks, social capital and ethnic identity of Caribbean young people in Britain

Tracey Reynolds

Introduction

The issue of young people as active agents, consumers and recipients of social capital who document their experiences in their own voices is a relatively new research area (see for example, Morrow, 1999a; Bassani, 2003; Schaefer-McDaniel, 2004; Leonard, 2005; Parker and Song, 2006a; Weller, 2006a; Holland et al., 2007). More recently research has started to explore young people's use of social capital in constructing identity across diverse ethnic and racial groups (Reynolds, 2006b; Parker and Song, 2006a). This article explores the experiences of second and third generation Caribbean young people in order to understand how their friendships networks act as a social resource in ethnic identity formation, which in turn strengthens same-ethnic friendships networks.

By drawing on the theory advanced by Putnam, the analysis indicates that these young people use 'bridging' social capital to develop inter-ethnic friendship bonds. More significantly, they also use 'bonding' social capital to establish same-ethnic/racial friendship networks within their local neighbourhoods. Indeed, the vast majority of the young people (26 out 30 respondents) stated that their three closest friends or 'best friends' shared the same ethnic-racial background. These friendships strongly matched the values closely associated with social capital: trust, reciprocity, emotional support, community, and identity. There were particular factors that facilitated these same-ethnic friendship networks which the analysis will address including: school, family, community and wider issues of social exclusion, which provide real and imagined social barriers to full participation of black and minority ethnic groups in Britain.

The discussion begins by briefly summarising the research context and reviewing the literature on ethnicity, friendships and social capital. The second part of the analysis examines young people's friendship networks and the forms of intra-ethnic social capital generated during their transitions into secondary schooling and adulthood. It also explores other social factors that shape and sustain Caribbean young people's same-ethnic friendship networks.

Research background

This article is based on research findings from the project entitled, *Caribbean Families, Social Capital and Young People's Diasporic Identities*. This is one of a number of projects within the Families and Social Capital ESRC Research Group at London South Bank University (see www.lsbu.ac.uk/families)[1]. The project is based on in-depth interviews with thirty second and third generation Caribbean young people (16-30-years-old), living in London, Birmingham, Manchester and Nottingham and fifty kinship/family members in these cities[2] and the Caribbean (Barbados, Guyana and Jamaica[3]) across all age groups. The interviews took place during 2003-2004 and the interview model with the young people and family members encouraged generational shifts and patterns to emerge in relation to social capital and ethnicity. Also highlighted in the analysis is the significance of transnational and cross-cultural family networks, rituals and celebrations in shaping ethnic identity (see Reynolds, 2004, 2006a and b; Reynolds and Zontini, 2006 and 2007).

Ethnicity, social capital and friendship networks

The quality of individuals' social relationships and the conditions that create bonding networks between people has long been a concern of social capital theorists such as James Coleman and Robert Putnam and it is necessary to consider briefly aspects of their writings related to the issues of ethnic identity. Putnam defines social capital as 'features of social life—networks, norms and trust—that enable participants to act together more effectively to pursue

1   The research forms part of the Families and Social Capital ESRC Research Group programme of work (ESRC Award Reference: M570255001). I would like to thank Professor Janet Holland and Dr. Susie Weller, Families and Social Capital ESRC Research Group for their comments on earlier drafts of the article.

2   A non-purposive method of sampling (snowballing) was used to select the sample across these contrasting urban locations in the U.K. where there is a high pattern of Caribbean settlement. In London interviews took place with 25 family members, in Birmingham and Manchester I interviewed 10 family members in each of these areas and in Nottingham interviews took place with 5 family members.

3   These countries also present an interesting contrast in terms of ethnic composition of the population. While Barbados is more or less mono-ethnic, comprising people of African descent, both Jamaica and Guyana are ethnically mixed. For example, 51% of the population of Guyana originate from the Indian sub-continent, African descendants are the second largest group and there exist small but substantial proportions of Amerindians, Syrians and Madeirans. In Jamaica people come from backgrounds as ethnically diverse as Africa, Europe, and South East Asia and China

shared objectives' (Putnam, 1994:2). He suggests that community members' participation in community affairs, or 'civic engagement', is a key aspect of social capital because their participation leads to various forms of collective action. Social capital is differentiated according to its capacity for 'bridging' (this is outward looking and involves relationships and networks of trust and reciprocity between different groups and communities) or 'bonding' (this is inward looking and involves relationships and networks of trust and reciprocity that reinforce bonds and connections within groups)[4]. Coleman adopts a functionalist approach to understanding social capital. He suggests that families and communities provide a social function that can be used as a resource by members to best represent their interests. Social capital is therefore embedded in family and community relations because it creates mutually beneficial relationships that are based on a normative expectation of obligation and reciprocity for its members (Morrow, 1999a; Winter, 2002). Coleman and Putnam both stress collective goods of reciprocity, trust and co-operation.

Social capital as a mechanism for integration and social cohesion has been utilised and applied to policy debates on 'race', multi-culturalism, diversity and the changing nature of British society. Several commentators have argued that our understanding of social capital embodies a moralistic and paternalistic concept of community that is sanctioned by the State (see for example, Amin, 2005; Furedi, 2006) and there is widespread concern over some minority ethnic groups unwillingness to integrate and actively participate in a wide range of civic and associational life (Faulkner, 2004; Runnymede Trust, 2004). A number of studies also implicitly and explicitly argue that different racial and ethnic groups' comparative failure to integrate and work across ethnic and religious groups to resolve common concerns has contributed to existing racial tensions and feelings of social exclusion in Britain today (for example see Parekh, 2000; Ousley, 2001). These studies reflect a wider preoccupation among policymakers concerning how to improve the active participation of marginalised groups in the democratic decision-making process and their connection to valuable external social resources (Strategy Unit, 2003; Fevre, 2004). Coleman's arguments concerning 'strong' and 'weak' social capital have been crucial in problematising different migrant communities (Goulbourne and Solomos, 2003; Zontini, 2004; Mand, 2006). So, for example, The Caribbean family is stereotyped as having 'weak' social capital and supporters of this viewpoint point to the limited

---

4   Woolcock (1998) adds a third dimension to Putnam's work: 'linking' social capital. This examines the capacity for social capital to develop relationships and networks of trust and reciprocity that allow individuals to access and link across different formal and informal resources.

participation of the Caribbean community in mainstream civic activities creating negative outcomes for individuals, family and community (Berthoud, 1999a/b and 2001). Despite the popular appeal of this weak/strong binary divide by policymakers and politicians alike, this oversimplification has been criticised by many writers who argue that social capital as a resource is shaped and constrained by structural divisions in society such as ethnicity, 'race', gender, social class and generation divisions (Goulbourne and Solomos, 2003; Edwards, 2004). Despite the high prevalence of inter-ethnic kinships networks within the Caribbean community, and compared to other ethnic groups, Caribbean people are unlikely to participate in public civic activities because of a generalised mistrust of society at the institutional level (Anwar, 1994). Yet they demonstrate strong 'bonding' social capital at informal interpersonal (e.g. family and friendship networks) and ethnic specific community levels (e.g. Caribbean welfare-based organisations) (McLean, 2002).

The concept of social capital is useful in capturing the essence of friendship networks in that issues of reciprocal trust, social support and social connectedness, which are typically understood as key features of friendships, are also understood as important social resources (Morrow, 1999b). Friendships are important for individuals' health, self-esteem and well-being. It is argued that people with close networks generally suffer less illness and social disorders compared to those with limited or 'loose' networks (Allan, 1989; Hall et al., 1999; Pahl, 2000). Similarly, friendships generate wider social contacts and networks, which may also benefit individuals (Pahl, 2000). A clear example of this is the way in which it has become a well-recognised practice that people draw on networks of friends to seek employment opportunities, hence the popular mantra *'its not what you know but who you know'.*

With regard to marginalised groups in society, same-ethnic friendship networks create the potential for community and group consciousness that may facilitate social and political mobilisation (Orr, 1999; Parker and Song, 2006a). They also provide a protective buffer and support mechanism in the face of exclusion and discrimination. However, steps to examine the collective values, actions and practices of same-ethnic friendships have been generally overlooked. Firstly in favour of debates that champion inter-ethnic mixing as a means to improve social cohesion (Phillips, 2006). Within this discourse, ethnically segregated networks are criticised as being 'too cohesive' and 'excessively bonded' (Parker and Song, 2006a). Secondly in favour of the individualisation thesis (Beck and Beck Gernsheim, 2002), which assess friendship networks within the context of changing social and moral values concerning family relationships and expressions of self-identity. On this note, it is claimed that friends provide individuals with a sense of self and important aspects of their personality are expressed through their friends (Pahl, 2000; Pahl and Pevalin, 2005). Further it is suggested that shifting circumstances of late modernity—migration, social and geographical mobility, young people as students and middle-income professionals living away from home, the rise of single-parent household and single-dwelling household to name but a few examples—have encouraged individuals' concern about self-identity, expression of personal choice and individual freedom to choose lifestyles (Weeks et al., 1999). Within this context of defining who we are as individuals, and with the emphasis on individual needs and meanings, it is argued that friends and non-kin family have become more salient in our understanding of self-identity (Weeks et al., 1999).

The analysis of Caribbean young people's lives illustrates that family are still important to their construction of ethnic-racial identity. However, in this study the young people's same-ethnic friendships networks are regarded as an equally important social resource. During the interviews the respondents characterised and categorised their friendships according to different degrees of intimacy, which also followed along racial-ethnic lines. Generally speaking, same-ethnic (also same-gender) friendships dominated the category of 'close friends'. These were also referred to as 'best friends'; 'good friends', 'bredrins/sistrens' and encompassed 'family friends' (i.e. networks of friends developed through parents/grandparents networks). In contrast, inter-ethnic friendship networks dominated the category of 'casual friends' and were also referred to as 'acquaintances'. The former category of friendship networks—'close friends'—were seen as representing a high degree of emotional intimacy, and involved issues of reciprocal exchanges, emotional support, trust, belonging, and equality of status whereas the latter category did not. However, the young people did have some degree of social investment with their 'casual friends' and these networks offered social support and connections, which at times functioned in instrumental and strategic ways.

An interesting feature of the young people's accounts was that whilst many of them recollected having 'mixed' and inter-ethnic friendships in the 'close friend' category as young children, by the time they entered secondary school at eleven-years-old these inter-ethnic 'close friends' tended to fall away. Similarly, by the time the respondents were young adults, entering university and/or the workplace, their 'close' friends, and indeed many of their friendship networks in the 'casual friends' category were almost exclusively African-Caribbean. Therefore, the next part of the analysis examines social capital in the context of young people's friendship networks and the forms of intra-ethnic social capital generated by the young people during their transitions into secondary schooling and adulthood, all of which facilitate same-ethnic friendship networks.

Social capital in the context of young people's friendship networks

The young people had high expectations of their close friends and they were strongly invested in these relationships. The themes of reciprocal exchanges, trust, equality, honesty, uncritical support, loyalty, mutual understanding and 'being there' for each other occurred repeatedly in the young people's accounts of friendship, mirroring many other studies that have explored this issue (Nestmann and Hurrelmann, 1994; Morrow, 1999a; Madood, 2004; Thomson and Holland, 2004; Weller, 2006a; Henderson et al., 2007). The following quotation provide some indication of this:

> I trust my friend Marcel. I know that if something bugs me and I tell her, that it will go no further, because she'll just keep that confidence. We've got that understanding that we don't need to say, 'Do not tell anyone'; it's just taken as read. It's like an unspoken rule type of thing.
>
> (Sharon, age 20 years, third generation, London, December 2003.)

Many of them valued stability and durability in their friendships networks and identified the ways that friends complemented specific aspects of their personality:

> It works with my best friends because we're so different, you've got Emma, who's, like, the goody goody and you've got me who's kind of like in between, then you've got Clare who's really naughty. And I find we kind of gel off each other in that sense. They're the type of friends who are constant, and who wouldn't just be [there] at the good times.
>
> (Carol, age 23, third generation, Nottingham, April 2004.)

In many of their accounts the young people expressed a generalised view of same-ethnic friendships framed around trust, support and reciprocal bonds. However, in both explicit and implicit terms they also identified how shared ethnic and racial bonds provided the context for these reciprocal trust relationships. These strong bonding ties established through shared a Caribbean ethnic identity encouraged natural affinity, familiarity and a sense of empathy between the young people and their same-ethnic friends:

> Ciara and Missy are my only two friends who are fully Jamaican, like both parents come from Jamaica, and that's what why we have a lot in common. The conversations I have with Ciara and Missy I couldn't have with my other friends. We talk about the kind of food we're eating. Ciara may say 'What are you having in your soup?' I'll know she's talking about dinner on Saturday because we both know that Saturday is soup day. And because we share the same background our conversations are deeper, we talk about our family here [U.K.] and Jamaica.
> (Patrice, age 19, third generation, London, October 2003.)

The young people valued the 'taken for granted' and the 'unsaid' aspect of their same-ethnic friendships, as a result of a shared cultural and ethnic background. This also encompassed an understanding between friends that they had shared similar experiences of social exclusion, racial discrimination and marginality in their everyday lives.

Despite the fact that these British born young people live in racially and ethnically mixed neighbourhoods, on one level it is perhaps unsurprising that the majority of young people in the study only had close friends who were also African-Caribbean. This finding resonates with a report from the Commission for Racial Equality, which claimed that more than 90% of white English people have no or few friends from black and minority ethnic groups (CRE, 2004). Likewise the same argument could be applied to other minority ethnic communities who also have limited number of close friends outside of their own ethnic groups (CRE, 2004 and 2005). One paradox with regard to the Caribbean community in the Britain is that compared to other minority groups they are more likely to have ethnically mixed families and recent Census figures suggest that 'mixed-raced' population, based on White/Black Caribbean partnerships, is the fastest growing black population (Platt et al., 2005; Owen, 2006). Yet, despite a greater propensity towards ethnically mixed families, many Caribbean people still choose their 'close friends' on the basis of a shared ethnic-racial background.

One reason for this could be that people choose friends very similar to themselves, who share similar social positions, resources and backgrounds, as a number of authors have suggested (see for example, Allan, 1996; Cotterell, 1996; Pahl and Pevalin, 2005). The data certainly support this fact. The young people were very uniform in their friendship choices in terms of ethnicity, gender, age and sexuality. As previously stated only four out of thirty respondents had close inter-ethnic friendship networks. Two of the thirty respondents identified a close friend of the opposite gender. Just one person, a female respondent, was a close friend with someone who had a different sexual orientation (e.g. male homosexual). The vast majority of respondents said that they had met their 'close' friends as children at secondary school, or later at college/university.

Some of the key writers in the field of friendship and social networks studies claim that the principle of equality is central in sustaining successful friendship networks and this is the main reason that people have friends that are very similar to themselves in terms of social background (Blau, 1977; Blau and Schwartz, 1984; Allan and Adams, 1999; Pahl, 2000). Moreover, those friendships that are generally marked by great social differences—such as, for example, ethnic divisions with inherent differences of status and perceived racial hierarchies and stereotypes that emerge out of this—are much harder to sustain and generally fade over time because it is more difficult to manage inequality.

Putnam's (2000) perspective on social capital regards people's civic participation in associational activities—for example members of a sports team or communities of interest—as a social resource in encouraging diverse people to interact with each other. It could be argued that this form of 'co-operative independence' (Blau, 1977) generated through civic participation has the potential to create the most conducive environment for the development of inter-ethnic friendships, because in pursuing a common goal, race or ethnic status of individual members is irrelevant (Blau, 1977). Some of the data in the study is certainly indicative of this and supports this viewpoint. For example, Videl, a second generation Indo-Caribbean was one of the few respondents who were actively involved in a diverse range of social clubs within his local neighbourhood. Videl was a keen sportsman and participated in the football and cricket team. He was also a member of the local environmental group, photography club and Stop the War coalition. He used these organisations to develop friendships with people across a broad spectrum of racial, ethnic and social backgrounds. Indeed, compared to the other respondents in the study, Videl had the most racially and socially diverse groups of friends.

However, whilst civic participation is a useful resource in developing inter-ethnic friendships and 'bridging' networks, sustaining enduring friendships bonds over a period of time is problematic because friendships developed within this context may only last as long as there is a common purpose and will fade thereafter (Pahl, 2000). Perhaps, this goes some way towards explaining why inter-ethnic friendships—which are induced by cooperative independence—are generally less stable and enduring over the life course compared to same-ethnic friendships.

At a policy level the explicit support and promotion of policies aimed at encouraging inter-ethnic mixing and friendships networks between diverse social groups have largely been in the areas of education and schooling (Weller and Bruegel, 2006; Phillips, 2006; Macleod, 2006). School is a primary arena where children develop social capital that is independent from their parents (Weller, 2006a). Weller and Bruegel's (2006) study exploring social capital in the context of children's school transitions found that inter-ethnic friendships developed at school are important social resources for bridging across different ethnic groups. Furthermore, young children at primary school in ethnically mixed areas were more likely to have inter-ethnic friendships and they rarely saw difference in terms of ethnic racial divisions. It was not until children later moved to secondary school that they developed this awareness of ethnic-racial difference and it was in secondary schools that they were more likely to develop same-ethnic friendships. Finally their study also reinforces the claim that common interest developed through sports, such as membership of the football team facilitates inter-ethnic friendships, a point previously highlighted in the analysis.

Another important research finding by Weller and Bruegel (2006) was that black and minority ethnic children in predominantly white schools or white classes at primary school were more likely to have white friends when they attended secondary schools that were ethnically mixed. In this study the Caribbean young people's retrospective accounts of their schooling experiences directly contradict this finding. What the data strongly indicates is that ethnically mixed secondary schools acted as a key catalyst for constructing identity in racial-ethnic terms. Developing same-ethnic friendships, and moving away from their white friends, was an important social resource of the young people to do so. The next part of the analysis explores the importance of secondary school for the Caribbean young people in developing ethnic identity and race consciousness. These accounts provide retrospective and reflective considerations of their schooling years, which they previously had not considered when they going through this stage of the life course. Critics may point to the authenticity of what is remembered in retrospective accounts. However, the value and benefits derived from understanding memories as a valuable social resource from which marginalised groups construct their narratives and redefine and negotiate identities far outweighs any criticism of this approach (see Plummer, 2001; Reynolds, 2005).

Same-ethnic friendships: culture, transitions and identity

In terms of constructing and reflecting on ethnic identity during these adolescent years key factors precipitated the young people's same ethnic-racial friendships. These included (i) children's transition to secondary school (ii) the family visit back home to the Caribbean, which re-affirmed ethnic and cultural identity (iii) transitions to higher education and the workplace, all of which are discussed in the following section.

Children's transition to secondary school

The vast majority of young people in the study had maintained close friendship bonds established in secondary schools and this is why it is important to consider children's transitions to secondary school and the way it relates to Caribbean young people's same-ethnic friendship networks in current times. All of the respondents identified one 'best' or close friendship formed during these schooling years. This finding goes against other studies into friendship networks and the claim that many adults have found it difficult to maintain their friendship networks from childhood (Mason, 1999; Pahl and Pevalin, 2005, Pahl et al., 2006). One reason that these Caribbean young people have been able to maintain their childhood friendships is because of established settlement patterns of Caribbean people into 'black neighbourhoods' and related to this, limited geographical mobility amongst the second and third generation compared to previous generations of Caribbean migrants (Reynolds 2006a). For example, many of the young people interviewed have never lived outside the area where they were born and went to school. Today, as young adults they either live at their parents' homes or within 30 minutes travelling time from those homes. Friendships bonds developed in the school context have been facilitated by this limited mobility.

The Caribbean young people experiences of school indicates that there were a number of factors, which facilitated the development of same-ethnic friendships when moving to secondary school. The transition from primary to secondary school usually occurs when children are eleven-years-old and they are entering the adolescent phase in the life-course. A number of studies show that adolescence is a crucial time for children to begin to explore issues of identity, separate to that of their family and parents (Cotterell, 1996; Morrow, 1999a; Lucey and Reay, 2000). For Caribbean and other black adolescents living in a white society, part of this identity making is articulated in ethnic-racial terms. This involves a process of race awareness, the development of a racial self and sensitivity to racial difference (Mirza, 1992; Tizard and Phoenix, 1993; Tatum, 1997; Weekes, 1997; Rumbalt and Portes, 2001). It was during adolescence that many of the Caribbean young people in the study remarked that for the first time they felt different to, or excluded from, white school friends and they had experienced direct (or open) racial discrimination. Consequently, the young people recollected that when they started secondary school they racially identified with other black children and they actively sought to interact with them on the basis that they were probably going through the same process of self-reflection and racial/ethnic identity formation. These friendship networks also acted as a protective buffer and support mechanism in the face of real (or perceived) instances of racial discrimination by other children and teachers. Moving to secondary school meant moving out of their local neighbourhoods into widening areas, which gave them the chance to meet a wider network of black children from neighbouring communities. The following quotation by Patrice recollecting her friendship networks in the context of her transition from primary to secondary school addresses some of these issues:

At primary school, all my friends were black and two of them were white. We [friends] all applied for [school] but I was the only one to get in. It was a good school and the majority of children that go there are white and middle-class. It was in a good area, not our area, but further out from where I lived. So I had to leave all my friends, and I had to make new friends. My main friends in secondary school were black because we had to stick together because they weren't many black girls in that school. They used to say we were a gang because we all hung around together and we were all black, whereas the majority of school was white. We used to get told off and always getting into trouble with the teachers, saying we was 'too loud' and we had 'too much attitude' but we were just sticking up for ourselves. Besides we were good at out work, I left with 10 GCSEs with four of them A* [grades] and my friends also got loads of GCSEs too so they [teachers] really couldn't tell us anything because we did get on with our work but

they [teachers] just didn't like us, they [teachers] couldn't relate to us.
(Patrice, age 19, third generation, London, October 2003.)

It is also useful to consider how aspects of the school curriculum and
the practice of streaming children according to academic ability could have
contributed to the salience of same-ethnic friendship networks in multi-ethnic
secondary school. Children's school friendship choices are mostly established
with children in the same year group and classes (Moody, 2001; Lahelma, 2002;
Weller, 2006a). This creates a potential situation whereby Caribbean children,
disproportionately concentrated in lower academic streams, are choosing other
same-ethnic friends who are also located within these groups. Similarly the
minority of Caribbean students situated in the higher academic stream may
band together for support and protection.

By and large it was the young people who attended comprehensive schools
in working class and multi-cultural communities that had greater tendency to
develop same-ethnic friendships. In contrast, the data suggests that the young
people who moved from predominately white primary schools to predominately
white secondary schools in affluent areas had ethnically diverse friends. Those
young people who attended privately funded secondary schools also had greater
tendency to develop multi-racial social networks of friends. Tellingly, these
young people either developed a racialised consciousness later in life, for example,
at university or the workplace or they utilised other social resources within
their social networks, such as transnational family and kinship relationships,
to construct ethnic identity. Two respondents, Justin and Anthony attended
private schools and they discussed these experiences during the interviews.
Justin, who was sixteen-years-old was still at school and Anthony, who is
twenty-years-old, had left school a few short years ago. Both Justin and Anthony
lived in professional two-parents middle-class households, in affluent outer
suburbs of London. In Justin's case, only a handful of black (mainly African)
children attended his school and his friends come from diverse racial and ethnic
backgrounds. On the advice and guidance of his parents Justin was very strategic
in selecting friends on the basis of developing future relationships and contacts
that could help him later in life. The additional economic resources available to
him at school also created greater opportunities to participate in extra-curricular
activity, which promoted inter-ethnic mixing. So for example, Justin was an
avid sportsman and represented his school in cricket, football, hockey, rugby
and swimming. He also attended the school's annual skiing trips to Austria

where he socialised with racially diverse networks. The bonding factor in Justin's friendship networks was shared-socio-economic status. In turn, Justin was able to use these bonds to bridge into inter-ethnic friendships.

Anthony's experiences provide a different perspective concerning inter-ethnic friendship networks established in privately funded predominantly white secondary schools. Anthony reflected that his parents had a race-conscious approach to childrearing and this was instrumental in him developing race awareness and ethnic identity at a very young age. In addition when Anthony was a small child, his father accepted a senior government post in Guyana and the entire family relocated here and this was where he completed his formative education. When Anthony's family migrated back to the U.K. in the mid-1990s he attended a secondary school where he was the only black child in his year group. Anthony felt that his experiences of living in the Caribbean during his formative years, alongside his parents' childrearing approach made him very aware of his ethnic-racial identity from a young age. These factors provided him with the confidence to develop multi-racial networks of friends whilst at the same time being embedded in his own ethnic-racial identity. His experiences show that strong bonding social capital within family and community networks can act as a precursor to bridging social capital in people's friendships bonds, allowing them to 'bridge out' and establish inter-ethnic friendships (Reynolds, 2006a).

The analysis also provides illustrative examples of the way in which parents facilitate their children's same-ethnic friendships networks. This influence was particularly strong when they were young children at school. However, even today as young adults the young people acknowledge that their parents still continue to influence their friendships choices, albeit to a lesser degree than when they were children.

Family visits home

The six week Summer holidays in the Caribbean as an adolescent was often mentioned by the young people as the first time they were allowed to visit without their parents, or when they travelled with their parents, were allowed greater freedom to move around local areas unsupervised with their siblings and cousins of a similar age. Generally, it was the young men who reported much greater personal freedom of movement. The gendered (and racial) policing of black female identity meant that the young women experience a higher degree of parental/ adult supervision as they moved through public spaces. Gender divisions aside, these family visits 'home', occurring at a life stage where adolescent are typically exploring issues of identity and belonging, acted as social resource in reaffirming a racial and ethnic identity and increased their awareness of living in, what they perceived as, a racist society. This further established their ethnic-racial difference from white children when they returned to school after these family holidays and encouraged them to develop same-ethnic friendship bonds.

Transition to higher education and the workplace

Higher education also played a crucial role in consolidating the young people's networks along racial and ethnic lines. Looking at the experiences of the young people who attended higher education, it was noticeable that they generally chose to go to local universities in black and urban areas where other black students also attended *en masse*, instead of institutions that may be better resourced (and may provide them with better opportunities) where there were limited number of black students (Reynolds 2006a). They studied courses where there were a relatively high number of black students and that provided a greater degree of success and future career opportunities:

> I wasn't really sure what social work was but I know that they had plenty of black people on the course and you see that other black people have careers in that area. I really wanted to do the librarian course at [university] but some subjects, you rarely find black people working in that area. Whilst in areas like social work and social housing there's more opportunities and you have a fair chance of completing and getting a good job at the end.
>
> (Angela, age 29, second generation, Birmingham, December 2003.)

The few young people who did venture out to institutions in largely mono-ethnic provincial areas found that they often felt isolated and alienated from their white peers and one strategy to cope with the situation was to actively seek out friendships with other black and minority ethnic students who they could rely on for support.

> Part of the process of us three getting together was when we was in college, we kind of got forced to be just friends, but it kind of lasted. We were the only black girls on the course, the rest were white [girls] and no-one wanted to work with us, so we did what we had to do and everyone was

like'we're not talking to them'. We became really close friends because of all the problems we were having in class and stuff, and so we all supported each other to get each other through the course because we were all going through the same thing.

(Emma, age 25, second generation, London, April 2005.)

University life also created the space, opportunity and networking possibilities for black students to meet and socialise with other black students and further explore issues of ethnic and racial identity through their participation in ethnic specific events, such as black student associations, and discussions and workshops concerning this issue. These experiences in the university setting created friendships networks for the young people that have survived after leaving. Parallels were also found in the work context where the young people who were in a racial minority participated in networking, support and mentoring events with other black colleagues. Not surprisingly, friendships emerged out of this shared experience. In the work setting same-ethnic friendships were also likely to develop because people generally make friends at work by selecting from the pool of colleagues they work with on regular basis and who share a similar status level of employment. Black people are concentrated and over represented in certain employment sectors and within this status, at status level (e.g. junior administrative posts in local and central government administration), whilst under-represented in others (Madood, 1997; Strategy Unit, 2003). Therefore within their categories and status level of employment they are more likely to socialise and develop friendship networks with other black colleagues.

Conclusion

In conclusion the notion of social capital is helpful in understanding how people choose and maintain their friendship networks. In the context of second and third generation Caribbean young people in the U.K., same-ethnic friendships networks generated important social resources for developing a sense of belonging and ethnic identity. Issues of particularised trust, emotional support, reciprocal care, mutual understanding and 'being there' that are provided by these same-ethnic friendships are all important to these young people because of the generalised mistrust, suspicion, social exclusion and discrimination experienced within wider society. The data shows that for these young people a shared ethnic bond and notions of ethnic belonging encouraged the acquisition and maintenance of particular sets of friendship networks and the displacement of other friendships which were outside these ethnic specific group boundaries and identities. As a result by the time the majority of respondents reached adolescence and had moved to secondary school most of their 'close' friends shared the same ethnic-racial background, although they did have inter-ethnic friends and associates.

Secondary school and the adolescent phase of the life-course were particular important to the young people in developing race consciousness and thinking about their identity in ethnic-racial terms. Same-ethnic friendships at school facilitated this process as well as providing mutual support and shared understanding concerning issues of racial discrimination and social exclusion. The family visits back home to the Caribbean, their experiences at university and the workplace further established ethnic group identity and ethnic-racial difference to their white peers and encouraged same-ethnic friendship bonds. Most of the young people's close friends were established in school or college and these friendships bonds have mostly endured across time. This factor is indicative of the strong bonding networks that are established through, and generated by, a shared ethnic identity and belonging.

Chapter 7

Religious identity based social networks as facilitators of teenagers' social capital: A case study on Adventist families in Finland

Arniika Kuusisto

Introduction

This article examines the social capital of families affiliated with religious minority denominations, using the context of Adventism in Finland as a case study. I have previously looked at Adventist young people's religious identity, and the present analysis is intended to take this one step further by examining the networks generated through the shared religious minority identity among denomination members. The perspective of the data analysed is based on the views of the Adventist parents of teenagers.

A religious minority provides an interesting context for research. The value system in a minority, especially a small minority like the Adventist community, is not only more cohesive—both in terms of value system and social networks—but it may also be more effective in producing social capital. Whereas parental values are increasingly fragmented in the contemporary postmodern society, within a more coherent minority setting the culture and lifestyle are more uniformly defined and child-rearing practices typically vary less.

Since social capital is significant for identity formation (Bourdieu, 1997), the present analysis is very much linked to some of my previous findings (summarised later). The main focus is on social ties and networks based on shared values within a minority setting, as well as the potential effects of religious membership on the teenagers' identities.

Identity development is closely connected with the socialisation process, i.e. the process of becoming a part of the group by learning its norms, customs and traditions. Furthermore, Pulkkinen (2002) has examined the link between socialisation and children's social capital, and introduced the concept of *initial social capital* into the field of developmental psychology. Her concept includes the developmental support received in the early socialisation context—primarily from the home and parents. In the context of this research, the denominational setting, and the particular social network within it, may also influence the socialisation process. After all, studies of religious socialisation among minority groups, and especially among Adventists in Finland, are very few. The present study, along with my previously reported findings (e.g. Kuusisto, 2003) will also contribute to a better understanding of such settings.

I will first examine *religious identity* as understood in this study, and then set a contextual framework by briefly introducing my previous findings on teenagers' religious identity in the research context. After that I will move on to looking at some notions of social capital, then to describe the methodological framework used here, followed by results and conclusions.

Religious identity

Identity is a concept with several connotations and varying uses in different fields of research. In social sciences, the notion has mainly been used as a means of understanding selfhood and individuality (Adams and Marshall, 1996, 429). In this regard, Levine (2003, 191) conceptualises identity as 'an ongoing psycho-social process during which various characteristics of the self are internalised, labelled, valued, and organised'. Even though this process continues throughout life, adolescence has been seen as a phase with special importance to identity development (e.g. Kroger, 1996, 1). The nature of identity as a process and object of constant negotiation over time is especially apparent when the values and expectations in the home differ greatly from those endorsed in the wider society (Schmälzle, 2001, 30; van Hoof and Raaijmakers, 2002, 201), or when the individual lives concurrently in different cultures (Sam and Virta, 2003, 213).

Religion, as a cultural phenomenon and an expression of spirituality, can also play a considerable role in structuring identity (Griffith and Griggs, 2001, 14; Heimbrock, 2001, 64[1]; Hunsberger et al., 2001, 365). However, although identity development in adolescence—particularly identity crisis—has been studied rather widely, there has been little research on any connection between religion and adolescent identity development and, hence, on any relation of religious identity to the adolescent's religious commitment. When measured in terms of church attendance, for example, more religious commitment has been linked with the identity statuses involving more general ideological commitment (Hunsberger et al., 2001, 367). [2]

---

1   Heimbrock (2001) sees the everyday usage of the concept 'religious identity' as problematic: he claims that religious experiences and theological reflections do not generally clarify 'a specific 'religious' dimension of a person's identity', and that linking religion and identity is based on a monolithic, simplistic concept of religion. Heimbrock's discussion of this issue is from a theological standpoint.

2   This refers primarily to statuses of achievement and foreclosure, as originally identified by Marcia (1966). Hunsberger et al., (2001, 367) refer to the studies of Markstrom-Adams et al., (1994) and Tzuriel (1984) as examples of those exploring the relationship between religious commitment and identity statuses.

Thus, *religious identity* here refers to the perceptions that people have concerning themselves as members of a particular religious denomination; a religious self-image and affiliation. It is perceived to include the individual's agency (Côté and Schwartz, 2002, 571; see also Coleman, 1988, 96) and, in line with social identity theory, to be essentially based on an individual's 'knowledge of his membership of a social group (or groups) together with the value and emotional significance attached to that membership' (Tajfel, 1981, 255). In this research it is seen as a personal association with the particular religious community in question.

Research context

Besides Sabbath (Saturday) observance and baptism through immersion, the life style choices emphasised within the Seventh-day Adventist minority culture[3] are also relevant to the research framework here. Adventism generally affects other spheres of life besides just personal devotion. The denomination also arranges various programmes for children and young people, and runs a network of schools and universities; in Finland there are presently four Adventist church maintained schools[4]. The social network of the denomination may also play an important role in socialising their young people. Thus the impact of the religious community (e.g. peers, teachers and other staff in denominational schools or summer camps, as well as members of the local congregation) as socialisers cannot be disregarded.

As a starting point for the present analysis, a brief introduction to some of my previously reported findings (Kuusisto, 2003; 2005a; 2006) from the same sample will help to set the framework. For Adventist teenagers, membership in the Finnish Adventist denomination is a significant component of their identity. Their religious identity was measured both in terms of direct responses to the survey statement, 'The fact that I am an Adventist is an important part of my identity', agreed with by 80% (f = 74; $M = 3.12$[5]; $SD=.52$) of these young people; and with a more extensive measure based on Phinney's (1992; 2004) MEIM[6] ($M = 2.85$; $SD=.50$). There was a statistically significant correlation between these two Adventist identity measures (.61**[7]).

3   Later referred to as Adventist/Adventism. The Adventist culture emphasises a healthy life style, often including vegetarianism, abstinence, avoidance of cigarettes and caffeinated drinks.
4   More on Adventist schools in the Finnish Education system in Kuusisto 2005c.
5   Mean on the scale 1-4, four representing the maximum in Adventist identity.
6   The *Multi-Ethnic Identity Measure*. This measure was extensively modified to fit the context of this research
7   Correlation is significant at the 0.01 level (2-tailed).

In order to further examine the nature of these teenagers' religious identity and their commitment to it, a more exploratory analysis was done by tagging the answers (on Likert scale 1-4) into three categories; depicting social (M = 3.09, SD = .62), cultural (M = 3.09, SD = .62), and spiritual (M = 3.10, SD = .58) aspects (Kuusisto, 2006, 138). Whether the religious minority identity is affected by the social context of the school they attend was also examined, i.e. whether the religious identity is context-specific[8]. The stated Adventist identity (.10) and the wider measure of Adventist identity (.16) did not correlate significantly with the social context of the school attended, and neither did the young people's self-esteem (.19). Thus, the teenagers' religious identity also seems to be rather independent of the social context (measured in terms of attending a mainstream versus a denominational school), which might, in line with Dunkel (2006), indicate the individual's sense of self-continuity and thus stronger identity commitment, and a sense of being the same person regardless of temporal and social contexts, emphasised by van Hoof and Raaijmakers (2002) as a central part of identity formation. Age did not have a significant effect on teenagers' Adventist identity, nor did gender (Kuusisto, 2005a).

Another set of data gathered among 15-30 year-old Adventists (n = 106) signifies that (a) religious membership affects young people's leisure, as 42% of these young people spend most of their free-time with other Adventist youth; and that (b) the religious minority can form rather tight social networks for the young people affiliated with it. In those data, 40% of the young people said that most of their friends are Adventists, and 22% stated that practically none of their friends are from outside the denomination. Moreover, for 71% the majority of their relatives also belong to the same movement, whereas only 12% stated that they have no Adventist relatives (Kuusisto, 2003, 289). Furthermore, this number of Adventist relatives may well affect the nature of socialisation; Bull and Lockhart (2007, 348-362), in their comprehensive analysis of Adventism in the United States, have found a link between the religious membership (measured with the number of succeeding Adventist generations) in the family history, and the individual's relationship to the denomination and her position in the society (e.g. educational level and socioeconomic status).

8   An analogous research design has previously been completed by Umaña-Taylor's (2004) looking at ethnic identity (also utilising MEIM) in relation to school social context.

Social capital

The notion of social capital has not been widely applied to the lives of children and young people (see e.g. Ellonen and Korkiamäki, 2005); although Bordieu (1980), who has particularly emphasised its role in group memberships, also considers social capital to be important in shaping children and young people's social development (see Coleman, 1990). Still, the concept can bring an interesting tool into examining the networking of young people who share religious values and an identity based on their affiliation with a religious minority. According to theories of social capital (e.g. Smith, 2001), the adolescent with a good 'stock' of social capital is more likely to reap other benefits such as better health; and may be able to utilise her networks in e.g. finding a place to stay when travelling.

There are numerous varying definitions of social capital. For Putnam, it refers to 'the norms and networks of trust and reciprocity that foster collective action' or 'connections among individuals—social networks and the norms of reciprocity and trustworthiness that arise from them' (2000, 19). Furthermore, Cohen and Prusak (2001, 4) write that, 'social capital consists of the stock of active connections among people: the trust, mutual understanding, and shared values and behaviours that bind the members of human networks and communities and make cooperative action possible'. Religious participation can be seen as an important source of social capital generating networks (Wuthnow, 2002; Putnam, 2000).

The notion of social capital has been divided into bridging (relationships across diverse social groups) and bonding (cementing homogenous groups) social capital (Putnam, 2000), both of which are applicable to the context of this study. Besides bonding the minority members together, when it comes to educational or ethnical background a denomination may be rather heterogeneous. Thus, a denominational network can also bridge together people who in the wider societal context represent different social positions. On the other hand, if the network encourages the individual to interact merely with people sharing a similar background, although bonding these people together, the religious affiliation may even prevent other — possibly more influential — contacts from developing (Wuthnow, 2002, 669; Putnam, 2000). In this regard, in relation to bridging social capital, Wuthnow (2002) distinguishes between two further sub-types: *identity-bridging social capital* (networks spanning culturally defined differences such as ethnicity or religious tradition) and *status-bridging social capital* (networks spanning vertical arrangements of power, influence, wealth, and prestige), he has examined the latter in relation to affiliation with religious groups. Wuthnow sees religious membership or affiliation as a social resource, producing social relationships and networks, which may help the community or an individual to accomplish their aspirations. However, although religious membership and congregational leadership positions are, according to Wuthnow's study, consistently associated with friendships with persons of wealth or those in positions of power, interestingly, the frequency of religious attendance was largely unrelated to these measures of social capital. Moreover, his data shows significant variations in levels of commitment between different religious traditions and different sized congregations.

Most explicitly for the context of this study, however, the notion of social capital has been applied to education and the family context by Coleman (1988; 1990). Coleman (1988, 100) regards social capital as essential for children's development and necessity for the creation of *human capital*, 'by changes in persons that bring about skills and capabilities that make them able to act in new ways'. Whereas, according to him, social capital 'comes about through changes in the relations among persons that facilitate action', and its worth lies in 'the value of these aspects of social structure to actors as resources that they can use to achieve their interests', or 'something of value has been produced for those actors who have this resource available and that the value depends on social organisation' (100-101). Although Coleman's research focuses on human capital as understood through academic education, there are many similarities between his findings and previous research on intergenerational value transmission—in terms of attachment between parents and children (Yli-Luoma, 1990, based on Bowlby, 1988 and Ainsworth, 1964), and the nature of relationships, such as parental authority in the family (Holm, 2001; Sundén, 1974; Kuusisto, 2003).

Furthermore, Coleman has investigated the importance of family social capital within the surrounding community; illustrated, for example, in the way that, in some living environments, the normative structure 'ensures that unattended children will be 'looked after' by adults in the vicinity'. He also states that, with close ties through family, community, and religious affiliation, trustworthiness is taken for granted, which eases the interaction (in his example the transactions in a wholesale diamond market). Any misuse of the network trust would cause a loss of family, religious and community ties. Coleman also emphasises the effectiveness of community norms as a form of social capital.

These can, besides facilitating certain actions (such as walking alone at night safely), also constrain others; his example of this is a community with strong and effective norms, restraining young people from—as he rather humorously expresses it—'having a good time' (Coleman, 1988, 99-100). This can easily be applied to the context of a rather coherent religious community, with its specific ideas of suitable behaviour and other matters such as appearance or what sort of music is appropriate for a young person to listen to.

Coleman writes about the value of networks by identifying several forms of social capital, mentioning issues such as information sharing in social relations (creating 'information channels' for individuals), norms and effective sanctions (e.g. those supporting and rewarding high academic achievement in the community or sanctioning crimes), which facilitate certain actions while constraining others (Coleman, 1988, 105). In the context of this study, the facilitated and constrained actions would be guided by the underlying religious values and denominational norms.

In the case of norms imposed on children by the parents, Coleman's notion of *intergenerational closure* (1988, 106), representing the relations between parents and children and their relations outside the family, is a particularly useful one when looking at socialisation in minority denominational settings. It illustrates, firstly, the relationships between peers in a school, meeting each other daily and having expectations towards each other, as well as developing norms for each other's behaviour. Whether the intergenerational closure is present in the community has to do with the parents' relations with each other—that is, whether the parents are friends of the parents of their children's friends (Coleman, 1988, 107). If they are members of the same community—in this case the Adventist denomination—they are likely to impose similar values and norms on their children, and the same set of sanctions monitors the behaviour of all their children. Therefore, the existence of intergenerational closure, in Coleman's words (ibid.), 'provides a quantity of social capital available to each parent in raising his children', which is important for both the existence of effective norms and the trustworthiness of social structures allowing the creation of obligations and expectations.

Coleman also examines the effect of a lack of social capital in terms of predicting that a young person will drop out of school before graduation (Coleman, 1988, 99-100). This analysis is interesting for the purposes of this research in that, if social capital helps the adolescent to stick with the school community, denominational networking may also help the Adventist young people to carry on with their religious affiliation after leaving the family home or denominational boarding school.

In this study, social capital is understood through the shared values and norms, and networks developed among those within the religious minority community. Thus, looking at the young people who have been socialised within this religious minority context in particular, the religious affiliation of an adolescent and her family can be seen as a social resource, creating social ties which are in turn an important source of networks for developing social capital.

Research questions

Based on the previous research literature as well as the findings of my previously analysed data depicting the significance of religious membership in Finnish Adventist teenagers' identities, this article aims to investigate whether this shared identity, in the form of denominational networks, also generates social capital for the teenagers and their families. More precisely, this article aims to examine the following questions:

1.   Does affiliation and the shared identity based network in the Finnish Adventist denomination create social capital for young people and/or their families? If so, what kinds of practical benefits does it bring?
2.   How do these social ties and networks affect young people's religious identity?

Method and sample

The study utilises mixed methodology[9] (Tashakkori and Teddlie, 1998), using both quantitative and qualitative approaches. The data includes survey and interview data gathered from teenagers, young adults and parents, as well as information from supplementary fieldwork.[10] This article features selected aspects and findings of the data gathered in 2004-2005 from the parents of Finnish Adventist teenagers.

The parental questionnaire was sent to the homes of 94 teenagers who had, in the previous survey, reported having an Adventist background. It was answered by 55 parents (37 mothers and 18 fathers) ages 36-67 (parental age $M=46$; median 45; SD 5.80). The Adventist generation represented—i.e. the number

9   Both sequential quantitative—qualitative (a survey followed by interviews) and qualitative—quantitative (interviews followed by survey and fieldwork data) methods are used. Each data set and the measures / instruments used cumulatively build on the findings from previously analysed data sets, and some of the sampling is done using a multi-stage sampling technique — for example, by including a question charting the willingness of the subject to be interviewed at the survey stage.
10   On methodological considerations here, see Kuusisto 2005b.

of succeeding generations of Adventism in the family history—was rather evenly split between first (f=16; 32%), second (f=16; 32%), and third (f=14; 28%); the sample also included a few (f=4; 8%) fourth generation Adventists. Of the 55 participants, 52 reported a baptismal age. Those fell in between ages 10 and 40, averaging age 18 (SD 7.66). Over half (f=30; 58%) had been baptised before the time they reached their legal majority (at the age of 18 in Finland); and the vast majority (f=44; 85%) by the age of 25.

The questionnaire started with a personal data section, and continued with two quantitative sections (statements on the Likert scale 1-4): the first on home education and the second on the relationship towards Adventist denomination as a cultural and a social network. The final section consisted of open questions. Those charted the parental views on (a) the choices and influences of school as a social context (denominational versus mainstream schools); (b) the possible effects of peer pressure on the adoption of the family value system (e.g. teenagers' willingness to participate in disco); (c) Adventist values, worldview and identity; (d) doctrines; (e) the denomination's effect on the parents' life choices; (f) the personal meaning of faith and the congregation; (g) possible benefits of social networking for the young people; (h) family practices on the Sabbath; and (i) the means of values education, to name a few.

Because of the relatively small number of respondents, in what follows I will generally present frequencies together with the percentages; the latter are only included for clarifying the proportion of a particular opinion in the data, and should be understood to be of an indicative value.

Results

The parents saw the denominational ties and networks as useful for their families in many ways. For the parents themselves, the social network of the congregation had been beneficial in practical matters such as finding a house, a job or a place of study for slightly over half (51%, f=26) of the respondents. The social networks were also rather significant for them; most of them (64%, f=33) said that most of their friends are Adventists, and for nearly a third of them (30%, f=16) most of their relatives were as well. When it comes to their children's individual social networks, most respondents (79%, f=42) considered their teenagers to have many friends outside of the denominational community as well.

Congregational membership as such also meant a lot to the parents. Personal faith, conceivably the core motivation for membership, was typically described as the mainstay or backbone of their life, their hope for eternal life, an inseparable part of life, and the foundation of everything else. The congregation was described as a 'family' or 'home'; a place for social encounters and intercession, creating togetherness, trust, and network of faithful, good friends, prayer friends; and a community which gave them a sense of belonging. For example, a 42-year-old mother defined her relationship to congregation and faith in the following way:

> Home. 'Roots'; to belong somewhere, to be something. Trust, hope for something better. Faith is like the air that I breathe, you do not come to think of that. It is a part of me like my heart is. What one feels, it is just life.   [37[11]]

The denominational framework was regarded as a good setting for bringing up children (f=51, 94%). Furthermore, it was seen by the vast majority of parents (f=48; 87.2%) as also protecting their children and adolescents from many bad influences. (Similar attitudes were also held towards the groups developed in mainstream school settings, presented later on.) However, besides dietary issues that affect some lifestyle choices, parents also see Adventist values as setting certain limitations on children's hobbies such as the football games, commonly played on Saturday; or dance lessons, because dancing may be considered inappropriate by some[12]. Furthermore, three quarters of the parents would not allow their teenager to go to a disco on the weekend. A quarter (f=13) would also not allow their teenage daughters to wear make-up. Still, nearly a half (f=25) of the respondents stated that they are aware of their teenagers experimenting with alcohol or tobacco.

Many activities organised for teenagers by the denomination were mentioned by the parents, including (a) mainly social events like ski trips and camps; (b) mainly religious events such as Bible studies and evening worship services; (c) international social and religious events like youth congresses and international pathfinder[13] camps; (d) evangelical events like choir concert trips and going out to sell an evangelical magazine together[14]; (e) charitable activities such as aid trips to orphanages and gathering money for charity, e.g. by ingathering[15] work;

---

11 Questionnaire number.
12 The questionnaire included these two examples in the statement in question.
13 Equivalent to scouts or brownies.
14 School classes may raise money for e.g. charity projects by selling the *Nykyaika* magazine. Some youth have also done it as a summer job to earn pocket money.
15 Voluntary money gathering for charity purposes; 50% of the profit goes to welfare work in Finland and 50% for relief and development work in the third world. The volunteers do not get paid.

(f) other social activities, often generated around a certain skill-developing theme such as guitar lessons or volleyball practices. Also the general benefit of having believing relatives, school friends from other believing families, Adventist dormitory deans and also neighbours around the denominational campuses were mentioned. These influences were considered to be important for 'rooting' the young people in the denomination and its social support networks. As one 44-year-old mother says, 'The youth activities in our congregation are important to our son. It is not easy to part from that circle of friends. The young people also support each other' [7]. Furthermore, a 58-year-old father saw the benefits of teenagers' networking as significant in terms of their long-term attachment to the denomination:

> Summer camps have a great significance, you gain acquaintances and you become a familiar face within the youth from around Finland; this still has an effect when you're a grown-up.   [44]

The parents also saw many other advantages in the denominational social ties and networks. Often mentioned items included spiritual, social and practical benefits such as personal and spiritual support, which came up in a good share of responses. For example, a 43-year-old father sees that the social network of the denomination has 'a lot [of advantages], if one wants to make use of it'. In his opinion, the main one is spiritual support, but he also sees that the network can help young people position themselves in society [13]. Another example comes from a 47-year-old mother, who sees that within the denominational social network:

> ... young people see that other people also lead Christian lives (learning through modelling); young people can undergo spiritual experiences, e.g. answers to prayers (learning through experience). Safety comes from God alone (sense of security). Also other members of the congregation can take part in providing a Christian up-bringing. [45]

Both bridging (ties between the members of different age groups here in particular) and bonding (mainly ties with peers within the denomination) social capital clearly appear in the data. This came up in different examples, including a statement by a 44-year-old mother who sees that 'if things go wrong at home' there will be some other adult in the congregation who can listen to the adolescent's woes [7].

The congregational network was also seen as supporting religious socialisation, both in terms of the parents more or less sharing each other's educational values—leading to family rules and expectations towards the teenagers within the community being more or less similar—which in turn supports parental authority and values taught in the home, in that it is easier for young people to stick with the religious value system of the home when other teenagers around them are more or less doing the same. The following extract illustrates one view regarding this kind of communal educational support:

> It is difficult for the parents to get things through to the adolescents, but other parents in the congregation give their support and their children have a similar up-bringing.   (Father, age 45.) [6]

The possibility of finding a future spouse within the same community was also frequently mentioned; e.g. a 40 year-old mother sees the congregational network as a provider of 'support in developing values for life and in choosing leisure activities, as well as in choosing a partner' [14].

Some other 'practical' uses of the network are illustrated in the following quote from a 45-year-old mother, saying: 'Through the other members of the congregation you can find a flat as a student or a summer job, or even a working place. At best the other congregation members can guide and encourage the young person in a good direction'. Other viewpoints included having Adventist friends to visit and stay with in different parts of the country and abroad. International education and trips abroad (e.g. with a volleyball team, a choir or school charity work projects) also came up more generally, and for example the opportunities to study abroad in Adventist universities, or to have a 'year off' as a student missionary, were seen as important by many.

Despite some minor reservations towards peer groups in general, there seems to be a general consensus that the peer group *within* (i.e. the social collective of relatively same-age intimates within the denomination) is at least more likely to have a positive influence than the peer group *outside* the minority (e.g. classmates in a mainstream school). This effect of social context was also evident in the data concerning how parents view differences of peer influence in denominational versus mainstream schools. For example, a 47-year-old mother says: 'Peer influence [is] strong. It seems to take over the home values at some age' (i.e. values of the peer group are transferred to the home) [1]. However, some other parents did not find notable differences in the peer group influences of different school types. A 41-year-old mother states: 'I haven't noticed any differences in that'. [5].

On the other hand, some parents viewed parental influence as being so dominant the school context, or going to school discos, made no difference.

Having the Sabbath off hasn't been a problem. Teachers know what religion we are affiliated with and the co-operation has worked well. We haven't allowed him to go to discos. Some situations that we have considered problematic we've tried solving together with the teachers and we've always found a solution so that the child has not been left completely out of everything. (Mother, age 44.) [7]

Parents were usually happy with the local public schools, and felt, for example, that the vegetarian diet[16] for the children was easy to arrange with the staff. Some even regarded the public school context as positive, in that it created some welcome discussions in the home. It was seen to have 'given options. With questioning it has in the end strengthened a positive Adventist identity' (Father, age 44) [8]. Nevertheless, most of the respondent families preferred to put their children in an Adventist school, at least at the primary school level, if there was one within a reasonable distance.

Rearing practices related to the religious up-bringing seem to culminate in the Sabbath. In some families this starts on Friday with special preparations, candles on the dinner table and so on. However, compared with previous data regarding 20-30-year-olds in the late 1990s, these notions were rather scarce in this data. As previous data also showed, the Sabbath afternoon was typically spent with the family as well as other Adventist families, dining well, spending time outdoors, and playing games.

Discussion and conclusions

The results indicate that the denominational network serves as a social capital generating social structure. It brings several benefits to young people and their families; both intangible things like lasting relationships and social support for developing and maintaining a value system and religious identity, and concrete benefits such as finding a summer job or a place to live. Social ties and networks

16 In Finland, all children throughout the school system are provided with a warm lunch, with no extra cost for the family.

can support religious identity by reinforcing the socialisation process (e.g. learning the values) and helping young people maintain the denominational value system (e.g. social support, norms). These findings, together with some of their implications, are discussed in more detail in the following.

According to the findings, religious identity and denominational membership are important for Adventist families; both for teenagers and their parents. The social ties and networks based on Finnish Adventists' religious affiliation are regarded as a notable benefit for both the teenagers socialised within it and for their families as a whole. In line with Putnam (2000) and Wuthnow (2002), these networks can well be considered as social capital generating. The 'capital' can here be exchanged for social, spiritual and mental support, as well as various practical assets which may help the individual to position herself in the society. Thus, as assumed in the beginning, the religious minority community, with its relatively cohesive value system and social networks, does seem to be rather effective in producing social capital for its members. The cohesiveness of the value system across the denomination can also be seen as an indicator of the existence of what Coleman (1988) calls intergenerational closure, further contributing to the family social capital. Intergenerational closure, in religious minority settings such as this one, can play an important part for the families in socialising the values and norms to the second generation.

For the teenagers of families poor in human capital, other denomination members can offer valuable alternative models for example to their academic attainment or career goals for the future, as a form of bridging social capital. In terms of human capital, the peer influence and networking may also encourage the young person to remain in education to reach the matriculation examination level[17] instead of leaving for a vocational school after completing comprehensive school[18], especially if the main body of peers continue with their education in the same denominational school (cf. Coleman [1988] on school drop-out behaviour). While this was not the direct focus here, it would be an interesting theme for further research. Besides human capital, for many young people, the denominational boarding school setting creates a strong network of friends around the country and even internationally,[19] which generates social capital for young people and is also likely to strengthen their religious commitment and identity—which, again, could be supposed to build up the ties within their social network in the denomination.

17 Sixth Form/A-level equivalent
18 GCSE equivalent

Despite all the benefits that a relatively tight denominational social network can bring for young people and their families, obviously no socialisation setting is without its problems, and also the cohesiveness of a community can have its downsides. For example, the trust given within the social network can be a problem if someone is to misuse it; or if for some reason a young person would be left out of the social network, she would not gain any of the network benefits. According to Coleman's (1988) theory, the latter could even lead to dropping out of education and losing community support in identity negotiations, leaving the young person very isolated indeed.

Additionally, although families with a strong tradition of membership in the family history and a wide circle of friends and relatives within a religious movement can help their offspring in gaining useful social relationships both to their peers and to the other adult members of the congregation, thus strengthening both 'bridging' and 'bonding' social ties (Putnam, 2000) *within* the community; they may well be lacking important social capital for developing networks in the wider society. Especially the teenagers attending denominational schools, boarding school in particular, may well be left with weak ties to their home neighbourhood and to the surrounding society (see also Weller, in this volume). Hypothetically, since this was not investigated in the present analysis, such setting could lead to reinforced contrasts between 'us' and 'them', which could make it more difficult for the young people to find their place in the society; an issue also occasionally brought up in the debate on the position of faith schools (e.g. Taylor, 2005).

However, the present findings do paint a picture of clear benefits in growing up within a community or support network with consistent parental values. Also, in the contemporary multi-valued society, learning a certain value system as a basis for one's personal worldview has been found in previous studies to be healthy for children and young people (De Ruyter, 2002); and by 'rooting' within a denomination—as expressed by the respondent—the youth will have an opportunity to feel belongingness and share an identity with the others within the community.

As stated in the beginning, religious minority membership certainly provides an interesting context for research on social capital. The findings do indicate that the value system in a small minority is cohesive in terms of both value

---

19 Some of the pupils come to Finnish Adventist schools from other countries, and these schools have co-operation agreements with sister schools around Europe and in the U.S.A.. These schools also offer their pupils possibilities for trips abroad with their choir, volleyball team, charity work group, etc. There are also sometimes student missionaries or other staff members from other countries.

systems and social networks, as well as being effective in producing social capital. Parental values, also reflected in the family lifestyle, are more defined than within a wider societal setting, and according to the findings here, this also generates intergenerational closure among the Adventist parents—their child-rearing practices typically vary rather little from family to family. This is an acknowledged form of social capital within the community, as parents trust the congregational network to support the socialisation of their children, both in the peer group between the young people, and in their social relationships between different age groups. Thus the network of Finnish Adventists, based on their shared religious identity, can well be seen as an important social capital generating structure for young people and their families. In other words, the shared religious identity, which to at least some extent is a prerequisite for entering these denominational networks, can here be seen as an important facilitator of social capital.

Chapter 8

Social capital and minority identity

Helena Helve

Tracey Reynolds' chapter illustrates that family is still important to British Caribbean second and third generation young people when they construct their ethnic-racial identity. The young people's same-ethnic friendship networks were an important social resource for them in their identity contruction. 'Best friends' were from the same ethnic background, even networks of friends developed often through parents/grandparents networks. Those 'close friends', were seen as representing emotional intimacy, and involved issues of reciprocal exchanges, emotional support, trust, belonging, and equality of status whereas the 'casual friends' and these networks did not.

Arniika Kuusisto's chapter presents her research about the identity of a Finnish religious minority group of Seventh-day Adventist young people. She illustrates rather tight social networks for the young people affiliated with it. Most of their friends came from the same religious group—even one fifth of them stated that practically none of their friends are from outside the denomination. The majority of their relatives also belonged to the same movement.

These previous two chapters show that studying the concept of social capital is important because it concerns the values and norms, which are collectively and socially negotiated ties and relationships of people like those coming from the same religious or ethnic background. In terms of social capital these young people shared a sense of identity, and they also had rather similar values and trust in each other. To research the social capital of minority young people is fundamentally important because it defines an individual's legal, political and social relationship to the wider society. There is an interest in this, because of the pressure towards system integration in Europe due to the convergence of economic institutions and expansion of the European Union.

In Pierre Bourdieu's studies (1986) the focus is on family and group relations by which a range of capital assets are transmitted over time, across generations. James Coleman (1990) focuses more on social capital as a resource that arises out of people's family and community relationships. Trust and reciprocity between people are manifestations of social capital (cf. Putnam 2000). As a new generation minority young people have a particular relationship to the social capital and social networks.

These chapters about minority young people also raise new questions: How do relationships and social networks enable minority young people to increase their social capital? Is social capital inherent in the structure of religious or ethnic family relationships, particularly intergenerationally? How does this differ for majority young people, and how do these minority young people form cohesive social and moral norms of trust and co-operation? Are strong family and kinship for them more important in their identity construction and formation of social capital than they are for other young people? Does the concept of social capital for these young people differ from that of majority young people? Are their networks for example more virtual, local or global?

The researched Caribbean young people live in the U.K. and the Seventh-day Adventists in Finland. Globalised and more 'flexible' labour markets and geographical mobility has had an impact on both of these societies. However, it seems that the researched minority young people still form their social capital in 'traditional' families and community relationships. But the individualisation of late modernity means that ethnic or religious minority young people also have their own life courses, values and beliefs which additionally contribute to the formation of their identity and social capital.

These two studies have a socio-historical and a cultural perspective which analyses the values and social capital of the young people and which look at the institutions like schools, summer camps etc. for special minority groups—in this case ethnic and/or religious ones—that stimulate their identity, values and beliefs and social capital. The identity formation of these minority young people occurs within their societal contexts. Their identity is embedded in relationships with others. This embeddedness derives from their subjective experiences of their own minority relationships in relating to the majority. Kuusisto and Reynolds show how important it is for the minority groups they studied to belong to a certain ethnic group or religion. In the minority position the term 'identity' seems to refer to the individual identity, the group identity, and the social identity of the minority group, leading to integration in the minority group with a strengthening of boundaries between 'us' and 'the others' i.e. 'bonding' rather than 'bridging' social capital (Putnam, 2000).

Social capital, as well as the potential of religious/ethnic membership, is significant for identity formation, and the social ties and networks are based on shared values within a minority setting. Identity development is closely connected with the socialisation process, i.e. the process of becoming a part of the group by learning its norms, customs and traditions. There is a link between socialisation and children's social capital (e.g. Pulkkinen's concept of *initial social capital*; Pulkkinen, 2002), in the early socialisation context; see also Helve, 1991 and 1993). In the context of the research of Kuusisto and Reynolds, the denominational settings, and the particular social networks within it, may also influence the socialisation process. Both religious and ethnic identity formation, in turn seem to strengthen friendship networks in the same minority groups. Both religious and ethnically segregated networks could be seen as being 'too cohesive' and 'excessively bonded' (c.f. Parker and Song, 2006b).

As shown in Holland's chapter in this volume, for young people from economically disadvantaged backgrounds, individual resources of ability and ambition do not transfer easily into success. Her longitudinal, biographical approach showed that the middle class young people are often well-resourced by their family and they are well networked regardless of circumstances. Also minority young people come from different economic and social backgrounds. Maybe their minority identity based on ethnicity or religiosity enables them to cope better with inequality and exclusion (c.f. findings from Field's work on the protestant and Catholic communities in Northern Ireland, Field, 2003). They have acquired their social capital from their ethnic and religious minority cultures and networks. Education helps them to bridge out into the broader majority communities. The articles of Kuusisto and Reynolds shows that minority young people have specific resources in bonding with family networks and communities which can also help them in bridging to networks of majority communities during transitions to education and work. Close social bonds bring both advantages and disadvantages (c.f. the chapter of Holland in this volume). The move from bonding to bridging in minority groups is a process requiring more research.

Social relationships work in different ways. There are also different kinds of interpersonal relationships with identities and identity formations which are based on personal, social and economic structures (see also Côté's chapter). In the transition to adulthood strong bonds to the family and to the minority communities can be negative leading to social exclusion within the wider society, in contrast to bridging leading to social inclusion in wider social networks and social integration and participation in society. Furthermore we need to know how important family and family relationships are to the well-being and transitions of minority young people when buildning bonding and bridging social capital.

Are some forms of social capital reinforcing the exclusion of minority young people and some providing a stable identity and are enabling them to bridge out of their minority communities to majority groups?

Part 4   Social networks in education

Chapter 9

Managing the move to secondary school: The significance of children's social capital

Susie Weller

Introduction

Successive British governments over the past two decades have promoted an education system based on market principles (Whitty et al., 1998; Chitty, 2004). The 1988 Education Reform Act saw the introduction of parental choice into schooling, thus challenging the 'one size fits all' comprehensive model promoted in the late 1960s. Since 1997 the New Labour Government has continued to regard schools as market competitors and has focused on modernising comprehensive schools by promoting the diversification of school types. In theory parents can choose from a wide range of schools including: specialist schools (focusing on, for example, science, Information Technology, languages, art or sport); faith schools; academies part funded by industry; single-sex schools; or community schools. A child can potentially attend one of any number of schools outside their immediate neighbourhood, and away from existing local networks. This process is not mirrored in a number of other European countries. For proponents of social capital such policy initiatives may be problematic, for as Robert Putnam (2000, 362) notes, neighbourhood schools can provide:

> ... unique sites for building social capital, friendship, habits of co-operation, and solidarity.

Research into secondary school choice in Britain over the last few years has increasingly included 'social capital' in its framework of analysis. This work has often focused on parent's perspectives with regard to the nature of complex admissions processes. A child's last year at primary school is widely viewed as a stressful and challenging time for many families as they compete for places at well-resourced schools. In practice, there are many inequalities within the system and research suggests that the social, economic and cultural resources of middle class families affords them a more advantageous position able to gain places at better-resourced, popular schools (see also Bagnell et al., 2003; Ball, 2003; Weller, 2006a; Holland et al., 2007). Families with poor networks often lose out on important opportunities and information.

Social capital is, however, a messy and often ambiguous concept defined and constructed in alternative ways by different authors. What is common amongst, what Nicole Schaefer-McDaniel (2004) refers to as, the 'theoretical fathers' of social capital, such as Robert Putnam, James Coleman and Pierre Bourdieu, is that children are not regarded as active agents. Despite its elusive definition, the concept has become increasingly popular in policy debates, particularly those around community cohesion within the U.K. and U.S.A. (Schuller et al., 2000; Franklin, 2004). Social capital also features heavily in debates on education. Both Bourdieu and Coleman utilise the concept of social capital to examine inequality. Coleman, for example, investigated why children in Catholic schools in deprived areas had higher levels of academic achievement than children attending state schools in similar areas. He proposed that the ethos of Catholic schools constructs an environment where students feel they are valued and that much is expected of them (Munn, 2000). Through the Catholic faith connections between the home, school and community are fostered, forming the basis for the development of social capital (Munn, 2000). Whilst Coleman (1990) does state that social capital *is* important for children, his focus on 'the family' constructs children as both passive in the formation of social capital (Morrow, 1999a) and as future beneficiaries of their parent's social capital through the advantages of academic achievement. Furthermore, although Bourdieu (1986) argues that capital is passed on through generations, he still centres discussion on children's future rather than present lives (Allatt, 1993; Edwardset al., 2003). Taking a community-based approach, Putnam (2000) also emphasises the importance of parental social capital and involvement on a child's development and educational achievement with little recognition of the influence of their own networks and their ability to generate and utilise social capital. Indeed, much parental social capital rests on the social networks built around the interaction of children.

More recently there has been a move towards considering children's own social capital. Authors such as Virginia Morrow (2000; 2001a; 2003) and Cherylynn Bassani (2003) have explored children's social capital particularly in relation to well-being in different cultural contexts. In her work with Japanese children, Bassani (2003) argues that children's social capital is more likely to develop through their own engagement with their local area, rather than by proxy through their parents or teachers. Moreover, Schaefer-McDaniel (2004) outlines a framework for conceptualising young people's social capital, which consists of social networks and interaction; trust and reciprocity; and sense of belonging or place attachment. This framework provides a useful basis from which to explore how children develop and deploy their own social capital.

Drawing on a four-year study, this chapter examines the role social capital plays in children's lives during the transition from primary to secondary school.[1] In the study social capital was defined as the resources individuals and collectives derive from their social networks; it is through social interaction that social capital is developed (Weller, 2006b). The project also critically engaged with Putnam's definition of social capital as consisting of bonding and bridging elements, whereby bonding social capital refers to exclusive, inward-looking connections amongst homogenous groups, whilst bridging social capital refers to outward-looking networks between different groups (Putnam, 2000; Field, 2003; Weller, 2006b). This chapter argues that social capital is a valuable lens through which to explore the transition to secondary school because it re-emphasises the 'social' in an education system that prioritises and validates individual achievement (see also Munn, 2000). For children themselves school is often equally or even more significant as a social encounter in which important 'lessons' about life, relationships and struggles are learnt (see also Morrow, 2001a). In policy terms, coping with the transition to secondary school is about an individualised experience in which students either achieve or struggle. The way in which children provide mutual support and other resources during this time has seldom been explored.

The study investigated a wide range of issues including parents' experiences of secondary school admissions, children's experiences of moving schools, travel changes, increasing independent mobility and the importance of friendships in discussions on social capital. The purpose of this chapter is to detail some of the key findings from the study arguing that contrary to dominant writings on social capital, children are active agents in the development and maintenance of social capital in families and neighbourhoods. Moreover, children actively use their own resources and networks to negotiate the transition to secondary school, to become more independent social actors who are able to settle in and 'get on' in their new schools. This chapter draws upon Willard Hartup's (1992) typology of the functions of friendship in order to illustrate the significance of children's

---

1 The 'Locality, school and social capital' project has been conducted by Dr Susie Weller and Prof Irene Bruegel. The research forms part of the Families and Social Capital ESRC Research Group's programme of work (Award ref: M570255001), see www.lsbu.ac.uk/families.

social capital in negotiating the transition to secondary school. Hartup (1992) argues that friendship provides cognitive, emotional and social resources. Firstly, cognitive resources refer to knowledge and sources of information. Secondly, emotional resources denote support and confidence when meeting new people. Finally, social resources convey the development of social skills (Hartup, 1992; Weller, 2006a). I extend Hartup's typology to include children's social networks more broadly. I begin by contextualising the study before examining the ways in which children develop and utilise social capital through their friendships and through their familial networks. Subsequently, I highlight the transition to secondary school as a significant time when children develop neighbourhood social capital, independent of their parents. Throughout the chapter I aim to illustrate the interactive nature of social capital within families and the wider social networks in which they are situated.

Contextualising the study

In order to identify suitable research sites a multi-stage sample selection procedure was adopted. The criteria focused upon areas with a relatively high level of deprivation in which there was some degree of competition for secondary school places. Ethnic and religious diversity was also significant given the importance Coleman attached to local ethnic solidarities in promoting educational attainment in the U.S.A. and more recent discussions of diversity as possible barriers to community bonding. As a result four Education Authorities located in a city in the Midlands (in central England), a New Town in the south-east of England and two inner London boroughs were selected. These sites represented areas where access to highly esteemed secondary schools was very limited. A more affluent outer London suburb was also chosen for comparative purposes. The study adopted a mixed method approach to explore the experiences of families from a number of different cultural, ethnic, religious and class backgrounds through the move to secondary school.

Fieldwork was conducted in two phases between 2003 and 2005 with 12 primary schools (4-6 classes within each research site) participating in the research. During the first phase 588 children in their final year of primary school (year 6) completed surveys examining, for example, what changes they believed the move to secondary school would bring, whether they had a role in selecting their new school and whether they would be moving schools with friends and/or siblings. At the same time 76 parents were interviewed to ascertain their views on issues such as secondary school choice, parental networks, their fears and concerns about their child's imminent move, parenting practices and values, trust in the local neighbourhood, as well as, their own educational experiences.

The second phase of the study focused on children's experiences post-transition. Participants moved from the 12 case-study primary schools to 103 secondary schools. Follow-up surveys were completed by 81 children in the first two years of secondary school (years 7 and 8). Focus group discussions were carried out with 75 children across a wide range of schools. Participants discussed changes in their daily lives, differences in friendship networks, the support offered by older siblings and their experiences in their local neighbourhoods. Many also completed 'friendship worksheets' which allowed comparisons to be made between the friendships detailed in their primary school surveys and their social networks at secondary school. The focus groups revealed much about secondary school transition from a peer group perspective. In order to compliment this dialogue a sample of 20 children, from a diverse range of backgrounds, were interviewed individually. These interviews provided more in-depth discussion of personal experiences, feelings, struggles and achievements and were conducted in participant's homes. On several occasions parents were present for part, or all of interview. In line with the children-centred ethos of the study children and parents provided written consent. A number of primary and secondary school teachers were also interviewed.

Friends as social resources

Whilst authors such as Ray Pahl (2000) have suggested that friendship is both a component and a consequence of social capital, the relationship between children's friendships and social capital has been relatively neglected. For many young people social capital *is* tied up in friendship (Whiting and Harper, 2003). Tess Ridge (2002, 142-143) argues that:

> Friendship plays an important role as a social asset; it is a valuable source of social capital, and an integral part of an increasingly complex and demanding social world ... Friendship for children, as for adults, is an entry point into wider social networks.

Moreover, the resources children glean from their friendships have, at best been overlooked and, at worst been regarded in a negative light particularly by the 'theoretical fathers'. Coleman (1961), for example, regards peer group interaction as having a negative affect on educational attainment, whilst Putnam (2000) also only affords children agency in the formation of destructive social capital, such as, membership of a gang. Contemporary work, including that of David Halpern (2005) also focuses on the 'youth problem' and ways to foster social capital amongst the young with little emphasis on children's own experiences. Viewing children's social capital in a negative light neglects the positive and constructive cognitive, emotional and social resources that friendships and wider social networks provide.

Within the context of this study children's social networks provided important 'coping' resources during the transition to secondary school. For many children, 'making new friends' and 'fitting in' were amongst their greatest anxieties even if they were excited about starting their new school (Graham and Hill, 2003; Pratt and George, 2005). Research by authors such as Kathryn Wentzel and Kathryn Caldwell (1997) and Helen Demetriou and colleagues (2000) suggest that children who are generally accepted by their peers tend to settle in and cope with school in contrast to those who inhabit a more peripheral position. In this study we explored the extent to which having friends already at their new school or moving to a new school with friends aided the transition. About a quarter of all children were unhappy not to be moving on with all their friends. The 10% of our sample, who were moving on alone, were decidedly less excited about their new lives. Seven out of ten of them still said they were excited to some degree, but this compares to over eight out of ten of the children moving up with a lot of friends. Amongst the children (14%) who knew no-one already at the school or going to the school, were newcomers to the area and other more isolated children who found themselves in less popular, poorly-resourced schools. It should also be noted that the secondary schools in our study adopted a wide range of policies with regard to placing children from the same primary school in the same class. Schools, therefore, have the potential to influence children's opportunities to maintain and develop social networks.

Participants drew on a number of cognitive, emotional and social resources from their friendships. Such networks were drawn on in a dynamic way with acquaintances, close friends and wider networks providing alternative resources in different scenarios. In the first instance children drew upon their social networks to provide practical or cognitive resources. During the focus group discussions participants highlighted the positive and negative initiatives their schools had used to help them settle in. At one school in East London students had not received maps straight away making it difficult for them to find their way around. One participant, Denis, however, tapped into his own networks to negotiate his new surroundings,

> On our fifth day we got a map of our school which shows you around the school ... and we got a guide book and it helped you going around the school 'cos you were like 10 minutes late for your lesson when you didn't know where you were going. Because I know older people in Years 9 and 10 and I can ask them where it is and they can just take me to that room.
>
> (Denis, focus group participant, mixed community school, East London.)

Participants also drew upon their social networks to provide emotional resources. Whilst at primary school some children forged allegiances with other children they knew would be moving to the same school. Such relationships were often instrumental and may be defined as *transitional* as they were frequently short-term bonds used to support children in the early stages of transition (see also Tampubolon, 2005). Our findings echo Rachel Brooks' (2005) research where young people at the tertiary college she studied behaved in a very instrumental manner making alliances with acquaintances they knew were applying for similar university courses or institutions (Weller, 2006a). This more instrumental use of acquaintances often provided participants with confidence in new and unsettling surroundings, since being seen on your own makes you stand out either as different or unpopular (Weller, 2006a). Being seen as part of a group during the first few days projects a more confident and popular persona to new peers. For as Pahl (2000, 162) argues:

> ... having someone as a friend is a form of power, which those without close friendships do not have.

One participant, Naz, reinforced the importance of having friends at secondary school:

> *Naz:* ...'cos you have to have your friends ... if you don't have friends it's not really 'In' [you don't fit in].
> *Susie:* Does it make life more difficult at secondary school if you don't have friends?

Naz: Yeah 'cos you get bullied!

    (Naz, individual interview, mixed community school, South London.)

Indeed fear of being bullied made it vital to have a solid friendship group. Friends acted as 'back up', ready to support and defend against bullying. Those without solid friendships were inherently more vulnerable (Weller, 2006a).

For the minority of children who found the move to secondary school challenging friends from primary school were particularly important. One girl, Sonia, had great difficulty settling in, even though her older brother attended the same school. After the first few months the situation was so problematic that she ran away from school. Her mother eventually managed to find her a place at a new school, attended by many of her old primary school friends. Despite starting this school three months late she settled in well with the help of her old friends from primary school. Those who find secondary school transfer particularly challenging seem to rely more on established social networks.

Participants also drew upon a wide variety of social resources during the transition to secondary school. Many children used and developed social resources through their networks that enabled them to 'settle in' and 'get on' at school. Old friends often provided a comfort zone in new surroundings and with new people during the settling in period. Some children phrased this in terms of being more confident with their old friends around them for support. One focus group participant, Ashley said that she could rely on her old friends to look after her and be nice to her. This highlights the importance of time in establishing relationships of trust and reliance. Whilst Ashley valued making new friends her old friends often represented solid foundations on which to fall back in times of difficulty or loneliness. Britney reinforced this view:

> … if you go to a school with your friends you don't feel as uncomfortable as you usually do 'cos you know each other and you can stick to each other like glue until you meet some new people.
>
>   (Britney, focus group participant, mixed community school, East London).

Moving schools with friends did not mean that children did not make new friends. Rather having a stable base of bonds to some children enabled many to bridge out to new friendships. Generally children were able to both maintain old friendships whilst making new ones. In some instances where children did move to a new school with their primary school friends they provided an important resource and support network during the early stages of the transition but as children settled in, became more confident and were split into different classes they made stronger attachments to new friends. In these terms children often used their bonded networks from primary school to bridge across into new relationships (see also Weller, 2006a).

Familial networks as social resources

By neglecting children's *own* social capital, the 'theoretical fathers' have failed to fully understand the relational nature of social capital within and across families. Coleman (1988) discussed the importance of parental involvement in children's lives in order to instil values and norms, and counter 'negative' peer group culture. He believed that children living in large families were likely to acquire less social capital than children living in smaller (two-parent) families because siblings have to compete for their parents' time (see also Edwards et al., 2006). Little attention has been afforded to the resources children provide for their siblings and wider family (Morrow, 1999a; Edwards et al., 2006). In our study older siblings, cousins and other relatives attending the same secondary school provided valuable cognitive, emotional and social resources. Kin who attended the school in the past were also able to provide some cognitive resources and 'insider information'. Just under a quarter of respondents in the primary school questionnaire had siblings already at the school to which they would be moving. After they had started secondary school we asked participants to reflect on what it was like having an older sibling at the same school.

Siblings and relatives provided cognitive resources in the form of practical help allowing access to the 'hidden curriculum'. Older brothers and sisters helped their younger siblings to become familiar with their new surroundings, negotiate relationships with teachers, peers and older students, as well as, offer help with academic work. Sarah, for example, reinforced the views of many participants:

> I think it's good to have brothers and sisters because, whenever you come, they tell you where things are if you get lost.
>
> (Sarah, focus group participant, mixed City Technology College, South London.)

Older siblings also helped children to practice and come to terms with the new school journey. For many this was particularly significant as it was the first time they had travelled without an adult. JP discussed the help his brother had given:

... he [older brother] helped me get to know my way around the places I didn't know ... like on the first day I hadn't made that many friends 'cos I was a bit shy and scared but I just went to my brother and he showed me around and on the second day I met new friends. On the first day and throughout the first week he came with me on the bus ... there to school and home so I know like where to get off and I know the route, just in case if I had to switch buses or anything.

(JP, individual interview, mixed community school, South London.)

The experience of older siblings is, therefore, a valuable resource in enabling children to gain confidence and settle in, as well as, learn day-to-day routines. Such support is particularly valuable during the first few days in a new school. Help is not, however, always a one-dimensional relationship in this context. Once JP had gained confidence within the school he was able to reciprocate the help he had received by standing up to a group of bullies who were tormenting his older brother. Younger children are, therefore, able to reciprocate the resources supplied by their siblings and other relatives. The examples highlighted thus far show the direct ways in which older relatives provide cognitive or practical resources. For some children, the mere presence of an older sibling in the same school provided more indirect resources even if the children had little contact. Lydia, for example, described leading a very separate life to her sister. At their school break-times for younger and older children were staggered and so there was little opportunity to mix with older relatives. Prior to starting the school Lydia had, however, made visits on several occasions to attend concerts in which her sister was performing. She was, therefore, already familiar with the school before she started:

Susie: Would you say that having your sister in the school was important in helping you settle in?
Lydia: Yeah it meant that I'd seen the school when she was playing in the orchestra and stuff so I'd already seen it then so I knew it quite well.

(Lydia, individual interview, girls' faith school, South London.)

Older siblings and other relatives often, therefore, imparted 'insider information' on practical issues, as well as, the expectations and norms within the school. With such 'currency' many gained a position of power as they were able to impart this knowledge to students with fewer connections.

In addition to cognitive resources siblings, cousins and other relatives also offered emotional support. For some children this was particularly important during the first few days of the transition, as JazzyB highlighted:

> *Susie*: What was it like when you first started?
> *JazzyB*: Well first I was a bit scared but 'cos my sister used to go there [she's left] I used to hang around with her and then I made friends in my form and I just ... I was alright after that.
> (JazzyB, individual interview, mixed community school, East London.)

Such help was particularly significant when a child felt lonely, as Zobia highlighted:

> I think it is good to have sisters at a school because if you like get hurt or something you can express your feeling to them.
> (Zobia, focus group participant, all girls' community school, East London.)

Importantly, sibling support or the resources they provide was frequently discussed in terms of 'back up'. Both boys and girls talked about the importance of sibling support if they had been bullied or had got into a fight. The status and stature of older siblings often warded off threats, as Lightbulb and Rachel discussed:

> *Lightbulb*: ... 'cos if someone starts to pick on you, you can go and see them [older siblings] and then they will sort it out.
> *Rachel*: I think it's better because if someone is picking on you really bad, your brother will go and sort it out (or your sister) and they'd support you so they probably wouldn't do it again.
> (Rachel and Lightbulb, focus group participants, mixed community school,
> SE New Town.)

As Edwards et al., (2006) discuss, even if siblings argue and fall out at home they are often a source of support and protection both in school and the wider community. In some circumstances siblings are able to offer help when children feel they are not getting adequate assistance from the school, as Jasmin infers:

Susie: What was it like having brothers and sisters in the school when you got there?
Jasmin: Protective [laughs] ... anything that happened to me ... I remember my sister ... an incident that happened and the person that did it to her ... it was very good 'cos they like got scared 'cos my brother was in the school and it all got sorted out but the thing is when you've told the Principal about something, it takes a long time for him to like ... he said to us he was going to send a letter and was going to sort it out and nothing happened.

(Jasmin, individual interview, mixed City Technology College, South London.)

Emotional support and 'back up' was for many children particularly reassuring on entering a much larger school with older and bigger students. Not only were many older siblings and relatives able to protect and nurture younger children but they also opened up networks into the wider school. In terms of social resources, siblings and cousins acted as 'bridges', providing a pre-established set of acquaintances or friends. Both Edisha and Aisha discussed how their familial networks had expanded their wider social networks within the school:

Edisha: ... I used to have a sister who comes to this school but she doesn't now ... I have a cousin here and she introduced her friends to me and her friends get to know me and their friends and it goes on and on...
Aisha: I think it's a ... my sister left when I come and I thought it would be better if she was still in the school but it's alright 'cos a lot of people in the school know her and know me from her and I don't really know them but they know me so it's alright ... when I'm passing them they say 'Hello' and I'm like... 'Who is this person?' so I have to say 'Hello' but it's all right. I think it's better if your sister had come to the school so you have people to talk to...

(Edisha and Aisha, focus group participants, all girls' community school, South London.)

Whilst Edisha and Aisha emphasise that some connections resulted in friendship and others in acquaintanceship, simply being known and accepted by older students is often reassuring. Another participant, Denis, illustrated how family bonds can open up friendship with children in a different year group:

Denis: I do have a brother in this school and he's in Year 8.
Susie: Was it good to have him here when you started then ... or not?
Denis: Yeah 'cos (I know loads of his friends anyway) and I've made more friends in Year 8 'cos there's loads of people that he knows that I'm beginning to join in (with).

(Denis, focus group participant, mixed community school, East London.)

In the majority of circumstances older siblings and relatives were regarded as positive resources during secondary school transfer. Such relationships were not always idyllic and it was beyond the realms of the study to ascertain older children's views on supporting their younger siblings. Some children did, however, describe the disadvantages of having older siblings in the school. It could be embarrassing or it could offer parent's greater surveillance (see also Edwards et al., 2006), as Asma discusses:

I hate coming to this school with my sisters 'cos, when I get in trouble (and I get in trouble a lot!), they find out really quickly and they tell my parents.

(Asma, focus group participant, girls' community school, East London.)

Having siblings at secondary school provides many children with networks and resources which have the potential to ease their transition to secondary school by giving them confidence. Gaining 'insider information' through familial networks provides many children with useful tools for getting by as well as enabling them to develop their relationships with new acquaintances by passing on this information. This social and cultural capital generally promotes children's status within their new school. Putnam (2000) talked of the networks and norms within schools. Siblings and other relatives often have knowledge of the norms and expectations within a school allowing new students to negotiate their behaviour with older peers and teachers.

Developing neighbourhood social capital

The government's emphasis on parental choice means that for many families, particularly those living in urban areas, children can seek to gain a place at a school some distance from their local neighbourhoods and away from their existing friendship networks. For many children secondary school transfer signals a time of growing independence, greater spatial freedom and expanded social networks. It is commonly regarded as a period involving many new challenges, particularly in terms of negotiating new places. It is also a time when many are afforded more opportunities to develop social capital independent of their parents. Social capital formation may, therefore, be seen as both a component and consequence of children's increasing independence. When children move to a new school they are likely to encounter new places and new people, and will often have to negotiate these surroundings unaccompanied by an adult. In our study participants transferred to a wide range of schools. Of the survey participants, the majority (83%) stated they would be travelling to secondary school unaccompanied by a parent or adult, compared to 48% of 11 year-olds at primary school. Of those 76 families we worked with more closely several children would be undertaking a substantial commute up to 17km from the family home.

Neighbourhood or community is a significant element of many dominant understandings of social capital. As Schaefer-McDaniel (2004) suggests social capital is concerned with a sense of place. In much work on social capital children's social networks coupled with their presence in public space has often been portrayed as threatening to others and negative for community social capital (Lee, 2001). But this negative stance on children's social capital is both damaging and ignores the complexity of their (changing) relationships with place. I argue that children play an active role in developing and fostering neighbourhood social capital. This role is particularly apparent during the period of secondary school transfer as children begin to develop their own relationship with the local community, independent of their families. In our study the period between the last year of primary school and the end of the first year of secondary school was considered by many parents as an important time to practice 'being streetwise' and to develop what Caitlin Cahill (2000) refers to as 'street literacy' or gaining and using knowledge about, and constructing the self through, experiences of the local environment. Over the summer vacation children frequently practice the new route to school. Whilst parents often increase their emotional monitoring of their child (see Stace and Roker, 2005), this period also marks a decrease in 'physical' control and surveillance. Several children in the first year of secondary school noted this:

> When I was in primary [school] I wasn't really allowed out that much
> but now I'm allowed like down the park whenever I want if I don't

have too much homework. I'm allowed to go to the cinema on my own.

(Ashley, focus group participant, community school, East London.)

Aside from simply growing older many parents suggested that it was the move to secondary school that encouraged or forced parents to 'let go':

It's only this year I've let her actually do it because before now I've not wanted her out of my sight but as she's starting secondary school when a lot of children do train rides and bus rides all over the place, we thought we had to let her do a bit more without us being there.

(Shelley, Mother, individual interview, outer London suburb.)

As a result children develop new networks and new understandings of their neighbourhoods. JP, described by his mother as 'a little home bird' whilst at primary school, discovered that moving to secondary school gave him a new found confidence. Rather than spending his leisure time at home he regularly 'hangs out' in the local area with a group of friends and has many local networks. Another participant, Jamie, attends a school some distance from the family home. After school he often spends a couple of hours 'hanging out' with friends in the area around his school acquiring new networks outside his immediate vicinity:

We walk around the area near the school and we like to go to the shops and hang around in the shopping centres and stuff.

(Jamie, individual interview, mixed community school, East London.)

Some children also developed new networks which they concealed from their parents. One participant, Michael, travels across several London boroughs unaccompanied by an adult to get to his popular and prestigious school. Despite being afforded the freedom to undertake a complex journey, he and his brothers have only just been allowed to play football in the local park. The park is within sight of the family home but his mother, Folami, was not keen for her sons to mix with local children.

Susie: So you know quite a few local kids through the park?
Michael: Yeah you get to know them all.
Susie: So in this area here, there aren't many children?

Folami: There is only one child here.

Michael: No there's two! My friend and then there's a family who have got two children.

Folami: Yeah but you don't see them?

Michael: I see them when I go and ride my bikes.

Susie: So you see some of them down the park?

Michael: Yes. I see quite a few people that come to the park regularly but most of them live sort of at the far back there and come from different estates around the area.

Susie: How do the local people treat children?

Michael: They actually treat you okay unless you do something that they don't really like and they'll tell you off but, apart from that, they're ...

Folami: How do *you* know that !?

Michael: No but I see other people getting told off.

(Michael, individual interview, selective faith school, Central London.)

Folami appeared shocked by revelations that Michael and his brothers were regularly meeting and mixing with other local children in the park. In effect Michael has developed more local social capital than his mother. Akin to Michael's experiences the lives of a significant proportion of children continue to be rigidly managed by their parents (see Valentine, 1995; 1997). Cultures of 'good' parenting, particularly amongst middle class families, compel parents to structure children's worlds (Valentine, 1995). Many were either involved in daily after school activities or had to return straight home. Such management of children's lives leaves them with limited opportunities for developing social capital situated in their local communities.

Despite such restrictions children were often instrumental in developing their parents' own social capital. For example, parents met more people in the local area through their children than by any other means either indirectly through antenatal classes, nursery and the primary school, or through direct links with their children's friends' families. Some of these friendships were extremely close. One couple detailed a holiday they had recently been on with the family of their daughter's friend. Another mother Beverley described her relationship with some of the parents she befriended at her child's primary school:

When we see one another on the street it's almost like an old brother or sister we haven't seen for a long while and it's a big excitement.

(Beverley, Mother, individual interview, East London.)

In helping their children to negotiate the new journey to secondary school several parents also increased their knowledge and understanding of the local area. Practising the new journey to school is significant in developing new local or wider geographies for many children. Indeed, this is also the case for some parents who also have little experience in using the local public transport system. Many parents, particularly those living in our suburban and new town research sites, travelled predominantly by car. In order to practice the new journey several parents had to research and find out about the local public transport before being able to impart the information to their children. Practicing the journey to school often opened up new insights into the local area for parents.

Children are, therefore, often instrumental either directly or indirectly in developing their parents' networks. In doing so, they instigate greater connections in neighbourhoods and communities. Ultimately, the building of social capital is an interactive process. One example of this is mother and daughter, Raveena and Kat, who live in a quiet residential neighbourhood, in a relatively deprived borough in East London. Raveena is fairly active in her local community, and enjoys living there. She has been involved in a number of campaigns for example on road safety. Her involvement and determination has been passed on to Kat, who is a class representative on the school council, and is currently campaigning for a girls' football team with the support of her mother and teacher:

Kat: I wanted to enter a football club though ... a local football club.
Susie: Is there a girls' team?
Kat: No. I'm writing a letter to Tony Blair.
Susie: Are you?
Kat: The teacher says 'I will help you write it'
Susie: You'll have to get a team together.
Kat: Mum's trying a lot of things like you know getting a local Youth Project teams and more girls stuff around here. It WILL happen one day!

(Kat, individual interview, all girls' community school, East London.)

The examples cited illustrate children's active role as generators of social capital at the neighbourhood level. The move to secondary school is an important period when children often begin to develop their own social capital independent of their families. At the same time, many children also play a key role in the interactive development of social capital in families and neighbourhoods.

Conclusion

Whilst to some degree it has been fruitful to draw upon the writings of the Pierre Bourdieu, James Coleman and Robert Putnam, contestations between the conceptualisations of social capital amongst the so called 'theoretical fathers' demonstrate the inherent difficulties in defining the concept. Research in this field has, to date, been particularly challenging for 'social capital' is often not tangible or easy to measure. Rather, it is perhaps now timely to focus on developing social capital theory informed by the growing number of studies which centre on the ways individuals and collectives develop, utilise and value the different resources acquired from their families, friends, and wider social networks. In doing so, the relational nature of social capital needs to be emphasised in order to highlight the role previously neglected groups, such as children, play in the generation of social capital within, for example, families, schools and neighbourhoods.

Social capital is, nevertheless, a useful lens through which to explore secondary school transfer as it re-introduces the 'social' into an education system that prioritises and validates individual achievement. It is, therefore, particularly important that the implications of schooling as a social encounter are fully acknowledged in policy debates and initiatives surrounding secondary school transfer. The transition to secondary school signals an important time when increasing independence affords many children more freedom to develop their own social capital. In these terms children are actively involved in the production and consumption of social capital within their schools, families and neighbourhoods.

The current focus of British education policy on parental choice means that children are in competition with one another for places at well-resourced schools. Such a focus often means that relationships such as friendship are sidelined and little attention has been given to the positive and constructive resources and experiences such networks can provide. Adapting Hartup's (1992) typology of the functions of friendship has been useful in highlighting the resources that children's relationships and networks confer during this period. Whilst Hartup's typology of cognitive, emotional and social resources is by no means exhaustive it does illustrate the different resources many children drawn upon and the dynamic nature of social capital. What is apparent is that children's own social capital during the transition to secondary school is important as many are able to draw upon, produce and reproduce such capital through their networks of friends, acquaintances and siblings in order to get used to the school, find their way around, learn the unwritten rules and practices, make new friends and expand their networks.

Chapter 10

Adolescents' and young adults' goal-related social ties

Katariina Salmela-Aro

Adolescence and young adulthood are life periods of many demands, challenges, and changes such as interpersonal and school-related transitions. It has been suggested that individuals are faced with more transitions and life-decisions in adolescence and young adulthood than at any other stage of life (Caspi, 2002). The transition to adulthood is a critical developmental period marked by a series of developmental tasks that include establishing an identity, experimenting with intimacy, forming stable intimate relationships and starting a family, making career decisions, and achieving independence from parents (Masten et al., 2004; Schulenberg et al., 2004). Adolescence and young adulthood is also a challenging period for social networks. Previous studies have found that during these time periods social ties change. The major tasks of adolescence and young adulthood relate to disconnections with parents and connections with peers and romantic partners on the one hand, and educational attainment on the other. For example, during adolescence parents' influence decreases, while that of peers increases. Across adolescence time spent with significant others such as peers and friends increases substantially (Rubin, Bukowski and Parker, 1998), and peers play a progressively more relevant role in adolescents lives (Helson, Vollebergh and Meeus, 2000). Moreover, at the end of the comprehensive school adolescents either follow the academic or vocational track. Resolution of these challenges is necessary for successful transition from adolescence to adulthood, whereas failure to leads to the risk of later developmental disadvantage and problems (Schulenberg et al., 2004).

Adolescents' and young adults' lives are embedded in the activities of others. The study of social relationships among adolescents' and young adults is concerned with exploring these relational aspects of human lives, and within this field increasing attention is being given to the motivational aspects of these relationships. In addition, research on motivation although traditionally focused on individual goals, has recently witnessed increased interest in the interpersonal aspects of people's motivation—shared motivation. Consequently, there is recent research where personality, motivational and social psychologists explore goals in their relational contexts (e.g. Berg, Meegan and Deviney, 1998; Brunstein, Dangelmayer and Schultheiss, 1996; Diener and Fujita, 1995; Harlow and

Cantor, 1994; Little, 1989; Little and Ryan, 1974; Ruehlman, and Wolchik, 1988; Strough, Berg, and Sansone, 1996). The purpose of this chapter is to illustrate how the personal goal perspective provides a new point for studying adolescents' and young adults' personal goals in their relational context during critical life transitions.

Personal goals

Personal goals refer to future states or outcomes that one strives to achieve or avoid (Emmons, 1986). Many concepts have been used to refer to personal goals, such as personal projects (Little, 1983), strivings (Emmons, 1986), and life tasks (Cantor et al., 1992). Life-span theories on motivation assume that the demands, challenges and opportunities people experience at a particular stage of their lives channel the kinds of personal goals they construct (Little, Salmela-Aro and Phillips, 2007; Nurmi, 1991; 1992); that personal goals play an important role in the ways in that people direct their own development (Brandtstädter, 1998; Heckhausen and Tomasik, 2002; Nurmi, 1993); that people adjust their personal goals on the basis of previous developmental transitions and life-events (Brandtstädter and Renner, 1990; Heckhausen, Wrosch and Fleeson, 2001; Salmela-Aro and Nurmi, 1997); and that such adjustment has consequences for their well-being (Heckhausen, Wrosch and Fleeson, 2001; Salmela-Aro, Nurmi, Saisto and Halmesmäki, 2001).

For those concerned primarily with interpersonal and relational issues, to think that the term 'personal goals' implies primarily *individualistic* goals, actions and pursuits would be a mistake. It has been shown that personal goals are imbued by the motives and aspirations of individuals and that some individuals may be primarily committed to the pursuit of self-focused and individualistic goals. For example, it has been previously found that those self-focused goals are actually related to low well-being (Salmela-Aro, 1992). However, it is important to emphasise that personal goals are not *restricted* to individualistic pursuits. Some people's lives are devoted to goals that are overwhelmingly focused on others. Moreover, interpersonal goals are among the most frequently evoked categories of goals that emerge when adolescents and young adults list their current and future pursuits. In addition, social goals are usually found to be related with high subjective well-being (Emmons, 1996, Salmela-Aro and Nurmi, 1997).

The role of the 'other' in the evocation, shaping, affirmation, management and termination of personal goals is a central component (Little, 1983) contributing to the social ecological contexts within which adolescents and young adults are embedded. Personal goals, in short, are inherently, deeply and pervasively interpersonal. Salmela-Aro and Little (2007) have suggested that other people play a critical role in the process of goal pursuit. First, other people play a critical role in the *inception* stage of goals. It might be, for example, that adolescents and young adults reject pursuing a certain goal because it will have a negative impact on others. In the planning phase others' role is critical. Adolescents' and young adults' goals might be mutually shared (Salmela-Aro and Kiuru, 2006). During the *action* phase of goals, other people may serve to facilitate or frustrate adolescents' goal pursuit. For example, other support might be critical to the goal action. Finally, in the *termination* phase of a goal, people may play an especially subtle role. The central proposition of the perspective is that it is through personal goals that individuals gain coherence in their lives through the balancing and juggling of internal and external influences that impinge upon them. These influences will change in nature and impact as the person ages, so the social ecological model is in essence a model for life-span developmental analysis.

How to measure goal-related social ties and networks?

The social shared aspect of personal goals is present in the first phase of goal elicitation in the Personal Project Analysis (PPA) matrix (Little, 1983). The important content domain is 'interpersonal goals'. This has been shown to also be true among adolescents' and young adults' personal goals (Salmela-Aro, 2001). Depending on the kind of respondents being studied this category can be further subdivided into goals relating to friends, peers, family, parents, intimate others, children, relatives or workmates (see for example Cantor et al., 1992; Chuef, Read, and Walsh, 2001; Langston and Cantor, 1989; Little, Lecci and Watkinson, 1992; Salmela-Aro and Nurmi, 1996). The number of interpersonal goals listed has been a major focus of research (see particularly Salmela-Aro and Nurmi, 1996; Salmela-Aro et al., 2000; Salmela-Aro and Nurmi, 2004). Moreover, in the appraisal phase, social goals are appraised by adolescents and young adults as more important than achievement goals (Salmela-Aro, 2001). Finally, the 'Open Column' in the original PPA matrix contained two columns in which individuals could provide information on 'With Whom' and 'Where' each project or goal was undertaken (Little, 1983). These questions facilitated exploration of the goal-related social network and ecology.

Interpersonal goals are those involving others on a personal level and include family, friends and intimate others. Typical examples among adolescents and young adults would be: 'spend more time with my family', 'hang out with my boyfriend' and 'visit my friends'. When we simply examine the number of such goals generated during the elicitation phase of PPA there is clear evidence that social goals are very common.

Adolescents' and young adults' social goals

Social, interpersonal goals are typical among adolescents and young adults. In the study among adolescents, friend-related personal goals were mentioned most often after school and future education related goals (Salmela-Aro, 2001). Later during the transition from school to work life, family-related personal goals were the third most often mentioned goals after education and work-related goals (Nurmi and Salmela-Aro, 2002). During young adulthood, in college student populations, the two highest frequency categories of personal goals were interpersonal and academic goals (Salmela-Aro, 1992), while among adults the goals related to occupation and family were predominant (Salmela-Aro and Nurmi, 2004).

When university students were asked to produce three personal goals, 14% of the subjects mentioned a goal related to family, 21% mentioned a goal related to the opposite, sex and 20% mentioned a goal related to friends (Salmela-Aro and Nurmi, 1996). Moreover, it seems that interpersonal goals are particularly prevalent before middle adulthood: among 25-34-year-olds about thirty per cent were more interested in family-related goals than older subjects (Salmela-Aro, Nurmi, Aro, Poppius and Riste, 1992). In short, although the types of interpersonal goals differ by age, the prevalence of interpersonal goals is notably high across adolescence and young adulthood.

Moreover, among adolescents and young adults personal goals may proceed unimpeded by and without impact on the goals of others. The interpersonal ecology of goal pursuit is likely to vary across different stages of the life span and on the nature of transitional periods as individuals move through the different behaviour settings that dominate phases of life. Transitional stages of life can be used to illustrate how a personal goal perspective casts light on relational aspects of development in adolescence and entry into adulthood.

Increasing attention is being given to the transitional period of adolescence and 'emerging adulthood' or young adulthood (Arnett, 2000; Bynner, 2006) and an important aspect of this transition are changes in the nature of interpersonal goals (Salmela-Aro, 2003; Salmela-Aro, Aunola and Nurmi, in press). Using latent growth curve analysis (Muthen and Muthen, 2004) Salmela-Aro, Aunola and Nurmi (in press) showed that the frequency of friend-related goals decreased across the time of emerging adulthood. Moreover, the number of family-related goals showed accelerating increase across the period. The results showed further that there was individual variation both in the level of family-related goals and accelerating increase in them across this transitional period.

However, when we turn again to the sheer frequency of interpersonal goals in the daily pursuits of individuals a different picture emerges. There is a rapidly growing literature concerning how social and interpersonal goals are related to high well-being. Salmela-Aro and Nurmi (1997) found in a longitudinal study that among university students, family-related goals predicted high self-esteem and a low degree of psychological distress. In turn, self-esteem predicted having interpersonal goals later on (Salmela-Aro and Nurmi, 1997). Salmela-Aro et al. (in press) found among emerging adults that the linear slope of depressive symptoms was negatively related to the quadratic trend for family related goals: the more depressive symptoms increased during emerging adulthood, the more deceleration the participants showed in family-related goals during the third decade of life; or the more depressive symptoms decreased, the greater the acceleration seen in family-related goals. Moreover, Salmela-Aro (2001) found that those young adults, who had many social, interpersonal goals during their transition from vocational school to work life, reported more positive mood states than others. Similarly, Emmons (1991) found that those young adults who sought to establish intimate relationships were more likely to experience positive well-being. Finally, Salmela-Aro, Nurmi, Saisto, and Halmesmäki (2000, 2001) found in a cross-lagged longitudinal study during transition to parenthood, that an increase in family-related personal goals during pregnancy and after the birth of a child predicted a decline in women's depressive symptoms. Moreover, the results show that interpersonal goals are related to high subjective well-being, while intrapersonal or more self-oriented goals are related to low subjective well-being (Salmela-Aro, 1992).

Examining the confidence that one has in interpersonal goals reveals consequences for young people's social relationships and well-being. Salmela-Aro and Nurmi (1996) have identified two groups of female young adults during university studies, the socially confident group, three quarters of them, with positive and confident appraisals (high on outcome and low on negative affects) of their interpersonal goals, and the socially uncertain group, one quarter, with negative and uncertain appraisals (low on outcome and high on negative affects). The results showed that the women in the socially uncertain group reported more negative interactions with their parents and in their intimate relationship, and also fewer new acquaintances, than the socially confident women. Moreover, those women who appraised their interpersonal goals in a negative and uncertain ways showed higher levels of depressive symptoms, stress and loneliness, and lower levels of self-esteem. In addition, their results revealed that young females with uncertain interpersonal goals become more depressed during the transitional period of starting university studies. Taken together, the research evidence suggests that being engaged and confident in interpersonal goals has a salutary effect on individuals.

Adolescents' and young adults' personal goals and social capital

Some individuals have considerable personal investment in goals that generate social capital (Putnam, 2000). Social capital refers to the social networks and ties that may provide access to resources and support. Underlying the concept is the notion that individuals benefit from their social ties and related resources (Lin, 2001). It has been suggested that it is not only social ties as such that are important but the kind of social resources that are accessed through them that makes a difference. It is assumed that social contacts' positions in societal structures are important, because they enable access to resources, such as information and social influence. Moreover, the composition of a person's network may play an important role in how s/he accesses resources and opportunities. Granovetter (1973) argued that networks characterised by weak ties, such as acquaintances, offer more new information than networks with strong ties, such as one's spouse and friends. Unlike strong ties, that bind interconnected individuals who then often share the same information, weak ties are often a bridge between different social groups and consequently enable access to new information. Bonding, in terms of strong social ties, means access to important resources which might help adolescents to respond to their daily problems. They allow adolescents and young adults to get by in their life. Bridging, in turn, refers to adolescents' and young adults weak ties. These weak ties bring adolescents and young adults access to useful resources that open the door to new opportunities, allowing individuals to get ahead in their lives. It might be argued that bonding would be more typical during adolescence and the transition period from comprehensive school to secondary education. Moreover, as it has been suggested that social ties change during life transitions, strong ties might decrease during transition from adolescence to adulthood. It has further been suggested that in consolidation periods social capital is more important than psychological capital, while at a time of crisis the psychological capital is more important than social capital. Conversely, individuals can be the recipients of social capital that is generated by others.

Individual needs for social support vary with age-related changes such as dependence on others, social roles related to occupational and social status (e.g. student, parent, employee, friend or spouse), and changes in residence (e.g. living with family, living on a college campus). As life circumstances change, both individuals' social networks and their needs for different types and amounts of support change (Colarossi, 2001). Gender differences in supportive relationships have been evidenced across the life span (Berndt, 1982). These differences have been suggested to be influenced by variety of factors, including gender role beliefs and behaviours related help seeking and use; support provides gender-biased perceptions about boys and girls need for support, their desire to provide support to them and actual differences in girls and boys support needs. Most researchers have found that girls receive more support, especially emotional support, than boys do (Colorossi, 2001). Colorossi (2001) found that female adolescents received more friend support than male adolescents, whereas male adolescents received more father support. However, they found that they did not differ in support from their mothers.

Social ties during transition from school to work

The relationship between social networks and social capital among young adults has been explored recently by Jokisaari and Nurmi (2005). In their study, the social capital framework was combined with that of personal goals to examine the kinds of social ties young adults have concerning their work-related goals when they face the transition to working life, and the role that social ties and resources related to them play in the outcomes of this particular transition. Personal goals relating to work were elicited from a group of students in the school to work transition period, and the respondents also completed a module which asked them to list people associated with the most important work goal. This included the strength of relationship to these people, their occupation and whether they helped or hindered that acquisition of the work goal. Jokisaari and Nurmi (2005) showed that the most often-named people were mother, spouse and friends. Moreover, young adults mentioned an increasing number of work-related social ties during the course of the transition to working life: supervisors and co-workers were mentioned more frequently at the later time point, whereas fellow students and school personnel were mentioned less frequently. Jokisaari and Nurmi (2005) showed further that students who had networks containing people of higher SES and weaker ties were more successful than others. Their results showed that goal-related social capital contributed to the prediction of employment status later on: higher social contact's SES at earlier time point was related to having a full-time long-term job which corresponded to one's education. Moreover, goal-related social relationships characterised by weaker ties contributed to the prediction of employment status later on: goal-related weaker ties between the young adult and his or her social contacts were related to getting a long-term job. Weak ties are valuable in working life, because they connect people with new social networks and enlarge information.

Transition from comprehensive school to educational tracks

To examine adolescents' goal-related social ties Salmela-Aro and her colleagues (2004-6) conducted a longitudinal study among those adolescents in the last year at comprehensive school. The aim of the study was to examine adolescents' education goal-related social ties during the transition from comprehensive school to educational tracks, either academic or vocational. In order to examine adolescents' goal-related social ties and changes in them during this educational transition, 874 adolescents (mean age 16) filled in the education goal-related social ties questionnaires twice, at the end of the comprehensive school and one year later. The results showed that the most often mentioned goal-related social ties among adolescents at comprehensive schools were parents, both mother and father. The next most often mentioned social ties were friends and siblings. The results showed further that after the transition from comprehensive school to secondary schools mothers, peers and boy/girlfriends increased as social ties. In addition, the results showed that adolescents' with higher grade point average (GPA), and those in the academic track mentioned parents, both father and mother, as social ties more often compared to those with lower GPA or those in vocational track. Moreover, gender differences in goal-related social ties emerged. Girls mentioned mother and friends more often than boys, while boys mentioned fathers more often than girls. In addition, the results revealed that family type was related to goal-related social ties. These results showed that in divorced and non-divorced families mothers were mentioned as often as a goal-related social tie, while in the divorced families father was mentioned less often as a social tie than in non-divorced families. The present study showed that the role of the father decreases in the case of divorce while that of mother stays the same. Finally, the results revealed that entrance to the academic track was predicted alongside education-related goal effort and progress, by strong social ties, such as the father. This study also provided evidence that close ties, rather than weak ties were of greater benefit to adolescents, but that this was particularly so for girls relative to boys. Consequently, bonding seems to play a key role during adolescent educational transitions, while bridging seems to be in a key role at young adulthood during transition from school to work.

Conclusion

Clearly the research agenda on personal goals, social ties, networks and social capital is both rich and complex. Personal goals are not purely individual processes; they are embedded in many ways in individuals' interpersonal relations. Many goals are shared with others and other people provide resources that contribute to an individuals goal attainment. Adolescents' and young adults' goals are closely embedded in their social relationships. When thinking about the future and related decisions, young people often negotiate with, ask advice from, use role models, or reject information given by their parents, teachers and peers. Other people may direct the goal development by communicating expectations and setting normative standards, they may act as role models and provide tutoring, information, support and feedback. Consequently, these underscore the fact that personal goals are not just private individual pursuits, nor intimate undertakings, but also actions with impact, enabling both individuals and communities to flourish.

Chapter 11

Education and juvenile crime: Understanding the links and measuring the effects.

Ricardo Sabates

Introduction

Education is a potentially large influence on young people's propensities to offend and possibly an important source of area-level variation in crime rates. Crime statistics for England indicate that crime rates are lower in areas with higher levels of education, which are also areas of higher per capita income and contain a higher proportion of families belonging to the highest socio-economic status (Home Office, 2003). Crime is more prevalent among young adults, as crime rates typically increases with age during adolescence, reach a peak during late teenage years, and decline thereafter.

A large body of literature has attempted to understand the process by which education is related to young adults' criminal behaviours. The human capital framework indicates that education increases human capital levels and wages derived from legal activities, which raises the opportunity cost of engaging in crime (Freeman, 1996; Farrington, 2001). It also increases the opportunity cost associated with incarceration since it increases the value of any time forgone. According to Lochner (2004) the relationship between education and crime depends on age and on the skills required to commit a particular criminal offence. Crime that required specialised skills tends to be committed by educated older adults (for example fraud) whereas crimes that require little skills tend to be committed by young, uneducated, individuals (for example stealing a mobile phone).

Sociological and psychological theories stress the importance of young people's learning experiences, the school as context for peer selection and for the formation of social capital, as well as the family context, as mechanisms through which education may affect decisions to engage in crime. Learning experiences impact upon children's self-esteem, self efficacy, sense of control over their lives and resilience, which in turn are features of the self that can moderate individuals' social behaviours. Learning may also enhance young people's cultural and social capital, which for Bourdieu (1993) consists of attainment of academic qualifications, use of language, forms of social etiquette and competence, as well as degree of confidence and self assurance, contacts and group memberships which provide actual or potential support and access to valued resources. Through its economic value in the labour market the forms of cultural and social capital described by Bourdieu can impact upon young people's decisions to engage in crime.

Learning is also a social activity which impacts upon youths' bridging, bonding and linking social capital formation. Marmot et al.'s (1991) findings from the Whitehall II study, which involved interviews with a large number of civil service employees, show that individuals in lower status jobs (who would have tended to have relatively low levels of education) had poorer social relations than those in higher status jobs (who would have higher levels of education). More individuals in lower status jobs reported visiting relatives once a month or more (greater bonding capital), whereas those in higher status jobs visited friends (greater bridging capital). Individuals with higher levels of education also have greater levels of linking social capital that is relations with other individuals in position of power.

During the school years, young people's social networks and social support systems are formed, developed and modified through their interactions with peers (Morrow, 1999a). Children's social networks start in the early years, though enjoyment in school life seems to be more important than social relations when children are very young. Socialising and making friends becomes more important in upper primary and secondary education, when children and young people's relationships outside the family environment assume greater importance (Farrell, Tayler and Tennent, 2004). Existing social networks are utilised to manage school transitions (Weller, 2007) and new networks emerge after each school transition. One may expect that peers are a protective factor against criminal behaviour but they can also promote antisocial and criminal behaviours, as peer effects are very strong in criminal decisions (Case and Katz, 1991; Calvo-Armegol and Zenou, 2004).

In addition, the school is the place to build important links with local communities as it involves teenagers in voluntary work, the value of education for society, and the importance of civic participation. Empirical studies have investigated the sense of connection with others as an outcome of education, as well as empathy, inter-personal trust, supportive relationships, sense of community, voluntary activity, and civic participation (Emler and Fraser, 1999; Ross and Mirowsky, 1999; Dench and Regan, 2000; Bynner and Egerton, 2001; Preston and Feinstein, 2004; Hammond, 2004). These outcomes are relevant here because social networks and links between adolescents provide protection for reducing criminal behaviour.

Theoretical models have also been used to interpret the ways in which parental education can protect young people from involvement in criminal activities. According to sociological theories, parents with more education are also more able to transmit social capital to their children through quality interactions, affective ties, and clear guidelines concerning socially accepted behaviours (Coleman, 1990). Families that invest in their children are more able to create social bonds, to foster social learning, and to increase moral values, which protect youths from accessing to, and engaging with, delinquent peers (Wright, Cullen, Miller, 2001). Economic models of fertility developed by Becker (1965, 1981), Becker and Lewis (1973), and Becker and Tomes (1976) provide similar explanations for the role of parental education. In these models parents are interested not only on the number of children but also in the well-being of each child. Parents with higher levels of education invest more in the well-being of their children which in turn protects them from engaging in crime and antisocial behaviour.

But not everything about education is positively related to reductions in criminal behaviour. For instance, education increases the earnings that one can derive from illegal activities and the skills learnt in school may be inappropriately used for crime (Levitt and Lochner, 2000). Socially disadvantaged adolescents may not benefit from low grade school achievements. For them, engagement in crime may be a better, though riskier, option (Morrow, 1999a). The school context is not always positive as some children subject others to acts of verbal or physical abuse and show other adverse forms of social behaviours (Farrell, Tayler and Tennent, 2004). Social capital may have adverse effects, as exemplified by groups of gangs, which are also social networks that provide access to resources and enforce conformity. In the long run, these groups may hold individuals down rather than raising each other up (Portes and Landolt, 1996).

While the theoretical arguments for educational effects on crime are well established, the empirical literature has only recently started to shed light on the causal effect of education (Penn, 2000; Lochner and Moretti, 2004). The objective of this paper is to provide empirical evidence on the impact of education on crime. In particular, we explore whether increasing participation in post-compulsory schooling has an effect on male juvenile convictions at the level of Local Education Authorities (LEA). To undertake the empirical analysis, we utilise the variation provided by the area-specific provision of

Educational Maintenance Allowances (EMA), a Department for Education and Skills (DfES) programme designed to increase participation in post-compulsory education. Unfortunately, we do not have area-level measures of young people's social capital to be able to analyse how social capital mediates or moderates educational effects on crime. Nevertheless, the relationship between education and crime is important as it has clear policy implications with indirect repercussions for young people's economic opportunities and social capital formation.

The paper is organised as follows: first, we describe the methodology to evaluate educational effects and then we present the results from our estimates of the change in conviction rates for burglary, thefts and other minor offences, for 16 to 18 year old males, in EMA areas relative to other areas.

To validate our results, we perform two sensitivity tests. The first test aims to capture the age-specific conviction rates reduction. If indeed the EMA is having an effect on crime, it will be through shifting (or preventing) 16 to 18 youths from criminal activities or potential criminal activities into education. Secondly, the EMA was extended to about one-third of all areas in 2001, so these areas are excluded from the analysis.

Methodology

The empirical estimation of education effects on crime is based on the evaluation of a U.K. government initiative, the Education Maintenance Allowance, which was piloted in 1999. The EMA programme was introduced in some LEA areas but not in others, so it is possible to assess the effect of this programme using an analysis along the lines of a programme evaluation. In this section, we describe the EMA programme, the data, and method used for the empirical estimation.

The EMA programme

In 1999, the Department for Education and Skills, (DFES), piloted the EMA programme in 15 LEAs, with a view to raising participation, retention and achievement in post-compulsory education among 16-18-year-olds.[1] The amount given to the recipient varied, between £30 and £40 a week plus achievement bonuses on completion of coursework. The full weekly allowance was payable if total parental taxable income did not exceed £13,000 per annum,

---

1   LEA areas where the EMA was piloted are: Middlesbrough, Walsall, Southampton, Cornwall, Leeds, Lambeth, Southwark, Lewisham, Greenwich, Oldham, City of Nottingham, Bolton, Doncaster, Stoke-on-Trent, and Gateshead.

while for those with a total parental income of between £13,000 and £30,000 (£20,000 maximum for the London pilot) support was progressively tapered, down to a minimum of £5 per week. In 2001, the EMA was rolled out to about one-third of LEAs, and in 2004 was rolled out nationally. The cost of the programme in 2001 was £109 millions, excluding evaluation and overhead costs, which was spent in 52 LEAs to assist around 52,400 students.

The EMA programme was piloted in areas with low participation in post-16 education. These areas have higher levels of deprivation, more families renting rather than owning their accommodation, and greater proportions of individuals without qualifications whose parents experience high labour market inactivity. The Ashworth et al., (2001 and 2002) and Heaver et al., (2002) evaluations of the first two years of the EMA programme indicate that overall, 63% of young people in low income families in pilot areas applied to the EMA programme in the first year and applications for the second year increased slightly by just 0.6 percentage points.

The offenders index data

Crime data come from the Home Office Offenders Index database (OI). The OI contains a history of criminal convictions from 1963 in England and Wales. The sample of individuals is a census of all court cases that occur during four weeks of the year. The sampling weeks are the first week of March, the second week of June, the third week of September, and the third week of November. Once a person is sampled, their complete history of convictions is recorded and they remain part of the sample in case of any future conviction. The period utilised for this paper is 1996 to 2002.

Offences were aggregated to the LEA-level. Linking petty crime areas, the area where the court has jurisdiction, to LEAs is not straight-forward. Some magistrate courts have changed over time, merging with others. Similarly, the categorisation of LEAs changed between 1996 and 1998. Therefore, we are constrained to perform the analysis from 1996 onwards. Additionally, we assume that no offences are committed across regions. This is a reasonable assumption for large areas, especially for juvenile crime. However, for London, we combined 13 LEAs and their respective courts into 4 main areas (North-East, North-West, South-East and South-West London). Apart from London, other LEAs had to be combined to match with the court level data into three areas. These were Bournemouth and Dorset; Bracknell Forest, Slough, Windsor and Maidenhead and Wokingham; and Essex, Southend and Thurrock. Excluding the LEA for City of London we were left with 132 areas for the analysis.

Convictions for burglary, theft and other minor offences committed by 16, 17 and 18-years-old males, between 1996 and 2002 were obtained for each LEA. The definition of burglary includes breaking, or attempting to break, into residential or non-residential properties. The definition of theft includes stealing from a vehicle, shoplifting and thefts or handling stolen goods. Other minor offences include attempt to steal, treason, perjury, aiding suicide, perverting the course of justice, failing to surrender, Revenue Law offences, among others, and exclude motoring offences. Grouping these sub-categories of offences in the OI data takes into account any changes in offence codes and disposal or sentencing codes between 1996 and 2002 to obtain a consistent treatment of the data over time (Home Office, 1998).

To standardise conviction rates for the size of population living in a particular LEA we utilised as a denominator the number of pupils aged 15 by LEA. This does not give quite the required rate per population of the specific aged but that information was not available to us by LEA. In order to account for population mobility, we factored in the growth rate of the population aged 15 to 19 by LEA. Essentially, conviction rates are measured per 1,000 pupils.[2]

Estimation method

The changes in male, juvenile conviction rates before and after the introduction of the government initiatives in treatment and non-treatment LEAs can be modelled using area fixed effects as follows:

$$C_{at} = \alpha_{\alpha} + \Phi EMA_{\alpha} * PolicyOn_{\alpha} + \Phi X_{at} + u_{at} \quad (1)$$

where C_{at} is the offence rate (burglary, theft or minor offences) in LEA a at time t; α_{α} are parameters to capture the LEA fixed effects estimation, EMA is a dummy variable equal to one for EMA areas, and *PolicyOn* a binary dummy variable indicating periods after the introduction of the initiative. The Φ parameter is the difference in means before and after policy introduction, i.e. the difference-in-differences. The matrix **X** contains area-level time-varying characteristics which

2   Age-specific conviction rates by LEA (16 to 18) are standardised by assuming that the number of 16 to 18 year old equal the number of 15-year-olds adjusted by population growth. For example, conviction rate for 16-year-olds in 1996 is equal to total convictions by 16-year-olds in 1996 divided by total number of age 15 pupils in 1995 times population growth for 15 to 19-year-olds from 1995-1996.

can be incorporated in the estimation to condition out time varying differences in treatment versus non-treatment LEAs.[3]

The difference-in-differences is an estimate of the effect of the EMA programme on male, juvenile convictions. This estimate is unbiased under the assumption that the programme is introduced randomly so that there are no differences between treatment and non-treatment areas with respect to the conviction rates (Sherman et al., 1998), that there are common crime trends before the introduction of the policy and that the introduction of the policy was not the result of a temporary increase in crime (Ashenfelter and Card, 1985).

Results

Table 1 presents results from the difference-in-differences estimates without controls using equation (1). Convictions considered are for males age 16 to 18 in terms of whether they were prosecuted and convicted for (i) burglary, (ii) thefts, and (iii) other minor offences not including motoring.

Table 1: Difference in Juvenile Convictions (16 to 18-years old males) per 1,000 pupils.

		Before EMA	After EMA	Within Group Difference
EMA Areas	Burglary	4.219	2.23	-1.989 (0.379)***
	Theft	14.366	9.563	-4.803 (1.102)***
	Other minor offences	10.441	8.596	-1.845 (0.612)***
Non-EMA Areas	Burglary	2.227	1.176	-1.051 (0.098)***
	Theft	7.643	4.817	-2.826 (0.260)***
	Other minor offences	6.592	5.4	-1.192 (0.195)***

---

3 Time-varying controls from 1996 to 2002 are (i) the unemployment rate for individuals under 25, (ii) the current, annual proportion of pupils eligible for free school meals (as a measure of area-level deprivation), (iii) the full-time equivalent number of qualified teachers, (iv) the percentage of pupils attaining no GCSEs at age 16, (v) the percentage of unauthorised half-day missed in secondary education, (v) the average pupil-teacher ratio, and, (vi) the full-time equivalent number of supplementary staff for ethnic minorities

		Before EMA	After EMA	Difference-in-differences
Between Group Difference	Burglary	1.991	1.054	-0.937
		(0.673)***	(0.525)**	(0.377)**
	Theft	6.723	4.746	-1.977
		(2.923)**	(2.007)**	(1.091)*
	Other minor offences	3.849	3.196	-0.653
		(2.148)**	(1.384)**	(0.620)

Note: Estimation based on 15 areas where the EMA programme was piloted. Before EMA is defined as 1996 to 1999 and after EMA post 1999. Asterisks (*), (**), (***) represents significance at 10, 5 & 1 percent levels, respectively. Estimations are weighted by population. Standard errors, in parenthesis, are clustered by LEA.

Table 1 shows a clear decline in juvenile convictions in all local education authority areas. The difference-in-differences estimator calculates difference in conviction rates both within and between EMA and non-EMA areas. For burglary rates committed by male youths aged 16 to 18, there is a reduction of 0.937 crimes per 1,000 pupils in EMA areas relative to non-EMA areas. The extra relative reduction for 16 to 18-years-old male thefts is nearly 2. These reductions are significantly different than zero at the 5% and 10% levels, respectively. However, there are not differences in convictions for other minor offences in EMA relative to non-EMA areas.

Results from the fixed effects conditional difference-in-differences model are shown in Table 2. The first column is the difference-in-differences estimate with the introduction of time-varying controls on convictions for burglary, and shows there to be a significant reduction in burglary in EMA areas relative to non-EMA areas (-0.93 convictions per 1,000 pupils). The significant effect previously found for theft is no longer statistically significant. In terms of other minor offences, the estimate continues to be statistically insignificant as we include time-varying controls.

Table 2: *Difference in differences in crime indicators for EMA areas*

	Burglary	Theft	Minor Offences
	(1)	(2)	(3)
TEMA* policy-on	-0.932	-2.031	-1.299
	(0.412)**	(1.332)	(0.967)
Controls			
Area fixed effects	Yes	Yes	Yes
Time-varying variables	Yes	Yes	Yes
Yearly controls	Yes	Yes	Yes
Cohort controls	Yes	Yes	Yes
R-Squared	0.53	0.53	0.53
Number of areas	132	132	132
Sample size	2,772	2,772	2,772

Notes: Notation follows from equation (1), where TEMA stands for LEAs where the EMA programme was piloted only, Policy-On indicates periods after the introduction of the initiatives.
Asterisks (*), (**) represents significant at 5 & 1 percent levels, respectively. Estimations are weighted by population. Standard errors, in parenthesis, are clustered by LEA. Controls defined as in footnote 2

Finally, Figure 1 shows the results from the fixed effects estimate with the inclusion of time-varying controls for different offences, by age and also excluding the rolling out of the EMA programme in 2001. The first line indicates the point estimate with confidence intervals for burglary for 16-18-year-olds, which is shown in Table 2. The next line is the estimated parameter for individuals aged 19 to 21 and the third estimate is for individuals aged 16 to 18 but excluding

Figure 1: *Difference-in-differences estimate in convictions for EMA areas, by age and excluding EMA rolled out*

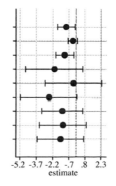

those LEAs where the EMA programme was rolled out. Similar results are shown for theft and for other minor offences.

Results for burglary show that offences committed by 19 to 21-years-old are not reduced more in EMA areas than in non-targeted areas. Excluding LEAs that rolled out the EMA programme, juvenile conviction rates for burglary (age 16 to 18) fell by approximately 1.1 convictions per 1,000 pupils in EMA areas compared to the rest of the LEAs. For thefts, there is an indication that conviction rates fell in EMA areas relative to other LEAs for the youngest group, both including and excluding the roll out of the EMA. But this result is only statistically significant at 10% level. For the 19 to 21 age group, there is no evidence that convictions for thefts were reduced by significantly more in EMA areas. Convictions for other minor offences do not seem to fall in EMA areas relative to non-targeted areas.

Conclusions

This paper evaluates the benefits that an educational programme may have in terms of crime reduction. The EMA programme was designed to increase participation in post-compulsory education and piloted in 15 LEAs in 1999. By providing financial support to youths from disadvantaged economic backgrounds, the EMA aimed to remove financial barriers to participation in education. Here, we investigate whether this programme has additional benefits in terms of crime reduction.

We discussed economic, sociological and psychological theories that explain the mechanisms by which, and the learning experience provided by, an educational programme such as the EMA can have an influence on juvenile crime reduction. These include the acquisition of skills which increases the opportunity cost of engaging in criminal activities; the impact on self-esteem, self efficacy, sense of control, resilience and cultural capital which are features of the self that protect against crime decisions; the formation of different levels of bridging, bonding and linking social capital; linking adolescents to the community and voluntary sector; and a potential future intergenerational effect as when these young people become parents they may be better equipped to have quality interactions with their children, affective ties, and to provide clear guidelines concerning socially accepted behaviours.

Empirically, we used area-level data on convictions for male juvenile burglary, theft and other minor offences (excluding motoring offences) for individuals aged 16-18-years-old, from 1996 to 2002. Using unconditional difference-in-differences estimation techniques, our results showed that male conviction rates for burglary offences fell more in the 15 LEAs that piloted the EMA programme than in other LEAs, about 1 fewer convictions per 1,000 pupils. There was some indication that convictions for thefts were also reduced, but this was not as clear as it was for the case of burglary convictions. Finally, we did not find any evidence that convictions for other minor offences fell in areas that implemented the EMA initiative compared to the rest of the LEAs.

The differential effect of education by type of offence committed found here may indicate that educational effects are linked to the skills necessary to commit crime (Lochner, 2004). Burglary and thefts require similar set of skills, usually low skills, than the broader set of skills required to commit the offences grouped under 'other minor offences'. These latter offences include attempt at stealing that require low skills to commit, but also Tax Revenue offences that require a more specialised set of skills to commit these offences. This may be one of the reasons why we found a stronger effect for burglary and theft convictions and no statistical effect for other minor offences. Lochner (2004) also found that property crime is mostly a problem for young uneducated men.

Still, we found that education effects are stronger for burglary than for thefts, which indicates that apart from the skills explanation there may be additional channels for the differential effects of education. One of such channels is perhaps through social capital and spending time in education. Burglary offences seem to require more planning (for example in trespassing a property) whereas thefts tend to be more opportunistic (for example stealing a mobile phone). Spending time in education and having positive peer groups may counteract the negative effects of the peer group involved in burglary and the timing required to commit the offence. However, these positive benefits of education may not affect thefts as stealing may happen as the opportunity arises.

A further explanation of the educational effects on burglary convictions at the area level may be the confounding effect of several crime and anti-poverty government interventions targeted in disadvantaged areas simultaneously. Feinstein and Sabates (2005) investigated the effect that during the same years of the implementation of the EMA, the U.K. Home Office initiated a targeted programme to reduce burglary in the worst performing areas of England and Wales. Some of these areas were also targeted by the EMA programme. Their results show important complementarities between the educational intervention and the direct intervention to reduce crime more effectively.

It is important to highlight some limitations of this research. Results presented here are based on participation in post 16 education, but this does not imply that there are differential effects of different types of schooling. For instance, in estimating the effects of education on crime, Lochner and Moretti (2004) focused on the effect of high school graduation on participation in criminal activities in the U.S.A. They used the exogenous variation induced by changes in state post-compulsory school attendance as an instrument to high school graduation. They found that completing high school reduces the probability of incarceration by about 0.76 percentage points for whites and 3.4 percentage points for blacks. They showed that the biggest effects of graduation are associated with violent crime, assaults and motor vehicle thefts. Interestingly, their results suggested that endogeneity of schooling decisions did not appear to bias estimates of the effects of education on crime. In other words, the possibility that the association between education and crime may be due to unobservable factors that affect both outcomes appeared to be, if any, small.

Other evidence from the U.S.A. showed the effects on crime reduction of an educational programme. The Quantum Opportunity Programme (QOP) was designed to increase the likelihood that youths would complete high school and enter a further education and training program. The program was also intended to improve grades and achievement test scores. It was founded on an explicit hypothesis that this would indirectly reduce risky behaviours such as substance abuse, crime, and teenage child-bearing (Taggart, 1995). The programme enrolled youths from disadvantaged backgrounds, especially those with a high probability of drop out from high school. The programme supplied the students with a tutor and supplementary school activities in educational and community projects. Financial incentives were also designed to encourage high school graduation. Two years after the programme completion, randomly-assigned participants were 34 percent more likely to achieve a high school diploma. Criminal activity, in the form of number of times participants were arrested, was 28 percent lower than for non-participants (Penn, 2000). This last result, however, was not consistent across all areas, for example, in Philadelphia crime increased whereas in Washington crime remained unchanged (Maxfield et al., 2003).

We also highlight that our indicator of crime is convictions, and not all crimes are prosecuted and convicted, only a proportion of total crimes. One may expect that the educational impact could be larger, but this does depend on the decisions made by the criminal justice system on who to prosecute. Finally, we do not have long-term data series of crime at the level of LEA, so we are not able to perform different sensitivity tests aimed at comparing targeted with non-targeted areas.

Chapter 12

Social networks in education

Jari-Erik Nurmi

An increasing amount of research during the past two decades has focused on social capital, and how such capital contributes to people's success in many life domains, such as socialisation, entrance into working life and overall well-being. The key notion in the field is that the social networks and ties people have formed in various contexts help them later on to successfully deal with various challenges and demands. Although the theories in the field vary according to what is exactly meant by social capital, most research have used sociological focus emphasising networks in various organisations and social niches, have focused on adulthood, have emphasised the importance of weak social ties instead of close relationships (strong ties), and have underscored people's active efforts in building up social networks.

The three chapters of this part of the book contribute to our previous understanding of social capital in four important ways. First, two of the chapters investigated social capital in the context of school transitions. Weller examined the functions of social capital in the transition from elementary to secondary school, while Salmela-Aro focused on the changes in goal-related social capital in the transition from comprehensive school to either academic (senior secondary school) or vocational post-comprehensive education. Also the chapter by Sabates deals with the role of education but, in his case, the focus is on how post-compulsory education impacts crime rates at community level.

Second, two of the chapters extend previous social capital research by reporting findings concerning close ties rather than weak ties, the latter being the major focus on previous research. Both of these chapters use open-ended measures that provide a possibility to explore the importance of different kinds of social ties in educational settings. The findings of Salmela-Aro showed that adolescents in comprehensive school mentioned their parents, friends, peers and siblings as major social ties with whom they talked about their education and occupation-related goals. The results were similar in post-comprehensive education: only boy and girl friends turned out to be a new category of social ties. In her chapter, Weller reported closely similar findings: besides friends also older siblings played an important role when children moved from elementary to secondary schools. Both of these chapters suggests that, at last during late childhood and adolescence, close interpersonal relationships, such as parents, friends and siblings, can function as important source of social capital. What is also interesting is that teachers were not mentioned as important social ties.

Third, the chapters discuss the role of children's and youth's agency in forming social capital. For example, Weller discussed this topic not only as a result of her study but also as the key limitation of previous research emphasising adults' social capital as a starting point of children's adjustment. She also stressed the fact that children actively try to connect to new friends, partly by using old friends and siblings as a basis for their new network building. Salmela-Aro's chapter focused on social ties related to one's personal goals, and therefore also emphasises the agentic nature of social capital.

Finally, all the chapters investigate social capital and networks in the context of broader societal forces. For example, Sabates examines whether the efforts of society in terms of building non-compulsory educational programs could reduce youth's problems behaviour, such as crime. The results showed that they do. Similarly, Salmela-Aro showed that divorce, being one of the recent historical trends in children's and adolescents' interpersonal environments, has consequences also to youth's social networks: divorce down played the role of fathers. Weller discusses the impact of 'market principles' being used in the development of secondary education in the U.K. as one important factor leading a substantial amount of variation in the kinds of secondary education available for children and families in present U.K.

Each of the chapters also provides an unique contribution to research on social capital. In her chapter, Salmela-Aro, for instance, reviewed several findings concerning how young people think about social capital concerning their personal goals. The framework was based on life-span theory of motivation but was complemented by some previous findings of the interpersonal nature of human motivation. Salmela-Aro interestingly described the role of social capital and social ties in three phases of motivation: inception, action and termination. The reviewed empirical findings, in turn, show that (1) interpersonal goals (family, friends) are closely associated to individuals' well-being, (2) that among young adults' weak-ties related to one's career-related goals contributed to people's success in goal attainment, and (3) that, in particular, goal-related strong ties played an important role in adolescence. Although the interpersonal nature of human motivation is an interesting research field, more research is needed in order to fully understand people's shared goals, the role of other people's support and encouragement in goal construction and goal-planning, as well as the role that other people play in the evaluation of goal attainment.

Weller's chapter focused on how children describe the role of other people in their transition from elementary to secondary school. Starting from some theoretical weaknesses of social capital theory, she ended up to emphasise children as active agents of their own development. The key idea of the chapter was that children actively use their previous network of friends to build up new social ties when entering into a new educational setting. Similarly, older siblings were used as a source of information, as well as a basis for new networks. The chapter applied qualitative approach to examine children's social capital. Although this is a reasonable approach in poorly examined field, there is an evident need in the future to complement the approach with more systematic and theory-driven approach as well.

Finally, Sabates deployed a framework of economics to examine whether building up non-compulsory educational programs can reduce youth's problems behaviour, such as crime. The results showed that such program were efficient in the case of some types of crime, such as burglary. The results were analysed at community level, although some discussion referred also to mechanisms operating at the level of individuals, such as the changes in self-esteem, self-efficacy, and resiliency, as well as to the ways in which participating education may provide opportunities to networking and building new social capital. Consequently, it looks as there is an evident need to complement the community-level research by examination of what is happening to individuals who participate various educational programs.

Overall, the chapters in this part of the book suggest that close relationships, such as parents, friends and siblings, play an important part in late childhood and adolescence. This is an important finding, because it complements some previous results among adults suggesting that weak ties, which are not based on close relationships, play a crucial role. This seems not to be case during childhood and adolescence. It is possible that interpersonal relations during childhood and adolescence have particular characteristics that are also reflected in the ways in which social capital functions at this particular age. Children grow up in families and start to spend an increasing amount of time with their peers. It seems that only when they move to live independently do they begin to be motivated and skilled to use less close social ties as the source of their social capital. Second, the findings show that the functioning of social capital and networks is not independent of the societal changes, and even social policy, and how they are reflected in children's and youth lives. Divorce, for example, was found to be reflected in kinds of networks adolescents reported. Similarly, goal-oriented educational programmes were shown to have consequences for adolescents' problem behaviour. Finally, the three chapters show that extension of the social capital framework to younger age periods does not only increase our understanding of different stages of human life-span but also suggests that some functions and processes operating in social capital may be age-specific.

Part 5	Transitions and potentials

Chapter 13

Social capital and social integration of young adults in changing times

Ingrid Schoon

Introduction[1]

A major task for young people in their transition to adulthood is the assumption of new social roles, such as entry into paid employment, and the participation in civic society (Arnett, 2000; Bynner, 2006; Shanahan, 2000). This process of social integration, describing the involvement of individuals in society, is set within a changing socio-historical context. Youth transitions have changed dramatically during the last 30 years, and there has been much discussion regarding changing labour market opportunities and socio-demographic transformations leading to prolonged periods of education, delayed entry into paid employment, and postponement of marriage and family formation (Arnett, 2000; Bynner, 2001, 2006; Furlong and Cartmel, 1997; Shanahan, 2000). Concerns have also been raised about declining membership in organisations and lack of political interest (Baron, Field, and Schuller, 2000; Bynner and Parsons, 2003). It has been argued that in the wake of increasing globalisation and uncertainty community values have given way to individualistic orientations and an erosion of social capital (Putnam, 1995). There are furthermore concerns regarding an increasing polarisation of youth transitions, with those being able to invest in their qualifications and skills reaping the greatest rewards regarding employment opportunities and social integration (Bynner, 2006; Jones, 2002). Despite a general educational expansion there are persisting inequalities regarding the participation in further and higher education, which remains more prevalent among young people from relative privileged backgrounds, who are able to draw on economic as well as social resources in their family for support (Bynner, 2001).

The aim of this chapter is to examine the links between personal, social and economic resources in shaping the social integration of young people in

1   The analysis and writing of this article were supported by grants from the U.K. Economic and Social Research Council (ESRC): L326253061 and RES-225-25-2001. Data from the National Child Development Study and the British Cohort Study are provided by the ESRC Data Archive. Those who carried out the original collection and analysis of the data bear no responsibility for its further analysis and interpretation.

a changing socio-historical context. To gain a better understanding of the mechanisms by which different forms of resources or assets are instrumental in achieving social integration, the usefulness of the notion of social capital will be explored. It is hypothesised that the social integration of young people into society is an outcome of investments at various levels, including investments in social relationships and in education.

The evidence presented here is based on data collected for two British birth cohorts born in 1958 and 1970 respectively, comparing the experiences of nearly 20,000 individuals in their transition to adult lives. Although born only 12 years apart, the two cohorts faced very different conditions and opportunities. The 1958 cohort was born during a 'boom period' of extraordinary economic growth which came to an end in the early 1970s, bringing with it the 'crisis decades' characterised by increasing insecurity and uncertainty (Hobsbawm, 1995). Between 1979 and 1986, and again between 1989 and 1993, Britain experienced the sharpest rises in unemployment since the 1940s (Gallie, 2000). The mid-1980s saw the virtual disappearance of the youth labour market (Hart, 1988) and a deepening economic recession. While most cohort members born in 1958 had completed their full-time education before the onset of the recession, members of the 1970 cohort reached minimum school leaving age right in the midst of the depression. The cohort data thus offers the opportunity to investigate how a changing socio-historical context influences experiences of social integration and civic participation.

Social inclusion and integration

Within the European context the Lisbon Summit committed EU member states to adopt the promotion of social cohesion and inclusion as a strategic goal in response to changing socio-historical conditions and increasing globalisation (EU, 2005; OECD, 2001). Globalisation, while creating the possibility for increasing interconnectedness throughout the world—through travel, trade and communications—can also bring with it centrifugal forces which dislocate traditional bonds, fragment societies and increase conflict and division (Green, Preston, and Janmaat, 2006). Calls for inclusion arise from the experience of exclusion and increasing disparities between groups in society related to lack of qualifications, lack of skills or capacity for employment (Atkinson, 2004). Research focusing on social inclusion of the socially marginalised through employment has generally paid less attention to the broader determinants of social integration across society as a whole. There is evidence to suggest that social inclusion extends from failure to engage with the labour market to general disengagement from society, as reflected in non-participation in community and civic activities (Bynner, 2001; Bynner and Parsons, 2003). Here thus a broader meaning of social inclusion will be adopted to cover the multidimensionality of the concept (Giddens, 2000). Furthermore a distinction is made between social inclusion measured at an aggregate level, and social integration which is measured at an individual level (Ravanera, Rajulton, and Turcotte, 2003). In the following social integration is gauged at the individual level, operationalised across different dimensions, including economic participation (being in paid employment), membership in organisations, and political participation.

Social and human capitals

In recent years the concept of 'capital' and its association with terms such as investment, ownership, and returns—originally derived from the field of economics—has been extended gradually to describe social, cultural and psychological assets and resources available for investment (Schuller, Bynner, and Feinstein, 2004). Classical analyses of capital as financial, physical or other tangible assets (including tools and machines for production) has neglected the value that lies in the importance of social networks, shared values, as well as of knowledge and skills (Aldridge, Halpern, and Fitzpatrick, 2002). The notion of human capital refers to the skills and capabilities of individuals, recognising the role of knowledge and education as important aspects of production (Becker, 1975; Schultz, 1961). The notion of human capital differs from that of social capital, which in turn is used to describe the social relations or networks individuals have (Bourdieu, 1986; Coleman, 1988). The term social capital was coined by Pierre Bourdieu and his colleague Jean-Claude Passeron in their classic work on social reproduction (Bourdieu and Passeron, 1977). Bourdieu's typology of capitals (differentiating economic, cultural and social capital) breaks with presuppositions inherent in the assumption of natural aptitudes that account for success or failure at school as well as the wider social system, and emphasises the embeddedness of individual achievements in a wider socio-cultural context. Bourdieu's conception of capital highlights the role of social inequalities in the production and reproduction of economic, cultural, and social resources. Drawing attention to an ecological or area-based component of achievement, Coleman proposed the notion of social capital reflecting community strengths based on shared attitudes and values, traditions and norms, which in turn is instrumental in the formation of human capital (Coleman, 1988). A more recent conceptualisation of the notion of social capital introduced a distinction between bonding and bridging social capital (Putnam, 1999). This distinction is useful in explaining the effects of relationships entered into by individuals. Close relationships, or bonding, focus inwards on relationships to a limited number of individuals, while bridging social capital is outward looking, creating connections across different heterogeneous groups.

Concerns about capitals

There has been some controversy about the use of the term 'capital' in such diverse terms (referring to financial, human, social, and cultural capitals), about its meaning and measurement across disciplines (Fine, 2001; Morrow, 2001b). The term investment is no longer confined to transactions in physical capital, but is used metaphorically to describe expenditures in the acquisition of skills and knowledge, as well as investments into social relationships involving commitment of time, energy and money. Returns associated with investment in human and social capitals not only involve financial returns, such as income, but can involve non-market or non-pecuniary returns. The measurement of such non-economic returns is however more difficult than those of more tangible assets and has let to criticisms of the viability of the terms, their inconsistent and varied definitions and assessment (Portes, 1998; Robinson, Schmid, and Stiles, 2002; Schuller, Bynner, and Feinstein, 2004; van Deth, 2004).

Another criticism of social capital theories is that although the notion of social capital takes into account that society is changing, the emphasis has been a conservative one, lamenting the decline in social capital and values. It is argued that mainstream thinking does not take on board theories of social change concerning the nature of intimate relationships and thus remains stuck in traditional paradigms with little understanding of the processes of how social capital operates (Edwards, Franklin, and Holland, 2007). Social capital is too often treated as an outcome, with little consideration for the processes that produce that outcome. Furthermore the nature of gender and generational relationships within families are assumed rather than investigated (Edwards, Franklin, and Holland, 2007).

Despite these criticisms, the concept of social capital has been useful in bringing the quality of social relationships to the attention of policy makers, and research inspired by an extended notion of capitals has opened up the communication between economic, sociological, and psychological perspectives on the role of social relationships and participation in the accumulation and realisation of assets and resources (Schuller, Bynner, and Feinstein, 2004).

Interdependence between capitals

The different forms of capital are not independent of each other, but are mutually interdependent (Schuller, 2001). Bourdieu's work, for example, suggests that economic capital generates cultural capital which in turn enables individuals to secure their place in society (Bourdieu and Passeron, 1977). Social capital can be transformed into the creation of human capital, for example where social capital in the family and in the community prevents early drop-out from school and aides the acquisition of skills and knowledge (Coleman, 1988). High levels of human capital may not be realised if the individual has no access to networks which provide opportunities for its use and application. Yet, it is not necessarily the case that high levels of social capital always lead to the accumulation of human capital, as for example in situations where the predominant social norms discourage educational aspirations and participation (Schuller, Bynner, and Feinstein, 2004). High level of social capital, especially bonding social capital, can depress the formation of human capital or the establishing of wider social networks. In a longitudinal study of disadvantaged young people MacDonald and colleagues could show that supportive local networks enable young people to cope with poverty, but paradoxically the same bonds can become part of the process in which poverty and class inequalities are reproduced (MacDonald, Shildrick, Webster, and Simpson, 2005). In the transition to adulthood strong bonds to the family and the community can be negative assets, associated with social exclusion, while bridging social capital is considered as positive, being associated with social inclusion and integration (Holland, this volume). The bonding form of social capital is based on exclusive ties of solidarity among homogenous groups, while bridging social capital refers to co-operative connections with the wider social context.

Dimensions of capital and social integration

In the following I will assess associations between human, bonding and bridging social capital in times of social change, aiming to contribute to a better understanding of the processes that produce social participation and integration. Human capital is conceptualised by the highest qualifications an individual has obtained, reflecting their investments in the acquisition of skills and knowledge. Bonding capital is operationalised through indicators of exclusive relationships young people have to their parents, intimate others (i.e. spouse and children), as well as to the community (indicated through number of household moves and church attendance). Both, links to the family and to the community (and their associated norms of reciprocity and trust) can facilitate or constrain certain activities associated with building bridges to the wider society (Coleman, 1988; Putnam, 1999). Bridging social capital is understood as the connections to wider social networks. It is operationalised across multiple domains to capture the multiple dimensions of social integration and participation, differentiating between an economic dimension (being in paid employment), a political dimension (voting in the last election), and social participation (membership in an organisation and/or a trade union).

It is hypothesised that social integration (i.e. connections to wider social networks) is the outcome of investment at various levels, including investments in the individual, the family, and the community. Two key assumptions will be tested. Firstly, does investment in human capital, i.e. in skills and qualifications, facilitate social integration? And secondly, does investment in close relationships (bonding social capital) undermine the development of bridging social capital? These two assumptions are tested through analytic models involving logistic regression with indicators of bridging social capital being treated as outcomes, and indicators of human and bonding social capital being considered as resources or assets.

The models will be run separately for the two cohort samples to assess cohort differences in the association between the different forms of capitals. Comparing social integration experiences in two cohorts, takes into account that society is changing, and allows the investigation of whether recent socio-historical changes have affected the mutual interdependence of different forms of capitals. Have the associations between different capitals changed for the two cohorts born 12 years apart? Has there been an increase or decline in the role of skills and qualifications in predicting social inclusion and integration? Has there been a change in the influence of close social bonds on the social integration of young people?

All models will control for variations in family social background. Previous research has established strong associations of social origin and social integration, with those born into less privileged families being increasingly excluded from educational and employment opportunities (Atkinson and Hills, 1998; Bynner, 2001; Schoon, 2006). There is furthermore evidence that social background is associated with social participation and values (Bynner and Parsons, 2003).

Furthermore, to take account of gender differences separate models are run for men and women in each cohort, which enables the assessment of gender specific associations.

Method

The study used data collected for the 1958 National Child Development Study (NCDS) and the 1970 British Cohort Study (BCS70), two of Britain's richest research resources for the study of human development. NCDS took as its subjects all persons living in Great Britain who were born between 3 and 9 March 1958. In five follow up studies data were collected on the physical, psycho-social and educational development of the cohort at age 7, 11, 16, 23, 33 and 42-years-old. The BCS70 has followed children born in the week 5—11 April 1970. Data collection sweeps have taken place when the cohort members were aged 5, 10, 16, 26 and 30 years.

The focus of this analysis lies on outcomes in early adulthood, at ages 30 (BCS70) and 33 (NCDS), when most cohort members have completed their education, established their working careers, and have started a family. The analysis is based on the cohort members who have taken part in both the birth surveys and the follow-ups at age 30 and 33, respectively. The samples comprise 10427 men and women in NCDS and 9820 in BCS70. An analysis of response bias showed that the achieved sample did not differ from the target sample across a number of critical variables (social class, parental education, and gender), despite a slight under-representation of males, and of the most disadvantaged groups (Plewis, Calderwood, Hawkes, and Nathan, 2004; Shepherd, 2004). Bias due to attrition of the sample during childhood has been shown to be minimal (Butler, Despotidou, and Shepherd, 1997; Davie, Butler, and Goldstein, 1972; Fogelman, 1983).

Measures

Gender (male/female)
Family social origin

Parental social class at birth is measured by the Registrar General's measure of social class (RGSC). The RGSC is defined according to job status and the associated education, prestige (OPCS, 1980) or lifestyle (Marsh, 1986) and is assessed by the current or last held job. It is coded on a six-point scale: I professional; II managerial and technical; IIINM skilled non-manual; IIIM skilled manual; IV partly skilled; and V unskilled (Leete and Fox, 1977)[2]. Class I represents the highest level of prestige or skill and class V the lowest. Where the father was absent, the social class (RGSC) of the mother was used in BCS70, and where there was no father at birth of NCDS cohort members, the mother's father's social class was used.

Human Capital.

The notion of human capital is operationalised by the highest qualifications obtained by cohort members in their early 30s, using a broad classification of academic and vocational qualifications based on a 5-point scale related to National Vocational Qualification (NVQ) levels (Makepeace, Dolton, Woods, Joshi, and Galinda-Rueda, 2003). NVQ 5 covers all post-graduate qualifications. NVQ4 refers to first degree-level qualifications and diplomas. NVQ3 encompasses the attainment of two or more A-levels, or their academic or vocational equivalent, which is comparable to the *baccalaureate* or to a U.S.A. High School degree. NVQ2 includes academic or vocational qualifications equivalent to a General Certificate of Secondary Education (GCSE) or ordinary (O-level) examinations grades A-C within the General Certificate of Education (GCE) examinations. NVQ1 covers other qualifications, such as lower grades of GCSE, O level or CSE and the lowest level of vocational certificates.

Bonding Social Capital.

Indicators of bonding social capital of cohort members in their early 30s include:
* Partnership status (single, cohabiting, married)
* Parenthood (no children, has children)
* Lives with parents (yes or no)
* Number of household moves since age 16 (none, 1-3; 4-7 and more than 8)
* Regular church attendance: cohort member visits a religious service at least once a month or not.

Bridging Social Capital.

Indicators of bridging social capital of cohort members in their early 30s include four dichotomous variables capturing economic, political and social participation:
* Employment status (in paid employment or not).
* Political participation (has voted in the last election or not)

2   The occupational categories used in the U.S.A. census and other European countries are similarly based on the skills and status of different occupations (Krieger, Williams, and Moss, 1997).

- Membership in any community organisation (yes or no)
- Membership of a Trade Union (yes or no)

Results

Table 1 gives the descriptive statistics of the sample, identifying prevalences for both cohorts and for men and women. In comparison to cohort members born in 1970, those born in 1958 are more likely to have left school without any or only few qualifications. In the 1970 cohort more men and women have obtained degree-level qualifications, yet in both cohorts there is a similar proportion of cohort members with post-graduate qualifications. Cohort members born in 1970 are less likely to be married by their early 30s, are more likely to be cohabiting or single than those born in 1958. The percentage of cohort members living with their parents at age 30 has more than doubled in the later born cohort, especially among men. Cohort members born in 1970 have moved less frequently, and are less likely to attend church on a regular basis than those born 12 years earlier. Regarding indicators of bridging social capital most cohort members (in both cohorts) are in paid employment. Cohort members born in 1970 are less likely to vote, are less likely to be a member of an organisation or Trade Union than those born in 1958.

Table 1: Descriptive statistics: Indicators of human, bonding and bridging social capital in the two Birth cohorts in %.

	NCDS All (n=10427)	NCDS Men (n=5084)	NCDS women (n=5343)	BCS70 All (n=9820)	BCS70 Men (n=4749)	BCS70 Women (n=5071)
Human Capital						
Highest qualification						
None (base)	12.0	10.9	13.1	9.1	9.6	8.7
NVQ1	13.2	13.4	12.9	8.1	8.3	7.9
NVQ2	31.3	27.8	34.7	27.7	24.3	30.9
NVQ3	16.0	18.8	13.3	20.4	23.4	17.7
NVQ4	23.8	25.0	22.7	30.9	30.5	31.3
NVQ5	3.7	4.1	3.2	3.8	4.0	3.6
Bonding Social Capital						
Marital Status						
Single (base)	19.7	20.7	18.8	32.0	35.6	28.7
Cohabiting	10.5	11.2	9.8	25.0	26.7	23.5
Married	69.8	68.1	71.4	43.0	37.8	47.8
Children						
Has children	68.9	61.6	75.9	45.5	36.3	54.1
Living with parents						
yes	5.6	7.8	3.6	12.0	16.4	7.8

	NCDS All (n=10427)	NCDS Men (n=5084)	NCDS women (n=5343)	BCS70 All (n=9820)	BCS70 Men (n=4749)	BCS70 Women (n=5071)
	Bonding Social Capital					
Number of moves						
None (base)	3.6	4.6	2.7	8.1	11.7	4.8
1-3	47.5	49.2	46.5	54.5	53.6	55.2
4-7	35.3	32.5	37.7	28.9	26.0	31.7
8+	13.6	13.6	13.1	8.5	8.7	8.2
Attends church regularly						
yes	11.0	7.3	14.5	8.1	6.1	10.0
	Bridging Social Capital					
Is in paid employment	79.7	91.3	68.5	81.6	90.0	73.8
Has voted in last election	77.1	75.6	78.6	62.2	59.6	64.7
Is member of an organisation	19.2	13.9	24.4	9.8	7.6	11.8
Is member of a Trade Union	29.2	35.0	23.6	20.2	20.2	20.1

Table 1 furthermore suggests gender differences in the indicators of human, bonding and bridging social capital. Women born in 1958 were more likely than men to have left school without any qualifications, while in the 1970 cohort this is no longer the case, and the number of women with degree level qualifications has increased considerably. Women are generally more likely than men to be married in their early 30s, are more likely to have children, and are less likely to live with their parents. Compared to men of the same age, they are generally less likely to be in paid employment, are more likely to have voted in the last election, and are more likely to be a member of an organisation. Regarding Trade Union membership, it appears that women born in 1958 were less likely to be a member than men, while women born in 1970 are as likely as men to be organised in a Trade Union.

It appears that the cohort data lends support to the assumption of a decline in social capital (Putnam, 1999), as reflected in the increase of cohort members in their early 30s living alone, a decline in community activities and political engagement. Yet, there also appear to be complex cohort and gender differences regarding social relationships and social participation, which will have to be explored further. For example, more young women are engaged in paid employment, indicating greater social integration of women through work—and more young people in the later born cohort, especially men are living with their parents, possibly suggesting closer links or greater dependencies with their parents.

In a next step the effects of human and bonding social capital on social integration are examined in multiple logistic regression models with the four indicators of bridging social capital as outcomes (separate models were run for each outcome). To take account of gender differences in the different forms of social capital separate models are run for men and women in each cohort, which enables the assessment of gender differences in the association between the different forms of capital. The results from the multivariate logistic regression model for men are given in Table 2, showing the odds of the event's occurrence for a specific category relative to the reference category, after controlling for social status of the family of origin. Odds greater than (or less than) 1 imply higher (or lower) probabilities of economic, political and social integration.

Table 2: Binary logistic regression (odds ratios) predicting indicators of economic, political, organisational inclusion for Men born in 1958 (NCDS) and 1970 (BCS70) in their early 30's (controlling for socio-economic status in family of origin)

	Paid employment		Voted in last election	
	NCDS	BCS70	NCDS	BCS70
Highest qualification				
None (base)				
NVQ1	3.01*	2.12*	1.31	1.27
NVQ2	3.09^	2.59*	1.87*	1.78*
NVQ3	5.21*	3.24*	2.24*	1.79*
NVQ4	7.88*	4.28*	3.28*	2.59*
NVQ5	18.43*	4.53*	3.63*	3.07*
Marital Status				
Single (base)				
Cohabiting	2.34*	3.57*	0.87	1.01
Married	4.67*	5.41*	1.12	1.67*
Children				
No Children (base)				
Has children	0.56#	0.40*	1.01	0.80#
Lives with parents	0.63#	0.66#	1.07	1.04
Number of moves				
None (base)				
1-3	1.02	1.05	0.85	0.87#
4-7	0.68	0.62#	0.74	0.64#
8+	0.42#	0.39*	0.41*	0.42*
Attends church regularly	0.91	0.69	1.13	1.54*

	Membership in any organisation		Membership in trade union	
	NCDS	BCS70	NCDS	BCS70
Highest qualification				
None (base)				
NVQ1	1.78#	1.57	1.65*	1.63#
NVQ2	2.33*	1.82#	1.39#	1.54#
NVQ3	2.57*	1.53	1.77*	1.54#
NVQ4	4.49*	2.90*	1.53#	1.90*
NVQ5	7.90*	3.49*	2.47*	1.32
Marital Status				
Single (base)				
Cohabiting	0.76	0.61#	0.98	1.04
Married	0.86	0.79	1.07	1.23
Children				
No Children (base)				
Has children	1.13	0.73#	1.09	0.89
Lives with parents	0.86	0.55#	0.71	0.98
Number of moves				
None (base)				
1-3	0.47#	0.69	0.67	1.37
4-7	0.52#	0.96	0.63	1.06
8+	0.75	1.05	0.46	0.75
Attends church regularly	2.08*	2.67*	1.34#	1.13

$* p < 0.001; \# p < 0.01$

Among men investment in human capital (as reflected in their highest qualifications obtained by age 30/33) is strongly and positively associated with all four indicators of social integration. The link is strongest for economic participation (i.e. being in paid employment) and being a member in an organisation. Yet, the association between qualifications and indicators of social integration is less strong for the later born cohort, suggesting that compared to men born in 1958 investment in human capital does not bring the same rewards.

Independent of the influence of highest qualifications there is a significant and positive association between marital status and employment, especially among men in the 1970 cohort. Being married is also positively linked with voting behaviour among men born in 1970. These findings might suggest that being married reinforces economic and civic engagement of men, especially for those in the later born cohort. Yet, men in a relationship are tendencially less likely to be a member in an organisation than single men, possibly reflecting more focused interests and attachment among men in a relationship. This effect is however only significant for cohabiting men in the 1970 cohort. Having children shows a negative association with employment status in both cohorts, after controlling for all other variables included in the model. This is a somewhat surprising finding, following the assumption of a male breadwinner role. Among men born in 1970 there is furthermore a slightly negative association between having children, voting behaviour and membership in an organisation. Living with parents is negatively associated with employment status in both cohorts, and with membership in organisation among men in the 1970 cohort. This finding might suggest that parents continue to play a role for young men establishing their independence, possibly especially in such situations where young people have difficulties in establishing themselves in the labour market. Frequent moves seem to undermine being in paid employment and voting behaviour, suggesting that the influence of community ties can be beneficial in finding paid employment and being engaged in the civic process. There is furthermore a significant negative association between frequent moves and membership in an organisation among men in the 1958 cohort. Regular church attendance is positively associated with being a member in an organisation (in both cohorts), with voting behaviour in the 1970 cohort, and Trade Union membership in the 1958 cohort.

Table 3: Binary logistic regression (odds ratios) predicting indicators of economic, political, organisational inclusion for **Women** *born in 1958 (NCDS) and 1970 (BCS70) in their early 30's (controlling for socio-economic status in family of origin)*

	Paid employment		Voted in last election	
	NCDS	BCS70	NCDS	BCS70
Highest qualification				
None (base)				
NVQ1	1.59*	2.18*	1.24	1.28#
NVQ2	1.76*	2.30*	1.69*	1.62*
NVQ3	1.60*	2.24*	2.95*	1.80*
NVQ4	2.56*	3.30*	2.45*	3.04*
NVQ5	3.59*	5.62*	4.20*	3.64*
Marital Status				
Single (base)				
Cohabiting	1.15	1.90*	0.87	0.91
Married	1.16	2.09*	1.64*	1.52*
Children				
No Children (base)				
Has children	0.16*	0.11*	0.95	0.96
Lives with parents	1.00	0.70#	1.22	0.88
Number of moves				
None (base)				
1-3	1.35	0.92	0.71	0.74
4-7	1.32	0.77	0.57#	0.58#
8+	0.98	0.51#	0.41*	0.44*
Attends church regularly	0.83#	0.64*	1.53*	1.62*

	Membership in any organisation		Member in Trade Union	
	NCDS	BCS70	NCDS	BCS70
Highest qualification				
None (base)				
NVQ1	1.21	1.84#	0.97	1.41
NVQ2	2.33*	2.05#	1.43#	1.83#
NVQ3	3.24*	2.69*	2.11*	2.14*
NVQ4	4.34*	3.81*	4.62*	4.92*
NVQ5	8.87*	4.71*	8.27*	3.96*
Marital Status				
Single (base)				
Cohabiting	0.93	0.78	1.00	1.33#
Married	0.94	0.92	0.96	1.62*
Children				
No Children (base)				
Has children	1.59*	1.22#	0.44*	0.62*
Lives with parents	0.92	0.71	1.29	0.90
Number of moves				
None (base)				
1-3	1.88	1.38	0.94	0.81
4-7	1.85	1.43	0.80	0.73
8+	2.66#	1.84	0.74	0.68
Attends church regularly	2.12*	2.46ᴬ	1.02	1.16

$* \, p < 0.001; \# \, p < 0.01$

Among women qualifications are also strongly associated with all indicators of social integration, especially employment status. While for men the role of qualifications in finding paid employment appears to have weakened, for women it has become somewhat stronger in the later born cohort. For the other indicators of social integration the role of highest qualifications is highly significant, yet weaker for women in the 1970 cohort than for those born in 1958, suggesting possibly increasing social participation of women with different educational backgrounds. This finding has however to be interpreted in the light of generally decreasing social participation in the later born cohort.

Being married showed no significant association with employment status among women born in 1958, yet among women born in 1970 it is a significant predictor of participation in the labour market as well as membership in a Trade Union. This finding could suggest changing gender relations, with men becoming more supportive or accepting of their partner's employment and membership in a Trade Union. Being married is also positively related to voting behaviour in both cohorts, suggesting that married women are politically engaged, exercising their civic rights (for which they had to fight very hard in the first place). Having children is negatively associated with being in paid employment and trade Union membership. On the other hand, having children is positively associated with membership in an organisation, suggesting that mothers might be less likely to participate in the labour market and Trade Union activities, but that they find other opportunities for social participation and engagement.

Living with parents shows a weak negative association with paid employment among women born in 1970. Frequent moves are also negatively associated with being in paid employment among women born in 1970 (as it is for men in both cohorts), possibly suggesting reduced employment opportunities due to a lack of social ties. On the other hand, frequent moves show a positive association with being a member in an organisation, which might suggest that women who are often uprooted in their living arrangements try to establish social links by becoming members of an organisation. This effect is however only significant for women born in 1958. Frequent moves are furthermore significantly and negatively associated with voting behaviour in both cohorts, possibly indicating a detachment from civic and political engagement due to weak ties to the community.

Women attending religious services on a regular basis are less likely to be in paid employment, but are more likely to vote and be a member in an organisation in comparison to those with no religious connection. It has been argued that religious affiliation is an indicator of bonding social capital capturing values in social capital that can bring both advantage and disadvantage (Ravanera, Rajulton, and Turcotte, 2003). Here we find that religious affiliation is associated with higher levels of social inclusion as reflected in civic and social participation, but a lower likelihood of being included through paid work.

Discussion

The aim of this paper was to assess associations between human and bonding social capital and social integration of young people in times of social change. Social integration was operationalised across three dimensions: economic, political, and social participation and assessed in two birth cohorts born twelve years apart. Although these dimensions do not completely cover all aspects of social integration, this analysis is an improvement on those focusing on only one dimension, such as employment. It contributes to a better understanding of the complexities and processes influencing the social integration of young people in changing times.

At a first glance it might appear that the findings confirm the assumption of a decline in social capital (Putnam, 1999), as reflected in the increase of cohort members in their early 30s living alone, a decline in social participation and political engagement. Yet, there also appear to be complex cohort and gender differences regarding social relationships and social participation, highlighting the need to take on board theories of social change, especially regarding the nature of intimate relationships and gender relations (Edwards, Franklin, and Holland, 2007), and to assess the processes underlying social integration in more detail.

Men and women are generally more likely to be included economically Women are more likely than men to participate in society through membership in organisations and making use of their right to vote. In the later born cohort there has been an increase of women participating in further education and in paid employment, yet a traditional gender division of labour appears to persist.

One of the key assumptions to be tested was whether investment in human capital, the acquisition of qualifications, skills and knowledge does facilitate social integration. The answer to this question is yes: those with higher level qualifications are more likely to be in paid employment, are more likely to vote, to be a member of an organisation or a Trade Union. Yet the findings also reveal that the rewards associated with higher qualifications are decreasing, especially for men in the later born cohort. This might suggest that post-16 education is becoming less effective as a means of breaking intergenerational cycles of disadvantage and social exclusion (Jones, 2002). An exception to this pattern concerns the economic participation of women in the labour market. Returns associated with investments in skills and qualifications are increasing with respect to women's employment opportunities in the later born cohort. This might be a reflection of the increasing number of women continuing in further education, as well as an increase of women, especially the highly qualified, participating in the labour market, even after they have made the step into family formation (Woods, Makepeace, Joshi, and Dolton, 2003). The finding might thus suggest that the expanded opportunities for education and work have different meaning and consequences for men and women.

This brings us to the other key question tested in this paper: does investment in close relationships undermine the development of bridging social capital and social integration? The answer to this question is not so straightforward. Strong bonds with like-minded individuals can bring both advantage and disadvantage, their influence changes with a changing socio-historical context, and differs by gender. Furthermore, the relationships between different forms of capital are interdependent. For example, the association between being in an intimate relationships and attachment to the labour market has increased for the later born cohort, and young men and women in a close relationship are also more likely to be in paid employment. This however can be a reflection of selection or causation effects. Close bonds to an intimate other can, on the one hand, encourage and support economic participation. On the other hand, it might be the case that economic participation facilitates the step into a relationship, that young men and women in paid employment are more attractive as potential marriage partners—increasingly so in the later born cohort. Among women born in 1958 the association between marital status and employment status is not significant. Thus, the findings could also suggest a shift in gender relations and changes in the nature of intimate relationships, as suggest by Edwards and colleagues (Edwards, Franklin, and Holland, 2007), and others (i.e. Beck and Beck-Gernsheim, 1995, 2002). The increasing insecurity and uncertainty of the 'crisis decades' appear have opened up new opportunities for family life, and men may have become more supportive or accepting of women's participation in the labour market. A married woman's place remains no longer in the home, and the so-called traditional division of labour with a male breadwinner role has been replaced with men and women sharing and ideally supporting each other in their role as worker (Crompton, 1999).

Having a child however, is negatively associated with paid employment status for women in both cohorts, and surprisingly also for men. Among men this finding might be a measurement error, as there are very few men in both cohorts who have children and who are not in employment. However, it might also reflect the continued risk for children in the U.K. to grow up in a workless household (UNICEF, 2007). For women this finding could imply that traditional gender roles still do apply after the birth of their children, or that women participating in paid employment are less likely to have children. This finding might illustrate that private issues can become public concerns. Persisting contradictions in intimate and family related roles might produce tensions and conflicts that are triggering changes in turn, bringing with them increasing demands of new kinds of relationships, and changes in the organisation of work and family related responsibilities (Beck and Beck-Gernsheim, 2002).

Having children is furthermore negatively associated with membership in Trade Unions among women. This finding might reflect that mothers are generally less likely to participate in paid employment (Woods, Makepeace, Joshi, and Dolton, 2003). The reduced rates of mothers being engaged in Trade Unions might furthermore be a reflection of childcare responsibilities and the non-unionised part-time employment that often goes with it (Bynner and Parsons, 2003). Among men having children is negatively associated with social and political participation in the later born cohort, while mothers in both cohorts are more likely to be a member in an organisation than women without children. These findings suggest that having children may have different consequences and meanings for men and women, underlining again the potential role of gender differences in the formation and utilisation of social capital. Fathers might find less time or energy for civic engagement in addition to their work roles, while women with children might be less likely to be in paid employment than those without children, but are participating in society through membership in organisations.

Another interesting finding is the increasing number of young people in their 30s living with their parents. The findings could be interpreted as indicating a generational change, where parents continue to play a central role in shaping their offspring's integration into the wider society, even after age 30. This might be a reflection of closer ties between parents and their children in the later born generation (Bengtson, Biblarz, and Roberts, 2002), or of extended financial and emotional dependence of young people on their parents (Jones, 2002; Jones, O'Sullivan, and Rouse, 2006). Living in the parental home at age 30/33 is negatively associated with employment status among men, which might suggest a negative influence of close family bonds on the development of economic independence. Yet, in interpreting this finding one has to keep in mind that those living with their parents at age 30 are possibly a select group, who have not yet reached economic independence (possibly due to extended education), or who had encountered difficulties in establishing themselves in the labour market. Furthermore, there is evidence that among those who still live at home in their early 30s there is an increased number of individuals who are ill or disabled (DiSalvo, 1996). The findings can thus also be understood to reflect the increasing burdens, pressures and demands posed on close family bonds.

Looking at the role of close ties to the community, as reflected in number of moves, the findings suggest that frequent moves are associated with reduced employment opportunities, and lack of political engagement among men and women. The findings might thus be indicative of advantages associated with stronger community ties regarding employment and political participation, where communities provide opportunities for economic participation and active citizenship. Yet, community ties of an exclusive nature, such as strong bonds with like-minded individuals who regularly attend religious functions, appears to lower the likelihood of being included through work. On the other hand churches and religious groups are organisations through which individuals mostly volunteer (Ravanera, Rajulton, and Turcotte, 2003), and might thus offer alternative (non-paid) forms of social integration.

In summary, the findings highlight the complexities and interdependence in the strategies used by individuals as they invest in and draw on the social, economic, and human resources available to them. Social inclusion, especially economic inclusion, is more likely among those with higher qualifications. Yet, the rewards associated with investment in human capital are changing for the two cohorts born twelve years apart, and have different consequences for men and women. Independent of the influence of academic qualifications, there are significant associations between social inclusion and close bonds to intimate others and ties to the community, suggesting that social integration across different domains calls for multiple levels of investment, not only for individual efforts at accumulating human capital. The study furthermore suggests that close social bonds can bring both advantages and disadvantages, and that for a better understanding of how different forms of capital are linked in bringing about economic, political, and social integration of young people into society, one has to take into account the multiplicity of ways that social relationship work, examine in more detail the impact of socio-historical change, and changing gender relationships. The notion of social capital is useful to gain a better understanding of the role and nature of social relationships in shaping youth transitions insofar that it differentiates between different aspects of social networks and helps to highlight the potential fungibility and interactions between different types of capital. What is still needed however is the consistent use of specific descriptions and definitions of social relationships, as well as the recognition of their malleability in response to a changing context.

Chapter 14

From newcomer to insider? Social networks and socialisation into working life

Markku Jokisaari

The author Saul Bellow looked back in his autobiography to how he got his first tenured post in the university: 'That promotion came thanks to Red Warren, [--] he twisted Joseph Warren Beach's arm and got him to advance me.' In this anecdote, Bellow had a connection to a person who in turn had a tie to another person who was in a high position and able to make a decision about who will be appointed to the job. This is an example, just one among many, of how social ties are often very important for career development and occupational mobility. Research too has shown how a person's connections are important in the labour market and for occupational mobility. In the literature an actor's social ties and the resources accessed through them have been conceptualised as social capital (Bourdieu, 1983; Burt, 1992; Coleman, 1988; Lin, 2001). Furthermore, a main premise in social capital theory is that social capital enhances the success of action. In other words, how an actor is situated in social networks often has important consequences to her or his career.

Social ties may be particularly important for recent graduates who face the transition from school to work. For example, recent graduates often have problems gaining recognition in the labour market and, consequently, they often need to get credentials, such as recommendations, through their network ties. Furthermore, just as employers use their networks and contacts to recruit new employees, it is important for job seekers to have network ties in the labour market in order to obtain information about job openings at the right time. Finally, graduates face various task and challenges when they enter an organisation. It is assumed that organisational socialisation plays an important role in how recent graduates adjust to work and assimilate to the organisation. Interaction with organisational insiders, such as supervisors, is the main channel for graduates to 'learn the ropes' in the organisation and working life in general.

Social capital, networks and resources

A central way to concretise the metaphorical use of the term social capital is to describe it within the framework of social networks and related resources. In this approach social capital consists of resources accessible through one's social ties (e.g., Coleman, 1988; Burt, 1992; Lin, 2001; Portes, 1998). In working life these resources may include information, credentials, influence and mentoring. Furthermore, in social capital theory two phases in the use of social capital are assumed: access to social networks and mobilisation of resources through these ties (Lin, 2001). First, access to various networks and related resources is not equally distributed. For example, a person's education and ethnicity has an influence on access to different networks. In addition, because resources are accessed through others, it is not self-evident how these resources should be mobilised. For example, whether a job seeker's acquaintance recommends him or her for a job is decision made by that acquaintance. Finally, the main premise in social capital theory is that the better access a person has to networks and related resources the more likely he or she will be to attain his or her aims (Burt, 1992; Lin, 2001). In other words, through social capital a person gets higher returns for his or her own investments, such as education, in different domains of life, such as working life. In addition, there are research findings which support this main premise of social capital theory (for review, see, Lin, 2001). For example, it has been shown that social ties and related resources are related to getting a job (e.g., Granovetter, 1995; Jokisaari & Nurmi, 2005), status attainment (Lin, 1999), promotion (e.g., Burt, 1997) and salary level (e.g., Burt, 1992; Lin, 2001). In other words, 'people who do better are somehow better connected'.

Social networks as a source of resources and opportunities

The social network approach has focused on two main explanations for how social ties are conduits of valuable resources: the structure of a person's network and whom a person reaches through her or his network ties.

It has been stated that network structure contributes to resource flow and localisation of opportunities (Burt, 1992; Granovetter, 1973). How a person's network members are connected to each other and to outside groups has consequences for resource flow, such as information. In this approach there are two important concepts: 'weak ties' and 'structural holes'. In his seminal paper Granovetter (1973) presented his 'strength of weak ties' thesis: networks characterised by weak ties, such as acquaintances, offer more new information than networks with strong ties, such as one's spouse and friends. Unlike strong ties, that bind interconnected individuals who then often share the same information, weak ties are often a bridge between different social groups and consequently enable access to new information. For example, Figure 1 shows three groups (A, B, C) and three persons (Kanerva, Kuutti, Kerttu) and their connections within and between the groups. In Figure 1 people are indicated by dots, strong ties between them by lines, and weak ties by dashed lines. In this example, Kanerva has weak ties in her network and she is in brokerage role between three groups: she is the only person who connects Groups A, B and C through her weak ties. Consequently, people whose networks include more weak ties are typically more likely to be a bridge between different groups than people with strong ties (Granovetter, 1973). Also Burt's (1992) concept of structural holes is based on resource benefits through networks. When a person's network includes people who don't know each other, there are structural holes in the network. A structural hole reflects a missing connection between persons. When there are structural holes in a person's network the person him- or herself is in a brokerage position between the people who are not themselves connected to each other. For example, in Figure 1 Kanerva has structural holes in her network and she is in a brokerage role between three groups, while Kerttu and Kuutti have all their ties within the same group, A, and these contacts are themselves connected to each other. Consequently, their personal networks contain no structural holes. It is assumed that structural holes and the related brokerage role bring information benefits. Like weak ties, a brokerage role connects a person to different people and more heterogeneous information. Another central advantage of the brokerage position is the timing of access to new information. Actors who are in a brokerage position are assumed to receive relevant information earlier than actors in more peripheral positions, because they are at the junction of the information flow (Burt, 1992). For example, the brokerage role may be related to the sending of a job application at the right time. When a person is in a brokerage role between people this may bring news

Figure 1. Brokerage role in network.

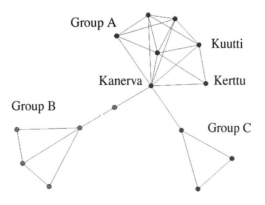

about job openings more rapidly as compared to more peripheral position in the network. Finally, a brokerage role between groups also brings access to referrals in different groups. As a broker has contacts in different groups these within-group contacts may in turn be a valuable source of recommendations within the group. Without contact in a group an outsider may be suspect, for example, when it comes to hiring someone. However, through the recommendations offered by a contact within a group an outsider acquires legitimacy within the group. In all, Burt (1992) assumes that a network characterised by structural holes is a mechanism for access to information and opportunities, i.e. a mechanism for social capital.

Another network mechanism with which to examine social capital is to ask with whom a person has contact. An influential theory in the field has been Nan Lin's social resources theory (Lin, 1982). The theory emphasises that the resources available through social ties depend crucially on the persons with whom a person has a connection. First, the higher position in the social structure a network person has, the more resources she or he will have. It is assumed that social contacts' positions in the societal structures are important, because they enable access to resources, such as information, credentials, and social influence (Lin, 1982; 2001). For example, a manager has more control over the resources in an organisation than a porter. Consequently, a person who has an opportunity to connect to a manager through his ties has more network-based resources available than a person who has a connection to a porter. A contact's resources are based on his or her position and the institution in which he or she is a member. In research an important indicator of social resources is the social tie's occupational prestige and socioeconomic status (SES) (Lin, 1982, 1999; Lin, Ensel & Vaughn, 1981).

Socialisation into working life and social ties

One of the most important transitions during early adulthood is that from school to work. How young adults manage to navigate through this particular transition may have many consequences for their well-being and later life course. Not only does a successful transition mean a secure job, financial security and a mark of independence, but research has also shown that the kind of work people do has an effect on their well-being, and on other life-domains, such as family life.

It might be assumed that social ties play a particularly important role when people enter a new societal field, such as the transition from school to work. For example, in the career development literature there has recently been an emphasis on the importance seeing a person's career development from a relational perspective (Blustein et al., 2004). Social relations have also been found to play a central role in individuals' narratives about their transition from school to working life. It might be assumed that when people enter the labour market they gain access to opportunities and related information, such as job leads, through social networks (Burt, 1992; Granovetter, 1995; Lin, 1999). For example, a job applicant may ask someone to write a letter of recommendation to a prospective employer. Social ties may also offer guidance, such as mentoring at the beginning of one's career (Higgins, 2001). In line with these assumptions we found in our research that graduates' social ties were beneficial for getting a job. Specifically, we investigated both the role of weak ties and social resources in obtaining a long-term job (Jokisaari & Nurmi, 2005). Our results indicated that both higher social resources and weaker ties contributed to getting a long-term job after graduation in Finland. Graduates' job search behavior and related activity was not related to employment after graduation.

However, the transition to working life is not only about getting a job but also 'learning the ropes' in an organisation. Organisational socialisation concerns the process through which a newcomer achieves the skills and knowledge in order to be a well-adjusted insider in the organisation. Graduates face various tasks and challenges when they enter into organisation. How they manage these tasks also has consequences for their work adjustment and career development (e.g., Saks & Ashforth, 1997; Schein, 1978; Wanous, 1992). A major task newcomers face during organisational entry is to acquire an understanding of the responsibilities and goals of a particular job during organisational socialisation. This understanding is then reflected in role clarity. Furthermore, newcomers need to develop relationships with their co-workers and to be included in a variety of workgroups. This aspect of socialisation should lead to increased social integration in the workplace. In addition, it has been assumed that low intentions to quit from an organisation reflect successful socialisation.

However, little is known about how organisation-specific social ties in graduates' personal networks may foster organisational socialisation and related adjustment to work. For example, graduates' pre-entry contacts with an organisation can take different forms. First, they may get first information about job opening in the organisation through their social ties. For example, they may have a friend or acquaintance in the organisation. Graduates may also have done their internship in an organisation and consequently may have had connections with that organisation as students. Following social network approach and social capital theory I assumed that graduates' existing connections in an organisation may contribute to their initial adjustment to work in that organisation. Specifically, I assumed that having supervisor-level contact in the organisation may particularly contribute to organisational socialisation and related work adjustment. In other words, supervisor-level contact typically ranks high in an organisational hierarchy, thus enabling the mobilisation of various resources. Also many organisational socialisation theories assume that one of the most important dyadic relationships for a newcomer is her or his relationship with a supervisor (e.g., Schein, 1978): the supervisor-newcomer relationship is an important interaction channel through which organisational socialisation is negotiated and implemented. For example, the supervisor often has formal authority in newcomers' role negotiations, and therefore, she or he has an opportunity to influence the newcomer's work assignments and goals. Furthermore, employee-level contacts in the organisation may also be beneficial for a graduate. For example, employee-level contact may be an important role in connecting and introducing a graduate to others in the workgroup and this may be indicated in higher social integration later on. Consequently, the research questions were: (1) To what extent is a supervisor-level contact in graduates' personal networks related to socialisation outcomes (role clarity, low intentions to quit from organisation) after organisational entry? (2) Is an employee-level contact in graduates' personal networks related to their socialisation outcomes (social integration) after organisational entry?

Methods

Participants and Procedure

The participants were graduates from four polytechnic schools in Finland. The schools represented three different occupational domains: technology (occupations such as software designer, telecommunications engineer, system manager), business and management (e.g., marketing manager, marketing assistant, sales manager), and health care (e.g., nurse, midwife, physiotherapist). Recruitment was arranged in co-operation with the school personnel, who informed students about the study. From the original list of names provided by the school administrations 422 (80 %) of the students agreed to participate in the study.

The participants were measured at two time-points.

(1) 422 students were examined during the last term of their last school year. They were asked to fill in the personal network inventory among other measures (Jokisaari & Nurmi, 2005). Thirteen students returned questionnaires which were not appropriately completed, and consequently they were excluded from the study. The remaining 409 participants were included in the study.

(2) About half a year after their graduation (Time 2), the participants were again asked to fill in the network inventory, an employment status inventory, and work adjustment questionnaire. The questionnaire was mailed to participants and they were returned by mail. Of the 343 participants who returned their questionnaires (response rate 84 %) 273 were employed.

Measures

Social ties. The participants were first asked to list their social ties concerning their work goals (Jokisaari & Nurmi, 2005): 'People often discuss their goals and related matters with others. The people with whom one has discussions may, for example, include school and organisation personnel or friends and relatives. If you look back over the last six months, who are the people with whom you have discussed important matters related to your work goals? Write below the first names or initials of three persons. Then, for each person describe what that person's relation is to you (e.g., spouse, supervisor). Next, give the occupation of this person.' After this instruction the participants were asked, first, to list the persons in their network by first name or initials; second, they were asked to describe the person's relation to them (e.g., spouse, supervisor); and, finally, they were asked to name the occupation of that person.

In addition, the participants were asked to indicate how close they were with the social contact, thereby reflecting the *strength of their tie* with the individual in question, i.e. whether it was weaker or stronger. This questions was answered using a 7-point scale (e.g., 'How close are you with this person?', 1 = *not at all close*, 7 = *very close*). I classified the social ties in the following way.

Organisation-specific social ties. I used dichotomised variables for each of the following categories to indicate the type of relationship named by the participant: mother, father, friend, spouse, boyfriend/girlfriend, sibling, schoolmate, school personnel, supervisor and co-worker. The supervisor category indicated *supervisor-level* contact (1 = supervisor-level contact, 0 = no supervisor-level contact) and employee category *employee-level* contact (1= employee-level contact, 0 = no employee-level contact) in an organisation.

Work adjustment. Intentions to quit were measured on a 3-item scale (Colarelli, 1984; e.g., 'I frequently think of quitting my job'). *Social integration* was assessed by three items (e.g. 'I feel comfortable around my co-workers'; Morrison, 1993). On both scales responses ranged from 1 (*strongly disagree*) to 5 (*strongly agree*). *Role clarity* was measured by using a 3-item scale ('Have clear goals and objectives been defined for your job?'; 'Do you know exactly what is expected of you at work?'; 'Do you know what your responsibilities are?'; Dallner et al., 2000). On this scale responses ranged from 1 (*never/seldom*) to 5 (*very often*).

Results

Analyses

To examine the effects of social ties at Time 1 on socialisation outcomes at Time 2, I used structural equation modeling (SEM). Structural equation modeling enables the prescribed relations between variables to be examined as in the case of the research question presented above, i.e., the extent to which supervisor-level ties and employee-level ties at Time 1 are related to socialisation outcomes (role clarity, social integration, intention to quit) after organisational entry (Time 2). The hypothesised model specifies the paths from supervisor-level ties to role clarity and to intention to quit, and from employee-level ties to social integration as shown in Figure 2. The role clarity, social integration and intention to quit scores were allowed to covary. The results showed that the hypothesised model fit the data well.

Social ties and socialisation outcomes

The results showed that social ties were related to recent graduates' socialisation outcomes in the organisation about six months after organisational entry (see, Jokisaari & Nurmi, 2005b). First, the results indicated, as shown in Figure 2, that supervisor-level contact in personal network was related to intentions to quit from the organisation and to role clarity. That is, graduates who had a supervisor-level contact reported a lower level of intentions to quit and higher level of role clarity than graduates without such a contact. The results further showed that an employee-level contact was related to social integration: graduates who had an employee-level contact in personal network reported higher level of social integration with co-workers in the workplace after organisational entry than graduates without such a contact.

Figure 2. Structural model. All numbers reflect standardised parameters with occupational domain and job tenure controlled for.

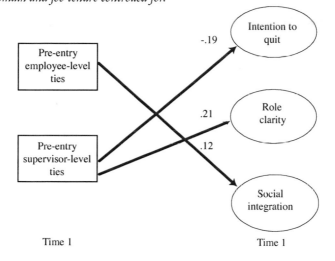

Discussion

In this chapter I examined social capital as a network-based resource. The social network approach has focused on two main explanations for how social ties are conduits of valuable resources: the structure of a person's network and whom a person reaches through her or his network ties. Furthermore, research has shown how social ties and related resources contribute in many ways to career development and occupational mobility (review, Lin, 1999). For example, getting a job after graduation is related to graduates' social ties and related resources rather than their own job search activity (Jokisaari & Nurmi, 2005). In addition, I discussed how organisational socialisation is a central part of the transition from school to working life. According to organisational socialisation theories recent graduates face different kinds of tasks and challenges when they enter an organisation. Finally, the preliminary results presented in this paper showed that graduates' social ties contributed to their organisational socialisation. The results showed that having a supervisor-level contact in their personal network contributed to graduates' lower intentions to quit from the organisation and higher role clarity after organisational entry. Furthermore, having an employee-level social contact in personal network was related to a higher level of social integration in the workplace.

Social capital and socialisation into working life

Research findings support the argument that a key process in the transition to working life and in organisational socialisation is the opportunity to make the kinds of social contacts needed to access and mobilise resources, ie. social capital (e.g., Gersick, Bartunek & Dutton, 2000; Jokisaari & Nurmi, 2005). The results presented here showed that having a supervisor level contact was related to role clarity and lower intentions to quit from the organisation. One of the most important tasks recent graduates face after organisational entry is to acquire an understanding of the responsibilities and goals of a particular job during organisational socialisation (e.g., Saks & Ashforth, 1997). This understanding is then reflected in role clarity. Supervisors often have formal authority in newcomers' role negotiations, and therefore have an opportunity to influence newcomers' work assignments and goals. In addition, supervisors play a central role in giving knowledge and feedback through which role expectations and performance are learned. In these ways the supervisor is able to contribute to newcomers' role clarity in their work. Furthermore, a supervisor typically has positional power to channel resources, tasks and opportunities in the workplace. Consequently, by having a supervisor-level contact a graduate has the potential for access to resources and opportunities; these in turn may contribute to successful socialisation after organisational entry, as indicated by higher role clarity and lower intentions to quit from the organisation.

Furthermore, the results showed that having an employee-level contact was related to social integration in the workplace. One explanation for this finding is that an employee-level contact may be a broker between the graduate and other employees in the workplace, i.e., he or she is able to introduce a graduate and oldtimers to each other. Furthermore, an employee-level contact may contribute to a graduate's reputation in the workplace by showing him or her, for example, to be a reliable person. One further possible explanation for these research findings is that organisation-specific social contacts may increase graduates' knowledge about an organisation. Earlier research has shown that pre-entry knowledge about an organisation is associated with employment quality (e.g., Kammeyer-Mueller & Wanberg, 2003). In other words, with pre-entry social ties to an organisation graduates may have more workplace-related information at their disposal and consequently their expectations about the workplace will not be unrealistically high. For example, employers tend to present their organisation in an overly positive way when they are recruiting new employees and this may generate unrealistic expectations among recruits (e.g., Wanous, 1992).

Practical implications

Social capital and network perspective also has practical implications for work transitions. In line with the earlier research (e.g., Lin, 1999), our earlier findings (Jokisaari & Nurmi, 2005) also suggests that social ties and connections should be considered as a factor in any program planned to help recent graduates in their entry into working life and organisations. For example, awareness of the role of informal channels and related social ties in obtaining employment could be of benefit to new entrants. Much of the information related to job openings is transmitted through social ties.

One further practical suggestion is that job seekers should be encouraged to channel their job seeking efforts through their social ties, if these have resources in and connections to the labour market. Employers often use their own networks to recruit and hire new employees (e.g., Fernandez & Weinberg, 1997). For example, over half of the organisations examined in Finland used their informal networks and connections to recruit new employees (Hämäläinen, 2004). One could advise the job applicants to mobilise their earlier contacts with supervisors, co-workers and other relevant acquaintances in order to locate appropriate people to write recommendations and act as referees. Recommendations may be particularly needed among recent graduates, because they often have problems to get recognition in labour market. It has also been found that job applicants recommended by employees within an organisation are more likely to be interviewed by employers and that same individuals receive more job offers than applicants without organisation-internal social ties (Fernandez & Weinberg, 1997). However, it is important to notice that social ties as such are not a channel for better employment, if there are inadequate resources available in the network. For example, I may have close and trusting relations in my network but the majority of the people in that network are unemployed. Consequently, capitalising on my network would be unlikely to find me a good job. Furthermore, as noted above, access to networks and related resources is not equally distributed. For example, there are findings which indicate that ethnic minorities use their ethnic networks to obtain a job and jobs obtained through these ties are lower paid than jobs obtained through other channels (e.g., Lin, 2001). Furthermore, research findings indicate that ethnic minorities often miss organisation-specific ties and consequently are disadvantaged in the hiring process (Petersen, Saporta, Seidel, 2000).

Research on the role of networks in labour market and employment outcomes challenge psychological assumptions about the importance of motivation and related job search behavior in employment. In psychology, the main premise typically is that finding a job is largely determined by a person's motivation to engage in job search and related activity (review, Kanfer et al., 2001). In other words, it is assumed that the more motivated and active a person is in seeking a new job the more likely he or she will be to find a job. However, little evidence has been found for the importance of motivation and job search behavior in finding employment (e.g., Kanfer et al., 2001). More importantly, in the psychological research tradition the role of social ties and informal channels in employment has typically not been taken into account and it has been assumed that information about jobs is available to all job-seekers in the labour market.

Given that social networks and related resources play an important role in many domains of life it is of paramount importance to develop interventions to see whether it is possible to assist persons to gain access new networks and mobilise related resources. As suggested in the literature, social groups, such as ethnic minorities and groups with low socio-economic standing, because of their positions and social ties, have different access to networks and related resources. Consequently, it is suggested that disadvantaged groups need help to access resources beyond their immediate social circles, such as thorough the provision of sponsors and mentors in career development and ties to institutions (e.g., Lin, 2001).

Finally, the results presented in this paper showed that having organisation-specific social ties, such as supervisors, in personal networks were related to graduates' role clarity, social integration and lower intentions to quit from the organisation after organisational entry. In other words, having organisation-specific social ties in personal networks seem to foster newcomer socialisation and related adjustment to work. These results suggest that social ties are not only beneficial in the hiring process but also in socialisation into the organisation. Perhaps the central message from the social capital theory and research in the labour market and career context is that the old saying 'man forges his own destiny' is not tenable; instead our employment and career prospects seem to be contingent on how we are located in social networks and related resources.

Chapter 15

Social capital and young people

Tom Schuller

Introduction

In this paper[1] I shall offer some reflections of a general kind on issues surrounding the status and utility of social capital as a research and policy concept; focus specifically on the gender-social capital link as a key dimension of young people's transitions; and offer some comments on young people's engagement in civic institutions. My approach tends to focus on the links between social capital and education or human capital (OECD, 2007). The paper is written from the perspective of one who is now primarily engaged in policy research, but I do not think this skews the argument too much.

As a preliminary to the more general comments, one could divide the youth social capital relationship into two related but distinct components, reflecting the multifaceted nature of social capital. First, there is the way in which social capital does (or does not) help young people to make whatever are considered to be the necessary transitions into adulthood, whether these be into adult employment, family life, or personal maturity. This might be called the instrumental dimension (though without this necessarily implying any degree of intentionality on the part of the people concerned—i.e. they are not necessarily deliberately exploiting their social capital to a specific end). Secondly, one could consider the extent to which young people themselves contribute to a society's stock of social capital, i.e. their levels of civic participation and the extent of trust which they exhibit. This might be called the intrinsic dimension. For the same groups, these two dimensions might exhibit very different profiles. A group of young people might use their networks very effectively and productively to progress into adulthood, successfully achieving a range of individual goals such as good jobs or high salaries; and yet exhibit entirely an individualist ethos and behaviour, eschewing any civic participation and displaying essentially atomistic attitudes.

---

1 This work is published in a personal capacity. The opinions expressed and arguments employed herein do not necessarily reflect the official views of the OECD.

Social capital as capital—a metaphor?

The emergence of social capital and other forms of capital has been chronicled many times (Baron et al., 2000). These uses of the term have sparked continuing debate amongst a range of disciplines, about how tightly 'capital' is to be defined. Roughly speaking, a continuum can be seen as running from a view of capital as a purely economic term that can strictly be applied to physical and financial resources, to a very loose approach that allows it to be attached to more or less anything which can be thought of as an asset of some kind and/or yields some kind of return or added value. Human capital comes closer to physical capital in terms of the acceptance of it in mainstream economics and the number of points of logical coherence that it has in common with physical capital. The point at which the line between a literal and a metaphorical application of the term is to be drawn varies enormously; so does the weight that might legitimately then be attached to any analysis involving the term.

Assuming for the moment that the concept of social capital is not immediately disqualified on the grounds of an illegitimate use of the term 'capital', there are at least three reasons why its use might be seen as potentially valuable in relation to both economic and social policies:

- it broadens the range of inputs to be considered in the processes which generate wealth and well-being, including successful integration into the adult world;
- it broadens the range of outputs to be used in measuring wealth and well-being, such that successful integration is considered a positive feature in its own right;
- it encourages a more dynamic approach to the analysis of social and economic issues, so that the interactions between different forms of capital are included. This is of course also a disadvantage in so far as it makes the analytical process more complicated.

In one sense, it does not matter whether or not the term 'social capital' is actually used, as long as the phenomena it refers to are adequately specified. But it may matter considerably, in at least two contrasting senses. First, on the positive side: using social capital may be a way of bringing together quite diverse elements which are nevertheless closely interrelated, such that analysis of one of them cannot be adequately undertaken without the others being taken into account. This is the thrust of the arguments linking human and social capital.

(OECD, 2001) Using social capital compels analysts and policy-makers to look at issues more in the round, and therefore, arguably, more realistically.

On the other side, it may be that lumping these different elements—trust, civic activity, political participation, network engagement, and so on—together under a single heading is not just conceptually clumsy but misleading, because it encourages analyses which attempt to cover too much. Here holistic approach meets analytical edge. One way out of this is to look rigorously at what is meant by a multi-dimensional approach; and to bring into play the notion of iterative triangulation: not only the use of multiple data types and sources, but their use over time in an iterative way, so that results and implications are continuously checked and refined.

From the policy angle particularly, the great advantage of human capital has been its fruitfulness in expanding the analysis of reasons why some economies perform more successfully than others. Could the same be true of social capital, with different application? The answer to this depends very largely on what models people operate with for approaching the analysis of economic and social performance. Putting it very crudely, if the search is for discrete independent variables which can be inserted into regression (or other) analyses to explain particular levels of performance, or differences in levels of performance, then 'social capital' as a concept is often likely to be both ill-specified and misleading.

If, on the other hand, the aim is to open up complex issues where multiple interactions are seen as inevitable, and different interpretations of these interactions as similarly inevitable and even desirable, then social capital may be a far better guide to sound analysis and valid policy prescription. Bringing social capital into the debate complicates matters rather than simplifying them. It does not supply a neat new tool of the same kind as previous tools but of higher calibre; rather, it entails a more multidimensional approach to analysis. But of course there will be no single figure answer to give as an end product of the analytical work, and this weakens its impact in the hurly-burly of short-term political decision-making.

Levels and context

What is the appropriate unit of analysis? Can we assess the volume/effects of social capital for an entire nation, or can it only be done at more local or neighbourhood level? The problem of aggregation has been frequently pointed out; it is compounded by the interaction between social capital at different levels. Halpern (2005) argued that intervention can operate at three levels:

- micro or individual level, through support for families, mentoring schemes, volunteering;
- meso or community level: promoting vibrant local government, building community-based asset schemes, building networks between firms, employees and community, and using ICT to strengthen neighbour interaction;
- macro or society level: promoting citizenship education, developing community credit schemes that reward volunteering, and developing genuine shared moral discourse to encourage mutual responsibility.

He goes on to draw up a quite complex 3-dimensional diagram for mapping different forms of social capital to these different levels. Conceptually this is very helpful. However it does not necessarily make the task of specifying and gathering data clearer, especially when, as Halpern himself recognises, the interaction between these different levels is extremely significant.

Awareness of context is always important in comparative work, but perhaps particularly so in relation to social capital. This applies to the cultural or ideological attitudes displayed towards the concept. These range from the enthusiasm shown in at least some academic and policy quarters in the U.S.A. to a quite widespread hostility in France. This latter stems from the general identification of social capital with 'communautarisme', which to French people of very different political persuasions signals an erosion of republican traditions of solidarity.

Context also covers perceptions of the state and its effect on social capital. In some contexts, social capital is seen as in some sense an alternative to or a counterweight to state provision, most obviously in the role of the voluntary sector. The state can be seen as the inhibitor of social capital; conversely social capital can be seen as some kind of safeguard against the inadequacies or even dominance of government. In others, notably in Scandinavian countries, the relationship is more of a positive sum game, with state and voluntary sectors seen as complementing each other; state support for citizens' study circles is an example. Specification of the significance and impact of social capital therefore depends on how the role of the state is defined and analysed, at different levels. Social capital may be a substitute or compensation for inadequate government; a challenge to the authority of government; or a positive complement—or, of course, a mixture of these.

Social capital and young people: gender and educational achievement

In the opening section I distinguished between instrumental and intrinsic forms of social capital, and observed in the abstract how these might apply to young people's transitions into adulthood. I now take up this issue again, through the prism of gender differences in educational achievement—one of the most remarkable trends in education over the last decade, and one which is certainly already having a major effect on youth transitions.

One of the most striking, and almost universal, educational trends of the last decade has been the shift in the relative achievements of males and females. In almost every single OECD country, girls now do better than boys at almost every level, up to and including doctoral, and in almost every single subject. In a few countries maths, engineering and physics still remain a male preserve, but even in these the picture is changing.

The flow of change began, naturally, with changes in school achievement and has now flooded through into higher education, including into graduate schools. The scale of the change is dramatic. For the 55-64 age group, 15% of women have attained tertiary education, on average across OECD countries; for men of that age group the figure is 21%. But for the 25-34 age groups that large superiority (if that is the right term) is turned into a significant lag (if that also is the right term): 33% of women compared with 28% of men. The trend is continuing for age groups currently preparing for higher education. In so-called 'high performing' education systems the difference seems to be biggest: for Finland the gap is 17 percentage points (47 to 30) and for Canada it is 13 (60 to 47).

Why is this happening and what are the consequences? It could be 'biology', once the sexist favouring of boys (by families and schools) disappeared, girls have simply come into their own as naturally superior students. It could be changes in teaching and assessment techniques. But the most plausible explanation is the peer group support which females give to each other. At school level, talking about their studies and their homework is a part of social communication among most girls, along with music, friends, and fashion and so on. The proportion of time devoted to it may be small, but it is there. It signals some kind of recognition that doing well at school matters, and is acceptable. We know the same is not the case in many male peer groups. Girls help each other to do well by building peer groups that reinforce educational achievement as valuable, and at the same time provide practical information and assistance. So the classic social capital recipe is present: networks of people who share similar values and who help each other to attain their goals. In other words, social capital may be the reason why women participate actively in post-compulsory education (at whatever level). And it may also explain why they are more likely to complete their courses successfully.

From this brief overview we can see how social capital helps some young people perform relatively well in education. The assumption is that this helps them to make a successful transition into adulthood. This assumption is, it should be noted, open to question; for example, it may be that continuously extending young people's participation in formal initial education at least partially infantilises them, and in effect simply postpones the entry into adult life. But at least high levels of social capital give them a better chance of using conventional means of establishing themselves.

Young people, civic participation and social attitudes

I turn now to a different question: do young people exhibit greater or lesser propensity than their elders to contribute to society's stock of social capital by taking active part in civic and political institutions, and do they exhibit greater or lesser trust in these institutions? I have no answer to this over-freighted question. In principle the answer should be yes, since both participation and trust are positively associated with education and educational levels having been rising from one generation to the next; but we know that there is no simple linear over-time relationship. The relevance of the question to the transition theme is twofold. First, engagement in civic institutions would generally be counted as part of integration into the wider society; and secondly, participation of this kind is a way of acquiring the skills and competences needed to play adult roles. Here I will just touch on a few of the issues.

First, there is no consensus on the kinds of participation which should be counted, and relatedly on the kinds of effect participation might be expected to have, on the individuals and on the wider society. One distinction is between what can loosely be called 'Putnamesque' and 'Olsonian' organisations, matching the distinction I draw earlier between intrinsic and instrumental forms of social capital. The former are groups, including youth groups, which allow their members to pursue common goals, in principle without imposing costs elsewhere. Olsonian organisations, by contrast, are ones designed to promote the interests of their members in some kind of a competitive context, such as pressure groups of various kinds, political parties and so on (see d'Hombres et al., 2007). The distinction is only loose, since much of Putnam's analyses include political participation as a positive indicator of social capital, but the conceptual distinction is easy to grasp.

Secondly, there is only a partial understanding of how changing participation patterns affect integration. Young people are more likely to participate in non-traditional forms of organisation, such as single-issue groups, or ones with a particular cultural affiliation. The shifting profile of organisational membership and cultural activity is accentuated by the rise of the Internet, with all the possibilities of virtual or electronic group membership (Bennet, 2007). One characterisation of the generational shift in domestic cultural practices has been to argue that young people's cultures are no longer sub-cultures or counter-cultures but co-located cultures; in other words, they co-exist with their parents' cultures, with generations sharing households on the basis of mutual acceptance, without the same levels of conflict which used to exist (Pasquier, 2007). This leads to a weakening of vertical patterns of cultural transmission. One consequence of this is an increased pressure on teachers, who are left isolated as the vertical transmitters of culture, at least as far as more traditional modes are concerned (e.g. through book-reading).

Thirdly, though, intergenerational influences remain relevant to the way young people acquire democratic habits and skills. In a large-scale study of Norwegian youth, Lauglo and Oia (2006) show that both the behavioural and attitudinal dimensions of social capital are influenced by family environments, but not merely or mainly through socio-economic status; it is the level of parental interest in civic affairs, and family conversation around these, which has the strongest effect. Moreover education matters—more than SES. The education includes, in the Norwegian context, extensive participation in school councils, so that active and informal learning is taking place alongside formal learning. The pattern will vary in other countries with less deep-rooted commitment to the school as a milieu for democratic learning.

Conclusion

As the previous papers in this section demonstrate, social capital can be conceptualised and applied in very diverse ways. For some this is a fundamental analytical weakness, for others it is a sign of versatility and strength. The transitions theme brings to the fore an essential aspect of social capital research: the need for a better understanding of the trajectories of social capital; how it grows and declines, and how it impinges on the paths over time of different social groups.

Chapter 16

Leisure life, identity and social capital

John Bynner

Leisure activity supplies the critical arenas in which young people begin to loosen their ties to the family and to find their own means of forging identity and building social capital of their own. The life styles and fashions of young people are not so much a sign of breaking with the family they grew up in as signalling a degree of autonomy in their own identity construction. Youth culture, though apparently pervasive in its impact on the young, takes many forms with variations marked by family structural influences such as class, ethnicity and gender (Bynner and Ashford, 1992b). The forms of leisure activity engaged in also change with age. The adult organised activities of childhood extend in early adolescence to church clubs and associations like Scouts and Guides. These in turn give way in the later teens to the commercial venues of the pub, club and pop concert.

Life Style and culture

The lifestyles associated with the cultural forms that young people want to express, as a basis of their group identity and social capital will also reflect to a certain extent their subsequent relationship to the labour market. This in turn impacts on decisions that have to be faced on whether to continue in education in the pursuit of qualifications or to leave at the first opportunity. Those young people on the fast track to the labour market, through dropping out of school at the earliest age and, to a lesser extent, those on vocational as opposed to academic tracks are likely to move from adult-organised activities to the more commercial expressions of youth culture and independence at a faster rate.

But more important are the values that are associated with their affiliation to a particular youth life style and group. Self appraisals based on feelings of efficacy and control, or depression, will link to leisure lifestyle, but social and political attitudes are more firmly based on the career trajectory the young person is on. Brake (1985), makes the useful distinction between two perspectives on youth culture; the intergenerational and the structural. The former represents youth culture as having an integrative function since the unconventional and in some ways antagonistic behaviour and values associated with it, serve as a means of helping young people find their niche in the prevailing social order. Sub cultures with a structural basis, as associated particularly with disadvantaged positions in education and the adult labour market, point to a more permanent basis for antagonism and hostility to the institutions of society.

Brakes' intergenerational explanation thought targeted principally at the reproduction of social inequality also has some affinity with developmental psychologists' conception of the processes of socialisation through which adult identity is formed through the teens. Much identity work (Coté and Levene, 2002) is apparent as the young person works through and resolves what Coleman (1993) and Hendry & Kloep (2002) describe as 'the focal concerns of adolescence'.

1. Developing a self identity in the light of physical changes.
2. Developing a gender identity.
3. Gaining a degree of independence from parents.
4. Accepting or rejecting adult values.
5. Shaping up to an occupational or unemployed role.
6. Developing and extending friendships.

Hendry (1989) sees leisure activities as the principle location for achieving these goals and emphasises the need for resolution of conflicts around relationships in three major areas: opposite sex, peers and parents. Each of these signifies an important transition point in progression towards adulthood and corresponds to a change in leisure style. Others have focussed on particular conflicts within the process e.g. Meeus, (1989) emphasises the 'teencentrism' (c.f. ethnocentrism) displayed by many teenagers as they attempt to break loose from adult controls and influences as reflected in hostility to institutions and groups outside that of the immediate peer group. Aitken and Jahoda's (1983) studies of young people's drinking behaviour in pubs shows how the rituals associated with 'round buying' cement relations in such peer groups reinforce social and gender identities and hence the social capital of the group as whole.

However as Brake's account also stresses there are structural features of these developmental processes that also need to be acknowledged. The changing nature of employment has increased the pressure on young people to gain qualifications and postpone entry into the labour market, extending the transition from school to work. This creates uncertainty about the future, a more 'individualized', as opposed to class-based response to the opportunities and risks involved, and a kind of moratorium on firm choices and decision making (Beck, 1986). The moratorium relates not only to occupation, but to the other long-term commitments and responsibilities of the adult world such as partnership and parenthood. The single life style prevails for much longer instead.

Diverging pathways

This transformation of young people's experience has led some to argue for the arrival of a new stage of the life course—'emerging adulthood' (Arnett 2004). However such a stage-based conception again tends to downplay the fact that such changes are highly differentiated with some young people taking the traditional route out of education to work at the first opportunity, and with the paths diverging for young men and young women as the possibilities of partnership, pregnancy and parenthood increasingly come into play (Bynner 2005).

'Navigating' this period of life effectively depends critically on access to different kinds of resources (Evans and Furlong, 1997). Its individualized features are thus constrained by structural factors such as class and gender and associated values (Furlong and Cartmel 1997). The extended transition to adulthood requires family support for much longer, not only financially, but in the form of advice and counselling to help ensure that the choices made will lead to fulfilling outcomes. And the advice given will in turn be conditioned by family aspirations based on values. Parents remain, typically, the most important source of advice about employment opportunities during the period (Banks et al, 1992) As Coleman (1988) argued in his original formulation of social capital, achievement also depends on the wider community of which the family is a part, supplying networks of mutual help, communal pressure for high quality educational provision and standards, and links to education and work opportunities. Such social capital though primarily vested in the parents is also accessible to the family as a whole. Good relations with the school and teachers are another key component. The access to opportunities through such contacts and the norms and values they imply, assure entry onto the achievement routes to middle class occupations as Bourdieu argued (Bourdieu, 1997).

In this scenario there is evidence of increasing polarisation between the educational 'haves' and 'have nots', the latter increasingly marginalised into patchwork careers comprising casual jobs interspersed with unemployment. The UK government's concern with the one tenth of young people over the period 16-19 not in employment education and training (NEET) is a reflection of the belief, shared in Finland, that dropout from all forms of education and training too soon must be avoided at all costs (SEU, 1999). The ConneXions counselling service was established to help such disadvantaged young people to keep engaged. The alternative can be 'Patchwork careers', comprising casual jobs interspersed with unemployment, extending possibly to wider manifestations of social exclusion such as drugs, crime.

The divergence of male and female paths over this period is another notable feature. Young women with poor educational careers leading to early leaving and minimal or no qualifications will tend to find the limited range of skilled jobs in factories and so on available to them, unsatisfying. The alternative route of early marriage and partnership is then likely to become increasingly attractive, with a career based on 'caring' for their own and other children. For boys limited opportunities in the labour market and poor prospects for progression in it, have almost the opposite effect of postponing commitments, extending what Wallace (1987), describes as 'perpetual adolescence'. Although such young men, for whom leisure supplies the main platform for achievement, will still be on average ahead of their counterparts pursuing higher education the pressure to settle and to establish a family is likely to prevail on them as well.

Social capital and the peer group

The peer group in the leisure context is also of course the other critical component of influence of growing importance through the teens. The group offers the basis of an identity which may be supportive of continuing educational engagement or working completely at variance with it. Such identity work as we have seen depends increasingly on the social capital of young people themselves. This supplies the means of refining and building the opportunities—protective and developmental—that underpins the Lifestyle experimentation that is taking place. The strengthening of the group's relational network focuses initially on the 'bonding' forms of social capital. 'Bridging' occurs more across the arenas where different roles are demanded—in the school setting as opposed to leisure context, for example.

As young people get older such networks and the strong and weak ties comprising them, extend to wider bridging and 'linking forms of social capital across the community (bridging across social groups) as well. With the new media and communications technology to which young people have increasing access, the links extend globally and to the virtual world as well. But again the idea of a relatively simple straightforward progression is an over simplification. Some teenage groups convert their bonding social capital into gang membership and through challenging and anti-social behaviour threaten the very basis of social cohesion on which communities depend. Those with a poor educational record, typically locked into unsatisfying jobs and unemployment, are most likely to convert their alienation into such networks, where violence becomes the means of resolving conflicts within the group and particularly with groups outside. In this sense social capital takes on the negative connotations (the 'dark side' in Putnam's terms (1990) in which bonding creates an impermeable barrier that sees all outsiders as a threat and ultimately an enemy to be vanquished.

Youth clubs

The question arises as to how to provide through leisure provision positive experiences, to help develop the bridging forms of social capital and links to opportunity structures outside those of the group. There is evidence to suggest that the type of leisure context can make a considerable difference. In work undertaken in longitudinal enquiries based following a large cohort of 12,000 individuals in Britain from birth in 1970 through to age 30 in 2000, it was found that age 16 leisure activity reflected a continuation of life patterns established earlier. The context of the leisure activity could also strengthen tendencies towards positive or negative outcomes in the economic, social and psychological health spheres at age 30 (Feinstein, Bynner and Duckworth, 2006).

Most notably, certain kinds leisure activity associated with churches, uniformed associations, such as Scouts and Guides and after school meeting places in school and community venues where hobbies and sports could be pursued, all tended to re-enforce trajectories leading to positive outcomes. The one exception was youth clubs of the traditional kind, which on balance predicted re-enforcement of negative tendencies leading to poor opportunities and various forms of social exclusion in the 30s. Such clubs typically offered unstructured provision where any formal curriculum gave way to casual games and conversation and the opportunity to 'hang out'. Comparable work in Sweden based on studying young people in similar 'Your Recreation Centres (*Fritisgardarå*) produced very similar results (Mahoney, Stattin and Lord, 2004). There was strong evidence that engagement in these clubs was on balance detrimental to the young people's later prospects.

The explanation of these somewhat counter-intuitive findings lies at the heart of the social capital debate. Young people from disadvantaged backgrounds, to whom the youth clubs in question are generally directed, tend to have poor educational records. The interactional setting of 'hanging out' may merely reinforce the negative feelings such young people have about schools and education and conventional (adult) frameworks of aspiration and achievement more generally. The youth workers in such situations will frequently not wish to intervene in the process of a developing group identity seeking often seeking to identify with it as serving to mitigate the sense of alienation and oppression that the young people feel.

The contrasting experience is in the other kinds of youth association and club based on activities like sport and where structures, in the form of goals and means of achieving them in accordance with rules, tend to be the norm instead. Sport is particularly significant in this respect because it is one of the few out-of-school contexts that has little connection with the socio-economic status of families or the educational achievements of the young people who engage with it. Consequently sport would appear to supply the basis for building the bridging and linking social capital and associated weak ties on which positive life paths can be built. Otherwise the interest may lie in reforming clubs with more structured provision capitalising more on what works in other venues. The goal should perhaps be less on sympathising if not identifying with young people's sense of oppression than giving them the means within a world they construct themselves, inside and outside the youth club, structured activity that will redirect their means of gaining self-esteem and fill them and the wider community with a sense of achievement. Finnish initiatives in such life management strategies have been exceptionally successful in this respect and provide the models of what is needed (Helve and Bynner, J. 1996; Helve, 1998).

The point this makes, as acknowledged by Putnam (1999), is that social capital is a *necessary* but not *sufficient* condition for community achievement and cohesion. At base, social capital is an expression of trust-based relationships in groups, the outcome of which will depend on the goals to which the group's life is directed. Youth culture is essentially inward looking defining its own generally short-term goals and the means of achieving them, while keeping the long term commitments of the adult world at bay.

Youth and media

But focussing on the negative side of youth culture as manifested in youth clubs or on the street, or at home, can disguise, of course, other features of it which both set young people apart from the adult generation in the current era and offer positive as well as negative contributions to the well-being of society as a whole. The use of media, especially ICT, offers opportunities for identity work and experimentation that were unknown to previous generations. Thus the internet, whether through chat rooms or formal structures such as Wikipedia, supplies the means of extending friendship patterns and forms of bonding outside immediate geographical locations and into virtual worlds as well. This brings the fundamental feature of social capital, 'trust', into the picture. To create relationships with people who are personally unknown to you, or who present personas that are not their own in web based interchanges, tests trust to the very limit. This compels participants to build their own sets of rules and values that individuals have to sign up to before they can join in. Such experimentation with new communities offers opportunities to which the previous generation has yet to be become fully aware. It also has clearly disturbing aspects to which media stories about internet seduction of vulnerable young people continually attest.

This takes us back to issues concerning the meaning and status of social capital, as applied to young people, which have recurred repeatedly through this book. Adult social capital as a coercive force through the serving of economic and sometimes sectarian goals, rather then personal fulfilment, is countered though youth culture expressed in leisure activity through which young people generate bonding forms of social capital for themselves. Bridging to the wider world takes place in the family and community including the school and the workplace and the church. With the growth of internet-based systems for the creation of communities and communications that are entirely self-determined bridging takes on new forms, extending the potential network of weak ties infinitely.

Conclusion

The information circulated thought websites has to be taken on trust not only by the community that produced it but by the wider population embracing all age groups, who through the internet have ready access to it. In this sense social capital resides in a system that offers new democratic forms with great liberating potential, but also the possibility of new forms of coercion as well. Youth social capital built through leisure life then becomes transmitted to the adult world: the reversal of the way resources were transmitted across the generations in the past. Young people's culture and the social capital that cements it may thus appear as a continuing threat to the adult world or a means of replenishing its developmental resources. The generations may then become more strongly linked through the opportunities that new technology provides. Are we seeing here in the new forms of youth social capital the foundations of the post modern world?

References

Adams, G. R. and Marshall, S. K. (1996), A developmental social psychology of identity: Understanding the person-in-context, *Journal of Adolescence*, 19: 429-442.

Adkins, L. (2002), *Revisions: gender and sexuality in late modernity*, Buckingham: Open University Press.

Adkins, L. (2005a), The new economy property and personhood, *Theory, Culture and Society*, 22(1): 111-130.

Adkins, L. (2005b), Social capital: The anatomy of a troubled concept, *Feminist Theory*, 6(2): 195-211.

Adkins, L. and Skeggs, B. (eds.), (2004), *Feminism after Bourdieu*, Oxford: Blackwell Publishing.

Aitken, P. P. and Jahoda, G. (1983), An observational study of young adult's drinking groups, *Alcohol and Alcoholism*, 18: 135-140.

Ainsworth, M. D. (1964), Patterns of attachment behaviour shown by the infant in interaction with his mother, *Merrill-Palmer Quarterly*, 10: 51-58.

Aldridge, S., Halpern, D., and Fitzpatrick, S. (2002), *Social Capital: A discussion paper*, London: Performance and Innovation Unit.

Alexander, C. (2000), *The Asian gang*, Oxford: Berg.

Allahar, A. and Côté, J. E. (1998), *Richer and poorer: The structure of inequality in Canada*, Toronto: Lorimer.

Allan, G. (1989), *Friendship*, London: Harvester/Wheatsheaf

Allan, G. (1996), *Kinship and friendships in modern Britain*, Oxford: Oxford University Press.

Allan, G. and Adams, R. (1999), (eds.), *Placing friendships in context*, Cambridge: Cambridge University Press.

Allatt, P. (1993), Becoming privileged: the role of family process, in Bates, I. R. and Buckingham, G. (eds.), *Youth and inequality*, Buckingham: Open University Press.

Allat, P. and Bates, I.. (1994), Arjen valinnat—Etnografinen tarkastelu kulttuurin vaikutuksista ammattiuran muotoutumiseen' (Routes and Daily Routines: Insights from ethnography into cultural influences on career trajectories), *Nuorisotutkimus* (Journal of Youth Research), 12(1): 29-38.

Amin, A. (2005), Local community on trial, *Economy and Society* 34(4): 612-633.

Anwar, M. (1994), *Race and elections: The participation of ethnic minorities in politics*, Coventry: Centre for Research in Ethnic Relations.

Arnett, J. J. (2000), Emerging Adulthood: A theory of development from the late teens to the late twenties, *American Psychologist*, 55(5): 469-480.

Arnett, J. J. (2004), *Emerging Adulthood: The Winding road from late teens through the twenties*, Oxford: Oxford University Press.

Ashenfelter, O. and Card, D., (1985), Using the longitudinal structure of earnings to estimate the effect of training programs, *Review of Economics and Statistics*, 67(4): 648-660.

Ashworth, A., Hardman, J., Hartfree, Y., Maguire, S., Middleton, S., Smith, D., Dearden, L., Emmerson, C., Frayne, C., and Meghir, C., (2002), Education Maintenance Allowance: The first two years: A quantitative evaluation, *Research Report No. 352*, UK Department for Education and Skills.

Ashworth, A., Hardman, J., Liu, W. C., Maguire, S., Middleton, S., Dearden, L., Emmerson, C., Frayne, C., Goodman, A., Ichimura, H. and Meghir, C., (2001), Education

Maintenance Allowance: The first year: A quantitative evaluation, *Research Report No. 257*, UK Department for Education and Employment.

Atkinson, A. B. (2004), *Joint report on social inclusion*, Brussels: DG Employment and Social Affairs, Social Security and Social Integration.

Atkinson, A. B., and Hills, J. (1998), *Exclusion, employment and opportunity*, London: Centre for Analysis of Social Exclusion, London School of Economics and Political Science.

Bagnell, G., Longhurst, B. and Savage, M. (2003), Children, belonging and social capital: The PTA and middle class narratives of social involvement in the North-West of England, *Sociological Research Online*, 8:(4), www.socresonline.org.uk/8/4/bagnell. htm, accessed 21st December 2004.

Ball, S. (2003), *Class strategies and the education market: The middle class and social advantage*, London: RoutledgeFalmer.

Ball, S., Maguire, M. and MacRae, S. (2000), *Choice, pathways and transitions post-16*, London: Routledge.

Banks, M., Breakwell, G., Bynner, J., Emler, N., Jamieson, L. and Roberts, K. (1992), *Careers and identities*, Buckingham: Open University Press.

Baron, S., Field, J. and Schuller, T. (2000), *Social Capital: Critical perspectives*, Oxford: Oxford University Press.

Baron, S., Field, J. and Schuller, T. (eds.), *Social capital: Critical perspectives*, Oxford: OUP

Bassani, C. (2003), Social capital theory in the context of Japanese children, *Electronic Journal of Contemporary Japanese Studies*, http:www.japanesestudies.org.uk/articles/Bassani.html, accessed 21st March 2005.

Bauman, Z. (2000), *The individualised society*, Cambridge: Polity Press.

Beck, U. (1992), *Risk society: Towards a new modernity*, London: Sage.

Beck, U., and Beck-Gernsheim, E. (1995), *The normal chaos of love*, Cambridge: Polity Press.

Beck, U., and Beck-Gernsheim, E. (2002), *Individualization: Institutionalized individualism and its social and political consequences*, London/Thousand Oaks/New Delhi: Sage.

Becker, G. S. (1964), *Human capital*, Chicago: University of Chicago Press.

Becker, G. S. (1975), *Human capital*, Washington D.C.: National Bureau of Economic Research.

Becker, G. S. and Lewis, H. G., (1973), On the interaction between the quantity and quality of children, *Journal of Political Economy*, 81(2): S279-S288.

Becker, G. S. and Tomes, N., (1976), Child endowments and the quantity and quality of children, *Journal of Political Economy*, 84(4): S:143-162.

Becker, G. S., (1965), A theory of the allocation of time, *Economic Journal*, 75(299): 493-517.

Becker, G. S., (1981), *A treatise on the family*, first ed., Cambridge, Massachusetts: Harvard University Press.

Bengtson, V. L., Biblarz, T. J., and Roberts, R. E. L. (2002), *How families still matter: A longitudinal study of youth in two generations*, Cambridge: Cambridge University Press.

Bennet, L. (2007), Changing citizenship in the digital age', paper to CERI meeting on New Millennium Learners, University of Florence, www.oecd.org/dataoecd/0/8/38360794. pdf

Berg, C. (1998), *The contextual-model for goals*, Presentation in the ISSBD congress, Bern, Switzerland, July, 1998.

Berg, C., Meegan, S. and Deviney, F. (1988), A social-contextual model of coping with everyday problems across the life-span, *International Journal of Behavioural Development*, 22(2): 239-261.

Berndt, T. J. (1982), The features and effects of friendship in early adolescence, *Child Development*, 53: 1447-1460.

Berthoud, R. (1999a), *Young Caribbean men and the labour market*, London: Joseph Rowntree Foundation.

Berthoud, R. (1999b), *Teenage births to ethnic minority women*, unpublished paper, Institute of Social and Economic Research, University of Essex.

Berthoud, R. (2001), Family formation in multi-cultural Britain: three patterns of diversity, paper presented at *Changing family patterns in multi-cultural Britain* one-day conference, ISER, April 3rd 2001.

Blackman, S. (2005), Youth subcultural theory: A critical engagement with the concept, its origins and politics, from the Chicago School to postmodernism, *Journal of Youth Studies*, 8(1): 1-20.

Blanden, J., Gregg, P., and Machin, S. (2005), *Intergenerational mobility in Europe and North America: a report submitted by the Sutton Trust*, London School of Economics.

Blau, P. (1977), *Inequality and heterogeneity: A primitive theory of social structure*, New York: Free Press.

Blau, P. and Schwartz, J. (1984), *Crosscutting social circles: testing a macrostructural theory of inter-group relations*, Florida: Academic Press.

Blustein, D. L., Schultheiss, D. P. and Flum, H. (2004), Toward a relational perspective of the psychology of careers and working: A social constructionist analysis, *Journal of Vocational Behavior*, 64: 423-440.

Bourdieu, P. (1983), Ökonomisches Kapital, kulturelles Kapital, soziales Kapital (Economic capital, cultural capital, social capital), in Kreckel, R. (ed.), *Soziale Ungleichheiten. Soziale Welt, Sonderband 2*: 183-198, Otto Schwartz and Co. Göttingen.

Bourdieu, P. (1986), The forms of capital, in Richardson, J. E. (ed.), *Handbook of theory of research for the sociology of education*, pp.241-58, New York: Greenwood Press.

Bourdieu, P. (1990), *The logic of practice*, Stanford, California: Stanford University Press.

Bourdieu, P. (1997/1986), The forms of capital, in Halsey, A.H., Lauder, H., Brown, P. and Stuart Wells, A. (eds.), *Education culture, economy, society*, Oxford: Oxford University Press, 46-58.

Bourdieu, P., (1993), *Sociology in question*, first ed., London: Sage.

Bourdieu, P., and Passeron, J. C. (1977), *Reproduction in education, society and culture*, London: Sage.

Bowlby, J. (1988), *A secure base: Parent-child attachment and healthy human development*, New York: Basic Books.

Brake, M. (1985), *Comparative youth culture*, London: Routledge and Kegan Paul.

Brandtstädter, J. (1998), Action perspective on human development in Damon, W. (Series ed.), and Lerner, R. (vol. ed.), *Handbook of child psychology: Vol. 1. Theoretical models of human development* (5th ed., pp. 807-863): New York: John Wiley.

Brandtstädter, J., and Renner, G. (1990), Tenacious goal pursuit and flexible goal adjustment: Explication and age-related analysis of assimilative and accommodative strategies of coping, *Psychology and Aging*, 5: 58-67.

Brooks, R. (2005), *Friendship and educational choice: Peer influence and planning for the future*, Basingstoke, Hampshire: Palgrave MacMillan.

Bull, M. and Lockhart, K. (2007), *Seeking a sanctuary: Seventh-day Adventism and the American dream,* second ed., Bloomington, Indiana: Indiana University Press.

Bullen, E. and Kenway, J. (2004), Subcultural capital and the female 'underclass'? A feminist response to underclass discourse', *Journal of Youth Studies*, 7(2): 141-153.

Bullen, E. and Kenway, J (2005), Bourdieu, subcultural capital and risky girlhood, *Theory and Research in Education* 3(1): 47-61.

Burt, R.S. (1992), *Structural holes: The social structure of competition*, Cambridge, MA: Harvard University Press.

Burt, R. S. (1997), The contingent value of social capital. *Administrative Science Quarterly*, 42: 339-365.

Butler, J. (2000), Critically queer, in Goodman, L. and de Gay, J. (eds.), *The Routledge reader in politics and performance*, London: Routledge.

Butler, N., Despotidou, S., and Shepherd, P. (1997), *1970 British cohort study (BCS70), ten year follow-up: A guide to the BCS70 10-year data available at the Economic and Social Research Unit Data Archive*. London: Social Statistics Research Unit, City University.

Bynner, J. (2001), British youth transitions in comparative perspective, *Journal of Youth Studies*, 4(1): 5-23.

Bynner, J. (2005), Rethinking the youth phase of the life course: the case for emerging adulthood, *Journal of Youth Studies*, 8: 367-384

Bynner, J. (2006), Rethinking the youth phase of the life-course: The case for emerging adulthood? *Journal of Youth Studies,* 9: 367-384.

Bynner, J. and Ashford, S. (1992), Teenage careers and leisure lives, *Leisure and Society*, 15: 499 519.

Bynner, J. and Ashford, S. (1992b), *Society and Leisure* 15 (2): 499-520. Presses de l'Université du Quebec.

Bynner, J. and Egerton, M., (2001), The wider benefits of higher education, *Report No. 01/46*, London: Higher Education Funding Council (HEFCE), and the Institute of Education.

Bynner, J., and Parsons, S. (2003), Social participation, values and crime, in Ferri, E., Bynner, J., and Wadsworth, M. (eds.), *Changing Britain, changing lives* (pp. 261-294), London: Institute of Education.

Cahill, C. (2000), Street literacy: Urban teenagers' strategies for negotiating their neighbourhood, *Journal of Youth Studies*, 3(3): 251-277.

Calvo-Armengol, A. and Zenou, Y., (2004), Social networks and crime decisions: The role of social structure in facilitating delinquent behaviour, *International Economic Review*, 45(3): 939-958.

Cantor, N., Acker, M., and Cook-Flanagan, C. (1992), Conflict and preoccupation in the intimacy life task, *Journal of Personality and Social Psychology,* 63: 644-655.

Case, A. C. and Katz, L. F., (1991), The company you keep: The effects of family and neighbourhood on disadvantage youths, *NBER Working Paper No. 3705*, National Bureau for Economic Research.

Caspi, A. (2002), Social selection, social causation and developmental pathways: Empirical strategies for better understanding how individuals and environments are linked across the life course, in Pulkkinen, L. and Caspi, A. (eds.), *Paths to successful* development: Personality in the life course* (pp. 281-301), Cambridge: Cambridge University Press.

Castells, M. (1996), *The rise of the network society*, Oxford: Blackwell.

Catan, L. (2004), *Becoming adult: Changing youth transitions in the 21st century*, Brighton, UK: Trust for the Study of Adolescence.

Chitty, C. (2004), *Education policy in Britain,* Basingstoke, Hampshire: Palgrave MacMillan.

Chuef, A., Read, S. and Walsh, D. (2001), A hierarchical taxonomy of human goals, *Motivation and Emotion,* 25: 191-232.

Cohen, P. and Ainley, P. (2000), In the country of the blind? Youth studies and cultural studies in Britain, *Journal of Youth Studies* 3(1): 79-95.

Cohen, D. and Prusak, L. (2001), *In good company: How social capital makes organizations work*, Boston, Massachusetts: Harvard Business School Press.

Colarossi, L. G. (2001), Adolescent gender differences in social support: Structure, function, and provider type, *Social Work Research,* 25: 233-241.

Coleman, J. S. (1961), *The adolescent society: The social life of the teenager and its impact on education*, New York: Press of Glencoe.

Coleman, J. S. (1987), Families and schools, *Educational Researcher*, 16(6): 32-38.

Coleman, J. S. (1988), Social capital in the creation of human capital, *The American Journal of Sociology*, 94(suppl.): 95-120.

Coleman, J. S. (1988), Social capital in the creation of human capital, *American Journal of Sociology,* 94, S95-S120.

Coleman, J. S. (1990), *The foundations of social theory*, first ed., Cambridge, Massachusetts: Harvard University Press.

Coleman, J. S. (1993), Adolescence in a changing world' in Jackson, S. and Rodriguez-Tomé, H (eds.), *Adolescence and its social worlds,* Hillsdale: Lawrence Erlbaum.

Coles, B. (1995), *Youth and social policy: youth citizenship and young careers*, London: UCL Press.

Coles, B. (2000), *Joined up youth research, policy and practice: an agenda for change?* Leicester: Youth Work Press

Commission for Racial Equality (2004), *Few black friends for whites*, news.bbc.co.uk/1/hi/uk/3906193.stm.

Commission for Racial Equality (2005), *Commission for integration and cohesion: A response by the Commission for Racial Equality*, London: CRE.

Côté, J. E. (1996), Sociological perspectives on identity formation: the culture-identity link and identity capital, *Journal of Adolescence*, 19: 419-430.

Côté, J. E. (1997), An empirical test of the identity capital model, *Journal of Adolescence*, 20: 577-597.

Côté, J. E. (2000), *Arrested adulthood: The changing nature of maturity and identity,* New York: New York University Press.

Côté, J. E. (2002), The role of identity capital in the transition to adulthood: The individualization thesis examined, *Journal of Youth Studies,* 5(2): 117-134.

Côté, J. E. and Levine, C. G. (2002), *Identity formation, agency and culture*, Mahwah, NJ: Lawrence Erlbaum.

Côté, J. E. (2005), Identity capital, social capital, and the wider benefits of learning: Generating resources facilitative of social cohesion, *London Review of Education,* 3(3): 221-237.

Côté, J. E. (2007), Youth and the provision of resources, in Helve, H. and Bynner, J. (eds.), *Youth and social capital*, London: Tufnell Press.

Côté, J. E. and Levine, C. (2002), *Identity formation, agency, and culture: A social psychological synthesis*, London and Hillsdale, New Jersey: Lawrence Erlbaum.

Côté, J. E. and Schwartz, S. J. (2002), Comparing psychological approaches to identity: Identity status, identity capital, and the individualization process, *Journal of Adolescence*, 25: 571-586.

Cotterell, J. (1996), *Social networks and social influences in adolescence*, London: Routledge.

Crompton, R. (ed.), (1999), *Restructuring gender relations and employment* Oxford: Oxford University Press.

D'Hombres B., Rocco, L., Suhrke, M. and McKee, M. (2007), *Does social capital determine health? Evidence from eight transition countries*, Institute for the Protection and Security of the Citizen, Luxemburg: European commission

Dallner, M., Elo A.-L., Gamberale, F., Hottinen, V., Knardahl, S., Lindström, K., Skogstad, A. and Orhede, E. (2000), *Validation of the general Nordic questionnaire (QPSNordic) for psychological and social factors at work*, Copenhagen: Nordic Council of Ministers.

Davie, R., Butler, N. R., and Goldstein, H. (1972), *From birth to seven: the second report of the national child development study (1958 cohort)*, London: Longman in association with the National Children's Bureau.

De Ruyter, D. J. (2002), The right to meaningful education: The role of values and beliefs, *Journal of Beliefs and Values*, 23(1): 33-42.

Deleuze, G., and Guattari, F., (2004), *A thousand plateaus*, London: Continuum.

Demetriou, H., Goalen, P. and Rudduck, J. (2000), Academic performance, transfer, transition and friendship: Listening to the student voice, *International Journal of Educational Research*, 33: 425-441.

Dench, S. and Regan, J., (2000), Learning in later life: Motivation and impact, *Research Report No. 183*, UK Department for Education and Employment.

Diener, E. and Fujita, F. (1995), Resources, personal strivings, and subjective well-being: A nomothetic and idiographic approach, *Journal of Personality and Social Psychology*, 68: 926-935.

DiSalvo, P. (1996), Who's at home at 33? In *NCDS User Support Group Working Paper 42*, London: City University, Social Statistics Research Unit.

Du Bois-Reymond, M. and Lopez Blasco, A. (2003), Yo-yo transitions and misleading trajectories: towards integrated transition policies for young adults in Europe, in Lopez Blasco, A., McNeish, W., and Walther, A. (eds.), *Young people and contradictions of inclusion: towards integrated transition policies in Europe*, Bristol: The Policy Press

Dunkel C. S. (2006), The relationship between self-continuity and measures of identity, *Identity*, 5(1): 1-32.

Edwards, R. (2004), Present and absent in troubling ways: Families and social capital debates, *Sociological Review*, 52(1): 1-21.

Edwards, R. Franklin, J. and Holland, J. (2003), Families and social capital: Exploring the issues, *Families and Social Capital ESRC Research Group Working Paper No. 1*, London: London South Bank University.

Edwards, R., Franklin, J., and Holland, J. (eds.), (2007), *Assessing social capital: Concept, policy and practice*, Cambridge: Cambridge Scholars Press.

Edwards, R., Hadfield, L., Lucey, H. and Mauthner, M. (2006), *Sibling identity and relationships: Sisters and brothers*, Oxford: Routledge.

Ellonen, N. and Korkiamäki, R. (2005), Sosiaalinen pääoma lasten ja nuorten näkökulmasta [Social capital from the perspective of children and youth], in Jokivuori, P. (ed.), *Sosiaalisen pääoman kentät* [The fields of social capital], Jyväskylä: Minerva.

Ellonen, N. and Korkiamäki, R. (2006), Sosiaalinen pääoma lasten ja nuorten hyvinvoinnin resurssina: Sosiaalinen pääoma-käsitteen käyttö kansainvälisessä lapsuus- ja nuorisotutkimuksessa (Use of the concept social capital in international childhood and youth studies), in Forsberg, H., Ritala-Koskinen, A. and Törrönen, M. (eds.), Lapset ja sosiaalityö, (Children and social work), Jyväskylä: PS-kustannus, 221-249.

Emirbayer, M. and Mische, A. (1998), What is agency? *American Journal of Sociology*, 103: 962-1023.

Emler, N. and Fraser, E. (1999), Politics: The education effect, *Oxford Review of Education*, 25(1): 271-272.

Emmons, R. (1986), Personal strivings: An approach to personality and subjective well-being, *Journal of Personality and Social Psychology*, 51: 1058-1068.

Emmons, R. (1991), Personal strivings, daily life events, and psychological and physical well-being, *Journal of Personality*, 59: 453-472.

Emmons, R. (1996), Striving and feeling: Personal goals and subjective well-being, in Gollwitzer, P. M. and Bargh, J. A. (eds.), *The psychology of action: Linking cognition and motivation to behavior* (p. 313-337): New York: Guilford Press.

EU (2005), *Working together for growth and jobs: A new start for the Lisbon Strategy*, Brussels: European Commission, Communication 33.

Evans, K. (2002), Taking control of their lives? Agency in young adult transitions in England and the new Germany, *Journal of Youth Studies*, 5(3): 245-269

Evans, K. and A Furlong (1997), Metaphors of youth transitions: Niches, pathways, trajectories and navigations, in J. Bynner, J., Chisholm, L. and Furlong, A. (eds.), *Youth, citizenship and social change*. Aldershot: Ashgate.

Fangen, K. (2001), *Pride and power: A sociological study of the Norwegian radical nationalistic underground movement*, Oslo: Institutt for sosiologi og samfunnsgeografi, Universitet i Oslo, Rapport 2:2001.

Farrell, A., Tayler, C. and Tennent, L. (2004), Building social capital in early childhood education and care: An Australian study, *British Educational Research Journal*, 30(5): 623-632.

Farrington, D. P. (2001), Predicting persistent young offenders, in McDowell G. L. and Smith, J. S., (eds.), *Juvenile delinquency in the US and the UK*, London: Macmillan Press Limited.

Faulkner, D. (2004), *Civic renewal, diversity and social capital in multi-ethnic Britain*, Runnymede Trust Occasional Paper no. 1, London: Runnymede Trust.

Feinstein, L., Bynner, J. and Duckworth, K. (2006), *Leisure contexts in adolescence and their effect on adult outcomes*, Wider benefits of learning Research Report No. 15, London: Institute of Education.

Feinstein, L. and Sabates, R. (2005), Education and youth crime: Effects of introducing the Education Maintenance Allowance programme, *Wider Benefits of Learning Research Report No. 14*, London: Institute of Education.

Fernandez, R. M. and Weinberg, N. (1997), Sifting and sorting: Personal contacts and hiring in a retail bank, *American Sociological Review*, 62: 883-902.

Ferri, E., Bynner, J. and Wadsworth, M., (eds.) (2003), *Changing Britain, changing lives: Three generations at the end of the century*, London: Institute of Education.

Fevre, R. (2004), *Social capital and the participation of marginalised groups in government, summary report*, ESRC funded project R000239410.

Field, J. (2003), *Social capital*, London and New York: Routledge.

Fine, B. (2001), *Social capital versus social theory: Political economy and social science at the turn of the millennium*, London: Routledge.

Flap, H. D. and Boxman, E. A. (2000), Getting started: The influence of social capital on the start of the occupational career, in Lin, N. Cook, K. and Burt, R. (eds.), *Social capital: Theory and research*, (159-181), New York, Aldine de Gruyter.

Fogelman, K. (1983), *Growing up in Great Britain: collected papers from the National Child Development Study*, London: Macmillan.

Franklin, J. (2004), (ed.), Politics, trust and networks: *Social capital in critical perspective, families and social capital, Families and Social Capital ESRC Research Group Working Paper No. 7*, London: London South Bank University.

Franklin, J. and Thomson, R. (2005), (Re)claiming the social: a conversation between feminist, late modern and social capital theories, *Feminist Theory* 6(2): 161-172.

Freeman, R., (1996), The economics of crime, in Ashenfelter, O. and Card, D., (eds), *Handbook of labour economics vol. 3*, Amsterdam: Elsevier Science.

Furedi, F. (2006), Taking the social out of policy—a critique of the policy of behaviour, *Diverse Britain: Social practice and social policy conference*, Families and Social Capital ESRC Research Group, London South Bank University, 8th September.

Furlong, A., and Cartmel, F. (1997), *Young people and social change: individualization and risk in late modernity*, Buckingham: Open University Press

Gallie, D. (2000), The labour force, in Halsey, A. H. and Webb, J. (eds.), *Twentieth century British social trends* (pp. 281-323), London: Macmillan.

Garbarino, J., Bradshaw, C. P. and Kostelny, K. (2005), Neighbourhood and community influences on parenting, in Luster, T. and Okagi, L. (eds.), *Parenting: An ecological perspective*, second ed., London: Lawrence Erlbaum Associates, 297-318.

Gersick, C. J., Bartunek, J. M. and Dutton, J. E. (2000), Learning from academia: The importance of relationships in professional life, *Academy of Management Journal*, 43: 1026-1044.

Giddens, A. (1991), *Modernity and self identity: self and society in the late modern age*, Cambridge: Polity Press.

Giddens, A. (2000), *The third way and its critics*, Cambridge: Polity Press.

Gillies, V. (2005), Raising the 'meritocracy': parenting and the individualization of social class, *Sociology*, 39(5): 835-854.

Goodwin, J. and O'Connor, H. (2005), Exploring complex transitions: looking back at the 'golden age' of school to work, *Sociology*, 39(2): 197-200.

Gordon, T., Lahelma, E. and Tolonen, T. (1995), Koulu on kuin...' Metaforat fyysisen koulun analysoinnin välineinä, ('School is like a ...' Metaphors as tools for analysing physical school), *Nuorisotutkimus* (Journal of Youth Research), 13(3): 3-12.

Goulbourne, H. and Solomos, J. (2003), Families, ethnicity and social capital, *Social Policy and Society*, 2(4): 329-338.

Graham, C. and Hill, M. (2003), Negotiating the transition to secondary school, *Spotlight*, No. 89, www.scre.ac.uk/spotlight

Granovetter, M. S. (1973), The strength of weak ties, *American Journal of Sociology*, 78: 1360-1380.

Granovetter, M. S. (1995), *Getting a job: A study of contacts and careers*, (2nd ed.), Chicago: The University of Chicago Press.

Green, A., Preston, J. and Janmaat, G. (2006), *Education, equality and social cohesion* London: Palgrave.

Griffin, C. (1993), *Representations of youth: The study of youth and adolescence in Britain and America*, Oxford: Blackwell.

Griffith, B. A. and Griggs, J. C. (2001), Religious identity status as a model to understand, assess, and interact with client spirituality, *Counselling and Values*, 46: 14-25.

Hall, P. (1999), Social capital in Britain, *British Journal of Political Science*, 29: 417-461.

Hall, S. and Jefferson, T. (1986/1976) (eds.), *Resistance through rituals: Youth subcultures in post-war Britain*, London: Hutchinson.

Hall, R., Ogden, P. and Hall, C. (1999), Living alone: Evidence from England and Wales and France for the last two decades, in McRae, S. (ed.), *Changing Britain: Families and households in the 1990s*, Oxford: Oxford University Press.

Halpern, D. (2005), *Social capital*, Cambridge: Polity Press.

Hammond, C., (2004), Impacts of lifelong learning upon emotional resilience, psychological and mental health: Fieldwork evidence, *Oxford Review of Education*, 30(4): 551-568.

Hämäläinen, H. (2004), Työvoiman rekrytointi toimipaikoissa vuonna 2003: Selvitys työvoiman hankintakanavista, rekrytointiongelmista ja toimipaikkojen tulevaisuuden näkymistä (Recruitment of work force in organisations in 2003). Helsinki: Ministry of Labour.

Hardt, M. (1999), Affective labour, *Boundary* 26(2): 89-100.

Harlow, R. and Cantor, N. (1994), Social pursuits of academics: Side effects and spillover of strategic reassurance seeking, *Journal of Personality and Social Psychology*, 66: 386-397.

Hart, P. E. (1988), *Youth unemployment in Great Britain*, Cambridge: Cambridge University Press.

Hartup, W. W. (1992), Having friends, making friends and keeping friends: Relationships as educational contexts, *Early Report*, 19: 1-4.

Heaver, C., Maguire, M., Middleton, S., Maguire, S., Youngs, R., Dobson, B. and Hardman, J. (2002), Evaluation of Education Maintenance Allowance pilots: Leeds. and London, first year evidence, *Research Report No. 353*, UK Department for Education and Skills.

Hebdige, D. (1979), *Subculture, the meaning of style*, London: Methuen.

Heckhausen, J. and Tomasik, M. J. (2002), Developmental regulation before and after a developmental deadline: The sample case of 'biological clock' for childbearing, *Journal of Vocational Behavior*, Special issue on the transition from school to work: societal opportunities and individual agency, 60: 199-219.

Heckhausen, J., Wrosch, C. and Fleeson, W. (2001), *Psychology and Aging*, 16: 400-413.

Heimbrock, H. G. (2001), Religious identity' between home and transgression, *Journal of Education and Religion*, II (1): 63-78.

Helson, M, Vollebergh, W, and Meeus, W. (2000), Social support from parents and friends and emotional problems in adolescence, *Journal of Youth and Adolescence*, 29: 319-335.

Helve, H. (1991), The formation of religious attitudes and world views: A longitudinal study of young Finns, in *Social Compass* 38(4): 373-392.

Helve, H. (1993), Socialization of attitudes and values among young people in Finland, in *Young, Nordic Journal of Youth Research,* 1(3): 27-39.

Helve, H. (ed.) (1998), *Unification and marginalisation of young people.* Helsinki: Finnish Youth Research Society.

Helve, H. and Bynner, J. (eds.) (1996), *Youth and life management: Research perspectives,* Helsinki: University of Helsinki Press.

Henderson, S., Holland, J., McGrellis, S., Sharpe, S., and Thomson, R. (2007), *Inventing adulthoods: A biographical approach to youth transitions,* London: Sage.

Hendry, L. B. (1983), *Growing up and going out,* Aberdeen: Aberdeen University Press.

Hendry, L. B. and Kloep, M. (2002), *Lifespan development,* London: Thomson Learning.

Hey, V. (2005), The contrasting social logics of sociality and survival: Cultures of classed be/longing in late modernity, *Sociology,* 39(5): 855-872.

Higgins, M. C. (2001), Changing careers: The effects of social context, *Journal of Organisational Behavior,* 22: 595-618.

Hobsbawm, E. J. (1995), *Age of extremes: The short twentieth century, 1914-1991,* London: Abacus.

Holland, J. (2006), Fragmented youth: Social capital in biographical context in young people's lives, in Edwards, R., Franklin, J. and Holland, J. (eds.), *Assessing social capital: Concept, policy and practice,* Cambridge: Cambridge Scholars Press.

Holland, J. (2007), Inventing adulthoods. Making the most of what you have, in Helve, H. and Bynner, J. (eds.), *Youth and social capital,* London: the Tufnell Press.

Holland, J., Reynolds, T. and Weller, S. (2007), Transitions, networks and communities: The significance of social capital in the lives of children and young people, *Journal of Youth Studies,* 10(1): 97-116.

Holland, J., Thomson, R., Henderson, S., McGrellis, S and Sharpe, S. (2000), Catching on, wising up and learning from your mistakes: Young people's accounts of moral development, *The International Journal of Children's Rights,* 8: 271-294.

Holm, N. G. (2001), Religionpsykologiska synpunkter på religiös fostran [Perspectives of the psychology of religion on religious upbringing], in Salminen, J. (ed.), Varhaiskasvatuksen uskontokasvatus [Religious education in the early years], Helsinki University, *Studia Paedagogica,* 24: 59-77.

Home Office (1998), The offenders index: Codebook, London: The Home Office.

Home Office (2003), Statistical bulletin recorded crime, England and Wales, 12 months to March, 2003, London: The Home Office.

Hunsberger, B., Pratt, M. and Pancer, S. M. (2001), Adolescent identity formation: Religious exploration and commitment, *Identity: An International Journal of Theory and Research,* 1(4): 365–386.

Jenks, C. (1996), *Childhood,* London and New York: Routledge.

Johnston, L., MacDonald, R., Mason, P., Ridley, L. and Webster, C. (2000), *Snakes and ladders: young people, transitions and social exclusion,* Bristol: Policy Press.

Jokisaari, M. and Nurmi, J.-E. (2005), Company matters: Goal-related social capital in the transition to working life, *Journal of Vocational Behavior,* 67: 413-428.

Jokisaari M. and Nurmi, J.-E. (2005b), The role of social ties in changes in socialisation outcomes among recent graduates, a paper presented at the *International social network conference, Sunbelt XXV,* 16-20 February: Redondo Beach, CA, USA.

Jones, G. (2002), *The youth divide: diverging paths to adulthood*, York: Joseph Rowntree Foundation.

Jones, G. (2005), *Thinking and behaviour of young adults 16-25: a review*, Annex A, Report on *Young Adults with Complex Needs*, London, Social Exclusion Unit, ODPM.

Jones, G., O'Sullivan, A. and Rouse, J. (2006), Young adults, partners, and parents: individual agency and the problem of support, *Journal of Youth Studies*, 9: 375-392.

Kammeyer-Mueller, J. D. and Wanberg, C. R. (2003), Unwrapping the organisational entry process: Disentangling multiple antecedents and their pathways to adjustment, *Journal of Applied Psychology*, 88: 779-794.

Kanfer, R., Wanberg, C. R. and Kantrowitz, T. M. (2001), Job search and employment: A personality-motivational analysis and meta-analytic review. *Journal of Applied Psychology*, 86: 837-855.

Karabel, J. and Halsey, A. H. (1977), *Power and ideology in education*, New York: Oxford University Press.

Kovalainen, A. (2004), Rethinking the revival of social capital and trust in social theory: possibilities for feminist analysis, in Marshall, B. L. and Witz, A. (eds.), *Engendering the social: Feminist encounters with sociological theory*, Maidenhead, Berkshire: Open University Press, 155-170.

Krieger, N., Williams, D. R. and Moss, N. E. (1997), Measuring social class in US public health research: Concepts, methodologies, and guidelines, *Annual Review of Public Health*, 18: 341-378.

Kroger, J. (1996), *Identity in adolescence: The balance between Self and Other* (2nd Edn), London: Routledge.

Kuusisto, A. (2003), Transmitting religious values in Adventist home education, *Journal of Beliefs and Values*, 24(3): 283-293.

Kuusisto, A. (2005a), How does school social context affect religious minority identity? Exploratory study on Adventist young people in Finland, in Kiefer, S. and Pederseil, T. (eds.), *Analysis of Educational Policies in a Comparative Perspective*, Linz: Schriften der Pädagogischen akademie des Bundes in OÖ, 30: 73-87.

Kuusisto, A. (2005b), Methodological issues and challenges in studying young people's religious identity, in Helve H. (ed.), *Mixed methods in youth research*, Finnish Youth Research Network/Society, 60: 197-212.

Kuusisto, A. (2005c), Adventist schools in the Finnish educational system, in Kiefer, S., Michalak, J., Sabanci, A. and Winter, K. (eds.), *Analysis of Educational Policies in a Comparative Educational Perspective*, Linz: Trauner, 130-137.

Kuusisto, A. (2006), Young people's religious minority identity and commitment: Case study among Adventist youth in Finland, in Tirri, K. (ed.), *Nordic Perspectives on Religion, Spirituality and Identity*, Yearbook 2006 of the Department of Practical Theology, Helsinki: University of Helsinki, Käytännöllisen teologian laitoksen julkaisuja [Publications of the Department of Practical Theology] 110.

Ladson-Billings, G. (2004), Critical race theory, in Ladson-Billings, G. and Gillborn, D. (eds.), *The Routledge Falmer reader in multicultural education* London: Routledge.

Lahelma, E. (2002), School is for meeting friends: Secondary school as lived and remembered, *British Journal of Sociology of Education*, 23(3): 367-381.

Lakoff, G. and Johnson, M. (1980), *Metaphors we live by*, Chicago: The University of Chicago Press.

Langston, C. A., and Cantor, N. (1989), Social anxiety and social constraint: When making friends is hard, *Journal of Personality and Social Psychology,* 56: 649-661.

Lauglo, J., and Oia, T. (2006), *Education and civic engagement among Norwegian youths,* Oslo: Norwegian Social Research

Lee, N. (2001), *Childhood and society: Growing up in an age of uncertainty,* Buckingham: Open University Press.

Leete, R., and Fox, J. (1977), Registrar General's social classes: origins and users, *Population Trends,* 8: 1-7.

Lefebre, H. (1991), *The production of space,* Oxford: Basil Blackwell.

Leonard, M. (2004), Bonding and bridging social capital: reflections from Belfast, *Sociology,* 38(5): 927-944.

Leonard, M. (2005), Children, childhood and social capital: Exploring the links, *Sociology,* 39(4): 605-622.

Levine, C. (2003), Introduction: Structure, development, and identity formation, *Identity: An International Journal of Theory and Research,* 3(3): 191-195.

Levitt, S. D. and Lochner, L., (2000), The determinants of juvenile crime, in Gruber, J. (ed.), *Risky behavior by youths,* Chicago, Illinois: University of Chicago Press.

Lin, N. (1982), Social resources and instrumental action, in Marsden, P. and Lin, N. (eds.), *Social structure and network analysis,* (131-145), Sage Publications.

Lin, N. (1999), Social networks and status attainment, *Annual Review of Sociology,* 25: 467-87.

Lin, N. (2001), *Social capital: A theory of social structure and action,* New York: Cambridge University Press.

Lin, N., Ensel, W, M. and Vaughn, J. C. (1981), Social resources and strength of ties: Structural factors in occupational status attainment, *American Sociological Review,* 46: 393-405.

Little, B. (1983), Personal projects: A rationale and method for investigation, *Environment and Behavior,* 15: 273-309.

Little, B. (1989), Personal project analysis: Trivial pursuits, magnificent obsessions, and the search for coherence, in Buss, D. and Cantor, N. (eds.), *Personality psychology: Recent trends and emerging directions (*pp. 15-31), New York: Springler.

Little, B. R., Lecci, L. and Watkinson, B. (1992), Personality and personal projects: Linking Big Five and PAC units of analysis, *Journal of Personality,* Special issue, The five-factor model: Issues and applications, 60: 501-525.

Little, B., Salmela-Aro, K. and Phillips, S. (eds., 2007), *Personal project pursuit: Goals, action and human flourishing,* Mahwah, New Jersey: Lawrence Erlbaum.

Lochner, L. and Moretti, E. (2004), The effects of education on crime: Evidence from prison inmates, arrests and self-reports, *American Economic Review,* 94(1): 155-189.

Lochner, L. (2004), Education, work and crime: A human capital approach, *International Economic Review,* 45(3): 811-843.

Lucey, H. and Reay, D. (2000), Identities in transition: anxiety and excitement in the move to secondary school, *Oxford Review of Education,* 26(2): 191-205.

Lury, C. (2003), The game of loyalt(o)y: Diversions and divisions in network society, *Sociological Review,* 51(3): 301-320.

MacCleod, D. (2006), Mixed primary classes are the 'key to integration, *EducationGuardian. co.uk,* Friday 25th August 2006, http://education.guardian.co.uk/raceinschools/ story/0,,1857678,00.html

MacDonald, R. and Marsh, J. (2005), *Disconnected youth? Growing up in Britain's poor neighbourhoods*, Basingstoke: Palgrave.

MacDonald, R., Shildrick, T., Webster, C. and Simpson, D. (2005), Growing up in poor neighbourhoods: the significance of class and place in the extended transitions of 'socially excluded' young adults, *Sociology,* 39(5): 873-891.

Machin, S. and Blanden, J. (2004), Educational inequality and the expansion of UK higher education, *Scottish Journal of Political Economy,* 51: 230-49.

Madood, T (1997) (ed.), *Ethnic minorities in Britain,* London: Policy Studies Institute

Madood, T. (2004), Capitals, ethnic identity and educational qualifications, *Cultural Trends,* 13(2): 87-105.

Mahoney, J., Stattin, H. and Lord, H. (2004), Unstructured youth recreation centre participation and anti-social behaviour development: selection influences and the moderating role of anti-social peers, *International Journal of Behavioural Development,* 28: 553-560.

Makepeace, G., Dolton, P., Woods, L., Joshi, H. and Galinda-Rueda, F. (2003), From school to the labour market, in Ferri, E., Bynner, J. and Wadsworth, M. (eds.), *Changing Britain, changing lives: Three generations at the turn of the century* (pp. 29-70), London: Institute of Education.

Mand, K. (2006), Social relations beyond the family?: Exploring elderly South Asians women's friendships in London, Special issue: Ethnicity and social capital, *Journal of Community, Work and Family,* 9(3): 309-324.

Marcia, J. (1966), Development and validation of ego-identity status, *Journal of Personality and Social Psychology,* 3: 551-558.

Markstrom-Adams, C., Hofstra, G. and Dougher, K. (1994), The ego-virtue of fidelity: A case for the study of religion and identity formation in adolescence, *Journal of Youth and Adolescence,* 23: 453-469.

Marley, B. (2001), Johnny Was (from the album *Rastaman vibration*), New York: Island Records, 548897, CD, 3mins 48secs.

Marmot, M. G., Adelstein, A. M., Robinson, N., and Rose, G. A. (1978), Changing social-class distribution of heart disease, *British Medical Journal,* 21(2): 1109-1112.

Marsh, C. (1986), Social class and occupation, in Burgess, R. G. (ed.), *Key variables in social investigation,* London: Routledge.

Mason, J. (1999), Living Away from Relatives: kinship and geographical reasoning, in McRae, S. (ed.), *Changing Britain: Families and households in the 1990s,* Oxford: Oxford University Press.

Masten, A., Burt, K., Roisman, G., Obradovis, J., Long, J. and Tellegen, A. (2004), Resources and resilience in the transition to adulthood: Continuity and change, *Development and Psychopathology,* 16: 1071-1094.

Maxfield, M., Castner, L., Maralani, V., and Vencill, M. (2003), *The quantum opportunity programme demonstration: Implementation and findings,* Washington DC: Mathematica Policy Research.

McGrellis, S. (2005), Pushing the boundaries in Northern Ireland: Young people, violence and sectarianism, *Contemporary Politics,* 11(1): 57-71.

McGrellis, S., Henderson, S., Holland, J., Sharpe, S. and Thomson, R. (2001), *Through the moral maze: A quantitative study of young people's moral values,* London: the Tufnell Press.

McLean, C. (2002), *Social capital, ethnicity and health: factors shaping African-Caribbean residents' participation in local community networks*, http://www/lse.ac.uk/depts/gender

McLeod, J. (2000), Subjectivity and schooling in a longitudinal study of secondary students, *British Journal of Sociology of Education*, 21(4): 501-521.

McLeod, J and Yates, L. (2006), *Making modern lives: subjectivity, schooling and social change*, Albany NY: Suny Press.

McNay, L. (2004), Agency and experience: gender as lived relation, in: Adkins, L. and Skeggs, B. (eds.), *Feminism after Bourdieu*, Oxford: Blackwell Publishing, 175-190.

Meegan, S. and Berg, C. (1998), *The interpersonal context of appraisal and coping with developmental life tasks*, Unpublished manuscript: University of Utah.

Meegan, S. and Berg, C. (2001), Whose life task is it anyway? Social appraisal and life task pursuit, *Journal of Personality*, 69: 363-389.

Mccus, W. (1989), Parental and Peer support in adolescence, in Hurrelmann, K. and Engel, U. (eds.), *The Social World of Adolescents*, New York: Walter de Gruyter.

Metcalf, H. (1997), *Class and higher education: the participation of young people from lower social classes*, London: CIHE in conjunction with PSI.

Metso, T. (2004), *Koti, koulu ja kasvatus: Kohtaamisia ja rajankäyntejä* (Home, School and Upbringing), Turku: Suomen Kasvatustieteellinen Seura, Kasvatusalan tutkimuksia, 19.

Mirza, H. (1992),, *Young, female and black*, London: Routledge.

Modood, T. and Acland, T. (1998), Conclusion, in Modood, T. and Acland, T. (eds.), *Race and higher education*, London: Policy Studies Institute.

Molyneux, M. (2002), Gender and the silences of social capital: Lessons from Latin America, *Development and change* 33(2): 167-188.

Moody, J. (2001), Race, school integration, and friendship: Segregation in America, *American Journal of Sociology*, 107(3): 679-716.

Morris, L. (1994), *Dangerous classes*, London: Routledge.

Morrison, E. W. (1993), Longitudinal study of the effects of information seeking on newcomer socialisation, *Journal of Applied Psychology*, 78: 173-183.

Morrow, V. (1999a), Conceptualising social capital in relation to the well-being of children and young people: A critical review, *Sociological Review*, 47(4): 744-765.

Morrow, V. (1999b), *Searching for social capital in children's accounts of neighbourhood and networks: a preliminary analysis*, Discussion paper series, Issue 7, Gender Institute, London School of Economics.

Morrow, V. (2000), 'Dirty looks' and 'trampy places' in young people's accounts of community and neighbourhood: Implications for health inequalities, *Critical Public Health*, 10(2): 141-152.

Morrow, V. (2001a), Young people's explanations and experiences of social exclusions: Retrieving Bourdieu's concept of social capital, *International Journal of Sociology and Social Policy*, 21(4): 37-63.

Morrow, V. (2001b), *An appropriate Capital-isation: Questioning social capital*, London: Gender Institute, London School of Economics.

Morrow, V. (2003), Conceptualizing social capital in relation to children and young people: *Is* it different for girls? Paper for presentation to *Gender and Social Capital Conference, University of Manitoba*, Winnipeg, Canada, May 2003.

Muggleton, D. (2005), From classnessness to clubculture: A genealogy of post-war British youth cultural analysis *Young*, 13(2): 205-219.

Munn, P. (2000), Social capital, schools and exclusions, in Baron, S., Field, J. and Schuller, T. (eds.), *Social capital: Critical perspectives,* Oxford: OUP, pp. 168-182.

Muthén, L. K., and Muthén, B. O. (1998-2004), *Mplus user's guide,* Los Angeles, CA: Muthén and Muthén.

Nayak, A. (2003), *Race, place and globalization: Youth Cultures in a Changing World,* Oxford: Berg.

Nayak, A. (2006), Displaced masculinities: chavs, youth and class in the post-industrial city, *Sociology*, 40(5): 813-831.

Nestmann, F. and Hurrelmann, K. (1994), *Social networks and social support in childhood and adolescence,* Berlin: Walter de Gruyter.

Nilsen, A. and Brannen, J. (2002), Theorising the individual-structure dynamic, in Brannen, J., Lewis, S., Nilsen, A. and Smithson, J. (eds.), *Young Europeans, work and family: futures in transition,* London: Routledge.

Nurmi, J.-E. (1991), How do adolescents see their future? A review of the development of future orientation and planning, *Developmental Review,* 11: 1-59.

Nurmi, J.-E. (1992), Age differences in adult life goals, concerns, and their temporal extension: A life course approach to future-oriented motivation, *International Journal of Behavioral Development,* 16: 169-189.

Nurmi, J.-E. (1993), Adolescent development in an age-graded context: The role of personal beliefs, goals and strategies in the tackling of developmental tasks and standards, *International Journal of Behavioral Development,* 16: 169-189.

Nurmi, J.-E., and Salmela-Aro, K. (2002), Goal construction, reconstruction and depressive symptomatology in a life span context: The transition from school to work, *Journal of Personality,* 385-420.

OECD (Organisation for Economic Co-operation and Development), (2001), *The well-being of nations: the role of human and social capital*, Paris: OECD

OECD (Organisation for Economic Co-operation and Development), (2007), *Understanding the social outcomes of learning* Paris: OECD

OPCS (Office of Population, Censuses, and Surveys) (1980), *Classification of occupations and coding index*, London: H.M.S.O.

Orr, M. (1999), *Black social capital: The politics of school reform in Baltimore, 1986-1998,* Kansas: University of Kansas Press.

Ousley, H. (2001), *Community pride, not prejudice: Making diversity work in Bradford,* Bradford: Bradford Vision.

Owen, D. (2006), Demographic profiles and social cohesion of minority ethnic communities in England and Wales, Special Issue: Ethnicity and Social Capital, *Journal of Community, Work and Family,* 9(3): 251-272.

Pahl, R. (2000), *On Friendship*, Cambridge: Polity Press.

Pahl, R. and Pevalin, D. (2005), Between family and friends: a longitudinal study of friendship choice, *British Journal of Sociology*, 56(3): 433-450.

Pahl, R., Pevalin, D. and Spencer, E (2006), Friendships over the lifecourse, paper presented at *British Sociological Association Annual Conference*, Harrogate International Centre, Harrogate, April 22.

Parekh, B. (2000), *The future of multi-cultural Britain*, London: Runnymede Trust.

Parker, D. and Song, M. (2006a), Ethnicity, social capital and the internet: British Chinese websites, *Ethnicities*, 6(2): 178-202.

Parker, D. and Song, M.(2006b), New ethnicities online: reflexive racialisation and the internet, in *The Sociological Review*, 54(3): 575-594, London: Blackwell Publishing.

Pasquier, D. (2007), Digital technologies, cultures, values and lifestyles', paper to CERI meeting on New Millennium Learners, University of Florence, www.oecd.org/ dataoecd/0/39/38359197.pdf

Penn, E. B. (2000), Reducing delinquency through service, *Fellow Report*, Washington DC: Corporation for National Service.

Pettinger, L., Taylor, R., Parry, J. and Glucksmann, M. (2005), (eds.), *A New Sociology of Work?* Oxford: Blackwell.

Petersen, T., Saporta, I. and Seidel, M.-C. L. (2000), Offering a job: Meritocracy and social networks, *American Journal of Sociology*, 106: 763-816.

Phillips, A. (2006), We must start small, *The Guardian*, August 26, http://education.guardian. co.uk/schools/comment/story/0,,1860757,00.html

Phinney, J. (1992), The Multigroup Ethnic Identity Measure: A new scale for use with adolescents and young adults from diverse groups, *Journal of Adolescent Research*, 7: 156-176.

Phinney, J. S. (2004), *The Multigroup Ethnic Identity Measure (MEIM)*, updated version, www.calstatela.edu/academic/psych/html/phinney.htm, accessed 15 June 2004.

Platt, L. (2005), *Migration and social mobility the life chances of Britain's minority ethnic communities*, Bristol: Policy Press for JRF.

Platt, L., Simpson, L. and Akinwale, B. (2005), Stability and change in ethnic groups in England and Wales, *Population Trends*, 121: 35 46.

Platt, L. and Thompson, P. (2007), The role of family background and social capital in the social mobility of migrant ethnic minorities, in Edwards, R., Franklin, J. and Holland, J. (eds.), *Assessing social capital: Concept, policy and practice*, Cambridge: Cambridge Scholars Press.

Plewis, I., Calderwood, L., Hawkes, D., and Nathan, G. (2004), *National Child Development Study and 1970 British Cohort Study: Technical report: changes in the NCDS and BCS 70 populations and samples over time*, London: Institute of Education, Centre for Longitudinal Studies.

Plummer, K. (2001), *Documents of life 2*, London: Sage publications.

Portes, A. (1998), Social capital: Its origins and applications in modern sociology, *Annual Review of Sociology*, 24: 1-24.

Portes, A. (2000), The two meanings of social capital, *Sociological Forum*, 15(1): 1-12.

Portes, A. and Landolt, P. (1996), The downside of social capital, *The American Prospect*, 26(May-June): 18-21.

Pösö, T. (2004), *Vakavat silmät ja muita kokemuksia koulukodista* (Young people's experiences of reform school), Helsinki: Stakes, Research no. 133.

Pratt, S. and George, R. (2005), Transferring friendship: Girls' and boys' friendships in the transition from primary to secondary school, *Children and Society*, 19: 16-26.

Preston, J. (2007), *Whiteness and class in education*, London: Springer.

Preston, J. and Feinstein, L. (2004), Adult learning and attitude change, *Wider Benefits of Learning Research Report No. 11*, London: Institute of Education.

Pulkkinen, L. (2002), *Mukavaa yhdessä: Sosiaalinen alkupääoma ja lapsen sosiaalinen kehitys, [Fun together: Initial social capital and child development]*, Jyväskylä: PS-Kustannus.

Putnam, R. D. (1994), Tuning in, turning out: the strange disappearance of social capital in America, *American Political Science Association Online,* www.apsanet.org/ps/dec95/putfig2.cfm.

Putnam, R. D. (1995), Bowling alone: America's declining social capital, *Journal of Democracy,* 6: 65-78.

Putnam, R. D. (1999), *Bowling alone: the collapse and revival of American community,* New York: Simon and Schuster.

Putnam, R. D. (1993), *Making democracy work: civic traditions in modern Italy,* Princeton: Princeton University Press.

Putnam, R. D. (2000), *Bowling alone: The collapse and revival of American community,* New York: Touchstone Books/Simon and Schuster.

Putnam, R. D. and Feldstein, L. with Cohen, D. (2003), *Better together: Restoring the American community,* New York: Simon and Schuster.

Puuronen, V. (1997), *Johdatus nuorisotutkimukseen* (An introduction to youth research), Tampere: Vastapaino.

Qvotrup Jensen, S. (2006), Rethinking subcultural capital *Young,*14(3): 257-276.

Raffo, C. and Reeves, M. (2000), Youth transitions and social exclusion: Developments in social capital theory, *Journal of Youth Studies* 3(2): 147-166.

Ravanera, Z. R., Rajulton, F., and Turcotte, P. (2003), Youth integration and social capital: An analysis of the Canadian General Social Survey on time use, *Youth and Society,* 35: 158-182.

Reay, D. (1998), *Class work: Mothers' involvement in their children's primary schooling,* London: UCL Press, Taylor and Francis Group.

Reay, D. (2000), A useful extension of Bourdieu's conceptual framework?: Emotional capital as a way of understanding mothers' involvement in their children's education? *Sociological Review* 48(4): 569-585.

Reay, D. (2005), Beyond consciousness? The psychic landscape of social class, *Sociology,* 39(5): 911-928.

Reay, D. and Lucey, H. (2000), 'I don't really like it here but I don't want to be anywhere else': children and inner city council estates, *Antipode,* 34(4): 410-428.

Reay, D., David, M. E., and Ball, S.J. (2005), *Degrees of choice: Social class, race and gender in higher education,* Stoke on Trent: Trentham Books.

Reynolds, T. (2004), *Caribbean families, social capital and young people's diasporic identities,* Families and Social Capital ESRC Research Group Working Paper No. 12, London: London South Bank University.

Reynolds, T. (2005), *Caribbean mothering: Identity and childrearing in the U.K.,* London: the Tufnell Press.

Reynolds, T. (2006a), Bonding social capital within the Caribbean family and community, Special issue: Ethnicity and social capital, *Journal of Community, Work and Family,* 9(3): 273-290.

Reynolds, T. (2006b), Caribbean young people, family relationships and social capital, Special Issue: Social capital, migration and transnational families, *Journal of Ethnic and Racial Studies,* 29(6): 1087-1103.

Reynolds, T. and Zontini, E. (2006), *A Comparative study of care and provision across Caribbean and Italian transnational families,* Families and Social Capital ESRC Research Group Working Paper No. 16, London: London South Bank University.

Reynolds, T. and Zontini, E. (2007), Assessing social capital and care provision in minority ethnic communities: A comparative study of Caribbean and Italian families, in Edward,

R., Franklin, J. and Holland, J. (eds.), *Assessing Social Capital: concept, policy and practice*, Cambridge: Cambridge Scholars Press.

Ridge, T. (2002), *Childhood poverty and social exclusion: From a child's perspective* Bristol: The Policy Press.

Robinson, L., Schmid, A. A., and Stiles, M. E. (2002), Is social capital really capital, *Review of Social Economy*, LX(1): 1-21.

Ross, C. and Mirowsky, J. (1999), Refining the association between education and health: The effects of quantity, credential, and selectivity, *Demography*, 36(4): 445-460.

Rubin, K. H., Bukowski, W. and Parker, J. G. (1998), Peer interactions, relationships, and groups, in Damon, W. and Eisenberg, N. (eds.), *Handbook of Child Psychology,* 5th ed., *Vol. 3. Social, emotional, and personality development,* (pp. 619-700), Hoboken: John Wiley and Sons.

Ruehlman, L. and Wolchik, S. (1988), Personal goals and interpersonal support and hindrance as factors in psychological distress and well-being, *Journal of Personality and Social Psychology,* 55: 293-301.

Rumbalt, R. and Portes, A. (2001), *Ethnicities: children of immigrants in America,* California: University of California Press.

Runnymede Trust (2004), Civic renewal and social capital, *Runnymede Quarterly Bulletin*, September.

Saks, A. M. and Ashforth, B. E. (1997), Organisational socialisation: Making sense of the past and present as prologue for the future, *Journal of Vocational Behavior,* 51: 234-279.

Salmela-Aro, K. (1992), Struggling with self: Personal projects of students seeking psychological counseling, *Scandinavian Journal of Psychology,* 33: 330-338.

Salmela-Aro, K. (2001), Personal goals during a transition to adulthood, in J.-E. Nurmi (ed.), *Navigation through adolescence* (pp. 59-84), New York: Routledge Falmer.

Salmela-Aro, K. (2003), Personal goals during emerging adulthood, Society for Adolescent research, *A poster in the First Emerging adulthood congress*, Harvard.

Salmela-Aro, K. and colleagues (2004-2006), Unpublished data, University of Jyväskylä, Finland.

Salmela-Aro, K. and Kiuru (2006), Shared goals, *Presentation in the Psychology Conference 2006*, Tampere, Finland.

Salmela-Aro, K. and Little, B. (2007), Relational aspects of project pursuit, in Little, B., Salmela-Aro, K. and Philips, S. (eds.), *Personal Project Pursuit: Goals, action and human flourishing* (pp. 199-220), Mahwah, New Jersey: Lawrence Erlbaum.

Salmela-Aro, K. and Nurmi, J.-E. (1996), Uncertainty and confidence in interpersonal projects—Consequences for social life and well-being, *Journal of Social and Personal Relationships,* 13: 109-122.

Salmela-Aro, K. and Nurmi, J.-E. (1997), Goal contents, well-being and life context during transition to university—a longitudinal study, *International Journal of Behavioral Development,* 20: 471-491.

Salmela-Aro, K. and Nurmi, J. E. (2004), Motivational orientation and well-being at work: A person-oriented approach, *Journal of Change Management,* 17: 471-489.

Salmela-Aro, K., Aunola, K. and Nurmi, J.-E. (in press), Personal goals during emerging adulthood: A 10-year follow-up, *Journal of Adolescent Research.*

Salmela-Aro, K., Nurmi, J.-E., Aro, A., Poppius, E. and Riste, J. (1992), Age differences in adults' personal projects, *The Journal of Social Psychology,* 133: 415-417.

Salmela-Aro, K., Nurmi, J.-E., Saisto, T. and Halmesmäki, E. (2001), Goal construction and depressive symptoms during transition to motherhood: Evidence from two longitudinal studies, *Journal of Personality and Social Psychology,* 81: 1144-1159.

Salmela-Aro, K., Nurmi, J.-E., Saisto, T. and Halmesmäki, E. (2000), Women's and men's personal goals during the transition to parenthood, *Journal of Family Psychology,* 14: 171-186.

Sam, D.L. and Virta, E. (2003), Intergenerational value discrepancies in immigrant and host-national families and their impact on psychological adaptation, *Journal of Adolescence,* 26: 213-231.

Schaefer-McDaniel, N.J. (2004), Conceptualising social capital among young people: Toward a new theory, *Children, Youth and Environments,* 14(1): 140-150.

Schein, E. H. (1978), *Career dynamics: Matching individuals and organisational needs,* Reading, MA: Addison-Wesley.

Schmälzle, U. F. (2001), The importance of schools and families for the identity formation of children and adolescents, *International Journal of Education and Religion,* 106, II(1): 27-42.

Schoon, I. (2006), *Risk and resilience: Adaptations in changing times,* Cambridge: Cambridge University Press.

Schoon, I., McCulloch, A., Joshi, H., Wiggins, D. and Bynner, J. (2001), Transitions from school to work in a changing social context, *Young: Journal of Nordic Youth Research,* 9(1): 4-22.

Schulenberg, J., Bryant, A. and O'Malley, P. (2004), Taking hold of some kind of life: How developmental tasks relate to trajectories of well-being during the transition to adulthood, *Development and Psychopathology,* 16: 1119-1140.

Schuller, T. (2001), The complimentary roles of human and social capital, *Canadian Journal of Policy Research,* 2: 18-24.

Schuller, T. (2004), Three capitals: A framework, in Schuller, T., Preston, J., Hammond, C. Brasset-Grundy, A. and Bynner, J, *The Benefits of learning: The impact of education on health, family life and social capital,* London: Routledge-Falmer.

Schuller, T., Baron, S., and Field, J. (2000), Social capital: A review and critique, in Baron, S., Field, J., and Schuller, T. (eds.), *Social capital: Critical perspectives,* Oxford: OUP, pp. 1-38

Schuller, T., Bynner, J., and Feinstein, L. (2004), *Capitals and capabilities,* London: Centre for Research on the Wider Benefits of Learning.

Schultz, T. (1961), Investment in human capital, *American Sociological Review,* 51: 1-17.

Seaman, P. and Sweeting, H. (2004), Assisting young people's access to social capital in contemporary families: A qualitative study, *Journal of Youth Studies* 7(2): 173-190.

Shanahan, M. J. (2000), Pathways to adulthood in changing societies: Variability and Mechanisms in Life Course Perspective, *Annual Review of Sociology,* 26:667-692.

Shepherd, P. (2004), NCDS and BCS70 update, *Kohort, CLS Cohort studies newsletter.*

Sherman, L., Gottfredson, D., Mackenzie, D., Eck, J., Reuter, P. and Bushqway, S. (1998), *Preventing crime: what works, what doesn't, what's promising,* Washington DC: U.S. Department of Justice, Office of Justice Programmes.

Shipman, A. (2002), *The globalization myth,* Cambridge: Icon Books.

Siisiäinen, M. (2003), Yksi käsite, kaksi lähestymistapaa: Putnamin ja Bourdieun sosiaalinen pääoma (One concept, two approaches: social capital by Putnam and Bourdieu), *Sosiologia* 40(3): 204-216.

Skeggs, B. (1997), *Formations of class and gender: Becoming respectable*, London: Sage Publications.

Skeggs, B. (2004), *Class, self, culture*, London: Routledge.

Smith, M. K. (2001), Social capital, in *The encyclopedia of informal education*, www.infed. org/biblio/social_capital.htm, accessed 13 February 2007.

Smith, S. S. and Kulynych, J. (2002), It may be social, but why is it capital? The social construction of social capital and the politics of language, *Politics and Society*, 30(1): 149-186.

Stace, S. and Roker, D. (2005), *Monitoring and supervision in 'ordinary' families* London: National Children's Bureau.

Stephenson, S. (2001), Street children in Moscow: Using and creating social capital, *The Sociological Review* 49(4): 530-547.

Strategy Unit (2003), *Ethnic minorities in the labour market*, London: Strategy Unit

Strough, J., Berg, C. and Sansone, C. (1996), Goals for solving everyday problems across the life span: Age and gender differences in the salience of interpersonal concerns, *Developmental Psychology*, 32: 1106-1115.

Sundén, H. (1974), *Barn och religion* [Child and religion], Stockholm: Verbum.

Taggart, R. (1995), *Quantum opportunity programme*, first ed., Philadelphia: Opportunities Industrialization Centre of America.

Tajfel, H. (1981), *Human groups and social categories: Studies in social psychology*, New York: Cambridge University Press.

Tamboukou, M. (2004), Nomadic trajectories in the unfolding of the self: Spaces of identity, *spacesofidentity.net*, 4: 3, www.uel.ac.uk/cnr/

Tampubolon, G. (2005), Fluxes and constants in the dynamics of friendship, *ESRC Research Methods Programme Working Paper No. 25*

Tashakkori, A. and Teddlie, C. (1998), *Mixed methodology: Combining qualitative and quantitative approaches*, Thousand Oaks, California: Sage.

Tatum, B. (1997), *'Why are all the black kids sitting together in the cafeteria?': And other conversations about race*, New York: Basic Books.

Taylor, M. (2005), Two thirds oppose state aided faith schools, *The Guardian*, 23 August, http://education.guardian.co.uk/faithschools/story/0,13882,1554593,00.html, accessed 30 May 2007.

Thomson, R. (2004), *Tradition and innovation: Case histories of changing gender identities*, unpublished PhD: London South Bank University.

Thomson, R. and Holland, J. (2002), Young people, social change and the negotiation of moral authority, *Children and Society*, 16: 1-13.

Thomson, R. and Holland, J. (2003), Hindsight, foresight and insight: the challenges of longitudinal qualitative research, *International Journal of Social Research Methodology*, *Theory and Practice*, 6(3): 233-244.

Thomson, R. and Holland, J. (2004), *Youth values and transitions to adulthood: an empirical investigation*, Families and Social Capital ESRC Research Group, Working Paper No. 4, London South Bank University.

Thomson, R. and Holland, J. (2005), 'Thanks for the memory': Memory books as a methodological resource in biographical research, *Qualitative Research*, 5(2): 201-219.

Thomson, R., Bell, R., Henderson, S., Holland, J., McGrellis, S. and Sharpe, S. (2002), Critical moments: Choice, chance and opportunity in young people's narratives of transition to adulthood, *Sociology* 36(2): 335-354.

Thomson, R., Holland, J., McGrellis, S., Bell, R., Henderson, S. and Sharpe, S. (2004), Inventing adulthoods: A biographical approach to understanding youth citizenship, *Sociological Review*, 52(2): 218-239.

Thornton, S. (1995), *Club cultures: Music, media and subcultural capital,* Hanover and London:Wesleyan University Press, University Press of New England,

Thrift, N. (1998), Virtual capitalism: The globalization of reflexive business knowledge, in Carrier, J. and Miller, D. (eds.), *Virtualism: A new political economy,* Oxford: Berg.

Tizard, B. and Phoenix, A. (1993), *Black, white or mixed race: Race and racism in the lives of young people of mixed parentage?* London: Routledge.

Tolonen, T. (1998), Everybody thinks I am a nerd: Schoolboys' fights and ambivalences about masculinities, *Young,* 6(3): 4-18.

Tolonen, T. (2004), Vanhemmuuden puutteen heijastuminen nuorten sosiaaliseen pääomaan (Missing parenthood and its effects on social capital of young people), *Nuorisotutkimus* (Journal of Youth Research), 22(4): 17-34.

Tolonen, T. (2005a), Sosiaalinen tausta, sukupuoli ja paikallisuus nuorten koulutussiirtymissä' (Social background, gender and locality in young people's educational transitions), in, Aapola, S. and Ketokivi, K. (eds.), *Polkuja ja poikkeamia — Aikuisuutta etsimässä,* (On and off the beaten tracks — Searching for adulthood), Helsinki: Youth Research Network and Youth Research Society, Publication 56: 33-65.

Tolonen, T. (2005b), Locality and gendered capital of working-class youth, *Young* 13(4): 43-361.

Törrönen, M. (1999), *Lasten arki laitoksessa* (The everyday life of children at institutions), Helsinki: Helsinki University Press.

Tzuriel, D. (1984), Sex role typing and ego identity in Israeli, oriental, and western adolescents, *Journal of Personality and Social Psychology,* 46: 440-457.

U.K. Social Exclusion Unit (1999), *Bridging the gap: Ne6ortunities for 16-18 year olds not in education employment or training,* London: The Stationery Office.

Umaña-Taylor, A. (2004), Ethnic identity and self-esteem: Examining the role of social context, *Journal of Adolescence,* 27: 139-146.

UNICEF (2007), *Child poverty in perspective: An overview of child well-being in rich countries,* Florence: United Nations Children's Fund. Innocenti Research Centre.

Valentine, G (1997), 'Oh yes you can,' 'Oh no you can't': Children and parents' understandings of kids' competence to negotiate public space safely, *Antipode,* 29(1): 65-89.

Valentine, G. (1995), Stranger-danger: The impact of parental fears on children's use of space, Paper presented at the *International Conference, Building identities: gender perspectives on children and urban space,* Amsterdam, The Netherlands, 11th-13th April.

van Deth, J. (2004), Measuring social capital: orthodoxies and continuing controversies, *The International Journal of Social Research Methodology: Theory and Practice,* 6(1): 79-92.

van Hoof, A. and Raaijmakers, Q. A. W. (2002), The spatial integration of adolescent identity: Its relation to age, education, and subjective well-being, *Scandinavian Journal of Psychology,* 43: 201-212.

Vanttaja, M. (2002), *Koulumenestyjät,* (School successors), Turku: Suomen Kasvatustieteellinen Seura, Research no. 8.

Walkerdine, V., Lucey, H., and Melody, J. (2001), *Growing up girl: psychosocial explorations of gender and class,* Basingstoke: Palgrave.

Wallace, C. (1987), *For richer or poorer: Growing up in and out of work*, London: Saxon House.

Wanous, J. P. (1992), *Organisational entry: Recruitment, selection, orientation, and socialisation of newcomers* (2nd ed.), Reading, MA: Addison-Wesley.

Weekes, D. (1997), Shades of blackness: young female constructions of black beauty, in Mirza, H. (ed.), *Black British Feminism*, London: Routledge.

Weeks, J., Donovan, C. and Heaphy, B. (1999), Everyday experiments: Narratives of non-heterosexual relationships, in Silva, E. and Smart, C. (eds.), *The new family?* London: Sage Publications.

Weller, S. (2006a), 'Sticking with your mates?' Children's friendship trajectories during the transition from Primary to Secondary School, *Children and Society*, online, 6 September.

Weller, S. (2006b), Skateboarding alone? Making social capital discourse relevant to teenagers' lives, *Journal of Youth Studies*, 9(5): 557-574.

Weller, S. and Bruegel, I. (2006), *Locality, school and social capital: Findings report*, Families and Social Capital ESRC Research Group, London South Bank University.

Weller, S., (2007), Managing the move to secondary school: The significance of children's social capital, in Helve, H. and Bynner, J. (eds.), *Youth and Social Capital*, London: Tufnell Press.

Wentzel, K. R. and Caldwell, K. (1997), Friendships, peer acceptance and group membership: Relations to academic achievement in middle school, *Child Development*, 68(6): 1198-1209.

Whiting, E. and Harper, R. (2003), *Young people and social capital*, www.statistics.gov.uk/socialcapital/downloads/youngpeople_final.pdf, accessed 9th October 2006.

Whitty, G., Power, S., and Halpin, D. (1998), *Devolution and choice in education: The school, the state, the market*, Buckingham: Open University Press.

Willis, P. (1978), *Learning to labour: How working class kids get working class jobs*, Farnborough: Saxon House.

Winter, I. (2002), *Towards a theorised understanding of family and social capital*, Working Paper 21, Melbourne: Australian Institute of Family Studies.

Woods, L., Makepeace, G., Joshi, H., and Dolton, P. (2003), The world of paid work, in Ferri, E., Bynner, J. and Wadsworth, M. (eds.), *Changing Britain, Changing Lives* (pp. 71-104), London: Institute of Education.

Woolcock, M. (1998), Social capital and economic development: towards a theoretical synthesis and policy framework, *Theory and Society*, 27(1): 151-208.

Wright, J. P., Cullen F. T. and Miller, J. (2001), Family social capital and delinquent involvement, *Journal of Criminal Justice*, 29(1): 1-9.

Wuthnow, R. (2002), Religious involvement and status-bridging social capital, *Journal of the Scientific Study of Religion*, 41(4): 669-684.

Yli-Luoma, P. V. J. (1990), *Predictors of moral reasoning*, Stockholm: Almqvist and Wiksell International.

Zhou, M., Bankston, C. L III. (1994), Social capital and the adaptation of the second generation: The case of Vietnamese youth in New Orleans, *The International Migration Review*, 28(4): 821-845.

Zontini, E. (2004), *Italian families and social capital: rituals and the provision of care in British-Italian families*, Families and Social Capital ESRC Research Group Working Paper No. 6, London: London South Bank University.

Index

Printed in the United Kingdom
by Lightning Source UK Ltd.
132757UK00001B/98/A